REBELS

OF THE WOODS:

THE I.W.W.

IN THE

PACIFIC

NORTHWEST

REBELS of the WOODS: the I.W.W. in the PACIFIC NORTHWEST

by ROBERT L. TYLER

University of Oregon Books

EUGENE, OREGON
1967

ACKNOWLEDGMENTS

Some parts of this history have been told by the author in the following articles, and the author is pleased to acknowledge the journals in which they appeared: "The Everett Free Speech Fight," *Pacific Historical Review*, XXIII (Feb. 1954), 1930; "The I.W.W. in the Pacific Northwest: Rebels of the Woods," *Oregon Historical Quarterly*, LV (Mar. 1954), 3-44; "Violence at Centralia, 1919," *Pacific Northwest Quarterly*, XL (Oct. 1954), 116-124; "The Rise and Fall of an American Radicalism: The I.W.W.," *The Historian*, XIX (Fall 1956), 48-64; "The I.W.W. and the West," *American Quarterly*, XII (Summer 1960), 175-187; "The United States Government as Labor Organizer: The Loyal Legion of Loggers and Lumbermen," *Mississippi Valley Historical Review*, XLVII (Dec. 1960), 434-451; "The Strike in Lawrence, Mass.: A View of Textiles and Labor Fifty Years Ago," *Cotton History Review*, II (July 1961), 123-131; "The I.W.W. and the Brain Workers," *American Quarterly*, XV (Spring 1963), 41-51.

Few Wobblies, of course, have left "papers," as important historical personages are wont to do. Consequently, the story of the I.W.W. has to be distilled from all the dead passion of its own newspapers and pamphlets and from such official organizational records as are available. But the I.W.W.'s antagonists have also left an equally passionate record, in state and federal government documents, in court records, in the contemporary news coverage of the commercial press and the non-I.W.W. labor press. The author has also gratefully used and acknowledged a number of well-researched monographs by other students which illuminate some tangential matters that still bear upon the I.W.W.'s history, the wartime deportation campaigns, the wartime Loyal Legion of Loggers and Lumbermen, the Haywood murder trial in Caldwell, Idaho, and other matters.

The author also expresses his appreciation to the University of Washington Library; the University of Oregon Library and its Oregon Collection; the University of Minnesota Library; the University of Michigan Library and its Labadie Collection; the Wayne State University Library and its Labor History Archives; the Clerk of the Supreme Court in Olympia, Washington; and Ball State University for tireless interlibrary loan service and some occasional financial help in making research trips. He also thanks the I.W.W. officers and members with whom he was privileged to talk and who helped him so graciously in letters or during his visits to the I.W.W. halls in Seattle and Chicago. He particularly thanks W. H. Westman, Carl Keller, Carlos Cortez, and the late John Kobe of Portland, Oregon.

ROBERT L. TYLER

CONTENTS

CHAPTER I

THE HOBO in the GARDEN

The history of the Industrial Workers of the World in the Pacific Northwest during the early years of the twentieth century is already encrusted by myth and legend. The survivors and the local-color regional writers tell the tale with nostalgia, with that esthetic distance peculiar to the folklorist. They intend, of course, some mute historical interpretation in their romance. They ask us to believe that the days of the Wobblies[1] and the "lumber trust" were good old days of simple issues and direct conflict. In those simpler days, bosses really bossed and workers were really virile Americans, not yet the aspiring Dagwoods nor redundant "other Americans" of today. The antagonists confronted each other honestly, like sheriff and gunman on the street in front of the saloon, without such latter day confusions and obstructions as the Department of Labor, the National Labor Relations Board, the Taft-Hartley Act, and all the rest.

The story of the I.W.W. does indeed return us to simpler days, and it can activate a nostalgic ache of time. But it also, as history rather than folklore, teaches us a sober lesson in cultural thrust and lag. A second- or third-generation frontier society, settling comfortably on its hard-won agrarian base and coalescing around its

---

[1] One version of the origin of this name for I.W.W. members ascribes it to a Chinese restaurant owner in Canada who catered to an I.W.W. clientele and who responded to criticism by saying, "I likee Eye Wobbly Wobbly." Stewart H. Holbrook, "Wobbly Talk," *American Mercury*, (Jan. 1926), p. 62.

aging wagon-train aristocracy, began suddenly in the late nine-teenth century to grow and change.[2] Small-scale agriculture and lumbering that had previously exported modest surpluses by freight wagon, river boat, or windjammer became the new com-mercial agriculture and the complex lumber industry of the twenti-eth century. The population of Washington and Oregon swelled, increasing faster than the population of the nation as a whole. The few original urban centers grew prodigiously, and new towns sprang up almost overnight. Strangers, whom the old settlers would never have encountered on the Oregon Trail—Scandinavi-ans, Finns, Germans by the thousands—poured into the region.[3] Business units and organizations grew in size and complexity. In-vestment capital flowed into the region in the wake of the rail-roads.[4]

As one might expect, the changing society clung to its values of hardy enterprise, agrarian simplicity and equality, self-reliance and individualism. However much this old society welcomed the flesh-pots of "progress" and "growth," it could not help but grow anxi-ous over the cultural changes such progress inevitably wrought. The older values of Jesse Applegate or Dr. David S. Maynard, early Oregon and Washington founders, became, in fact, less and less appropriate to the new urban and industrial society.

The various political protest movements of the turn of the cen-tury had their roots in this change, the Populists with their hyper-sensitivity to Eastern "exploitation," the Progressives with their concern over the threat from both plutocracy and the anarchism of the lower orders, and all the wild array of radicalisms that bloomed and died around the shores of Puget Sound. One protest movement, the I.W.W., appeared in the region during this era and for a brief period during the first world war grew to alarm-ing proportions. I.W.W. members preached the most "advanced" radicalism of the day, an Americanized anarcho-syndicalism, as they closed in combat with the developing capitalism of the Pacific

[2] Dorothy Johansen and Charles M. Gates, *Empire of the Columbia: A History of the Pacific Northwest* (New York, 1957), pp. 383-399.

[3] Oscar Osburn Winther, *The Great Northwest: A History* (New York, 1960), pp. 418-420.

[4] Johansen and Gates, *op. cit.*, p. 460. "The lumber industry thus illus-trates very clearly the way the Pacific Northwest was expanded and changed under the new conditions of industrialism and finance capitalism . . ."

2

Northwest. Yet, ironically, the culture of the I.W.W. revealed much the same agrarian distrust of "nonproducers," much the same frontier ethos of individualism and simple equalitarianism from which sprang its most implacable opposition in small town and rural Washington and Oregon. Both sides, in a curious sense, hearken back to the same ancestral *virtu*. Indeed, a kind of myopic misunderstanding seems to be present—at least from our perspective of fifty years—between the bumptious Wobblies and the local Commercial Club valiants who harried them out of town. The vigilantes, of course, were unaware that a revolution in the economy of their region had fated more drastic change than any the Wobblies would every bring. On the other hand, the Wobblies, preaching doctrines of proletarian solidarity, so apparently "un-American," were unaware that their behavior, their style, reflected the frontier virtues that their enemies also espoused.

Hence, the story of the I.W.W. in the Pacific Northwest is, on one level, a kind of romance with gun battles, manhunts, courtroom and jailhouse drama. This story has its picaresque heroes, its knights of the road, its soap box revolutionaries, its ragged troubadours. But the history of the I.W.W. in the region also reveals how a pioneer American society adapted, with some pain and confusion, to rapid social change. The transformation of an agrarian society by railroads, by large-scale enterprise, by urbanization, by new patterns of hired help and employer, fostered an anxious and violent conservatism and an equally desperate radicalism. The story in this perspective is perhaps a prototype of much of American history in other regions and other eras, a clash of threatened and mythic "Americanism" with a "Bolshevism" of one kind or another. When the first machine marred the American garden before the Civil War, the scene was set for such a social conflict. By the time Westward expansion and settlement had created its myth—later made into a canonical interpretation of all of American history by Frederick Jackson Turner—it had also created the possibilities for the kind of social tensions of which the I.W.W. story in the Pacific Northwest is an example. Perhaps the third generation of any "settlement"[5] in the American experience has within it

---

[5] Professor Mario S. De Pillis of the University of Massachusetts, in a paper delivered at the April 1965 meetings of the Mississippi Valley Historical Association in Kansas City, Missouri, suggested a conceptual change in

the possibility of severe conflict. The hardening "frontier" ideology is confronted suddenly by railroads, by factories, by cities. The "left" responds more or less appropriately with programs to manage the change and to preserve as much as possible of the old values. Some conservatives are tempted to a kind of know-nothing reaction, a defensive hoarding of the old that can find no better outlet in action than violent attacks on the "left."

If the key to understanding both the antagonists of our history is to be found in the rapid social change within the Pacific Northwest after the 1880s, it would be appropriate to look at some of the evidences of that change. In 1880, the population of Oregon was 174,768 and that of Washington, still a Territory, was 175,116.[6] By 1910, only thirty years later, the population of Oregon had increased to almost three-quarters of a million, and that of Washington to over a million.[7] Portland, the undisputed capital of the region in 1880, controlled much of the trade of Washington as well as of Oregon because of its favored position athwart the river traffic of the Columbia and its tributaries.[8] Seattle challenged this pre-eminence in the next two decades. In 1883, the Northern Pacific Railroad, aided by generous federal land grants, made connections with Puget Sound, founding new cities as it came. In the late 1890s, the Alaskan gold rush siphoned people, money, and trade through Seattle.[9] By 1910, Seattle had grown to 237,194, and Portland, hard-pressed, to 207,426.[10] In 1880, the two cities had had populations of only 3,533 and 17,577 respectively.[11]

---

the traditional "History of the West," or "Western Expansion." He suggested rather a "History of Settlement." One interesting field for research in such a new "conceptual field" of American history would be the adaptations of the succeeding generations to the changing social and economic conditions of the "settlement," whether it be Jamestown of 1607 and after, or, presumably, Levittown of the 1940s and after.

[6] *Statistics of the Population of the United States at the Tenth Census, June 1, 1880,* (Washington, 1883), p. 3.

[7] *Thirteenth Census of the United States, Taken in the Year 1910; Abstract of the Census,* (Washington, 1913), p. 24.

[8] Winther, *op. cit.,* p. 195.

[9] Murray Morgan, *Skid Road: An Informal Portrait of Seattle* (New York, 1951), pp. 159-168.

[10] *Thirteenth Census of the United States,* pp. 64, 75.

[11] *Statistics of the Population of the United States at the Tenth Census,* pp. 304, 362.

4

The coming of the railroad, of course, stirred this growth in population, this rapid economic change. The railroad connected the region to the Midwest and, indeed, to the whole rapidly expanding national market that the United States was fast becoming. People and goods could flow more easily in and out of the region. Expanded enterprises became a possibility for the first time. The lumber industry, the fisheries from Alaska to the mouth of the Columbia, the horticulture of the Yakima region and the Hood River valley, the mining industry in Idaho and Montana, grew with the expanding markets, undergoing far-reaching changes in capitalization and organization as they grew.[12]

The I.W.W. in the Pacific Northwest was most active in the lumber industry. Although Wobblies could be found spreading their gospel of discontent among migrant farm workers and hard-rock miners, they worked most numerously in the logging camps and, secondarily, the lumber mills. The lumber industry, consequently, is the principal stage for our story of the I.W.W. This industry—one of the first industries on almost all of America's frontiers—has a history in the Pacific Northwest almost as long as the history of settlement. The Hudson's Bay Company built the first sawmill near Fort Vancouver on the Columbia only a few years after the founding of that fort.[13] In the 1850s, the founding fathers of Seattle came to plan their little town site around the primitive Yesler sawmill, the first industry they succeeded in attracting. Logs came down the first "skid road" from the primeval forests around Seattle to this early waterfront mill.[14] In 1853, the Maine-based firm of Pope and Talbot, merchants, sea captains, and lumbermen, transferred themselves to Puget Sound, bringing the first sophisticated sawmill machinery to the settlement they established at Port Gamble.[15]

This early lumber industry, in the pioneer decades, grew most rapidly on Puget Sound. Exporting lumber was much easier from the placid waters of Puget Sound than it was through the still dangerous bar of the Columbia River's mouth. Primitive operations

---

12 Johansen and Gates, *op. cit.*, pp. 383-399.

13 *Ibid.*, p. 160.

14 Murray Morgan, *op. cit.*, pp. 28-29.

15 Ralph W. Hidy, Frank Ernest Hill, and Allan Nevins, *Timber and Men: The Weyerhaeuser Story* (New York, 1963), p. 217; William B. Greeley, *Forests and Men* (New York, 1951), pp. 158-159.

sufficed to supply the limited local market and the export markets in California and the mining West, in South America or the Sandwich Islands. After falling and bucking, the logs were pulled by horses or oxen, under the profane exhortations of the "bull of the woods," over greased skid roads of logs to nearby sawmills, or to water where they could be floated in rafts to sawmills. By the early twentieth century, logging railroads had been built into some timberlands, extending the range of operations between logging camps and mills. But the typical operation was small, with about a $25,000 capitalization.[16] Nationally, the economic center of the lumber industry still lay in the upper Midwest and Great Lakes region.[17]

But the lumber industry, from New England to Wisconsin, has been a voracious consumer of its raw materials. By 1890, logging operations had ravished most of the virgin timberland of the Great Lakes states. The great lumber tycoon of the Midwest, Frederick Weyerhaeuser, began to look for new timberlands. In 1894 and 1896, upon the invitation of promoters, he visited the South to investigate opportunities in the yellow-pine region. But certain factors—the heat and malaria of the South, for instance—made Weyerhaeuser pass over the resources of the South. In 1900, a group of investors led by Weyerhaeuser purchased 900,000 acres of timberland from the Northern Pacific Railroad, putting down a staggering $5,400,000.[18] A large tract of railroad land grant in Washington thus, for the first time, came under the control of a really large lumber enterprise. Weyerhaeuser became one of the three biggest owners of timberland in the United States, sharing the honor with the Northern Pacific Railroad and the Southern Pacific Railroad. In 1914, the Pacific Northwest held almost half of all the privately owned timberland in the country, and a fourth of that vast empire was owned by these three great landlords.[19]

Until about 1915, none of these great owners made any effort to enter the manufacturing end of the lumber business. Weyerhaeuser, through his newly appointed regional manager, George Smith

---

[16] Johansen and Gates, *op. cit.*, p. 389; Hidy, *et al.*, *op. cit.*, p. 217.

[17] Hidy, *et al.*, *op. cit.*, pp. 143-157.

[18] *Ibid.*, pp. 212-213.

[19] Dept. of Commerce and Labor, Bureau of Corporations, *The Lumber Industry* (Washington, 1913-1914), Vol. I, xx.

Long, continued to buy land, but he built only one sawmill, in Everett, Washington. This mill served mostly as a kind of laboratory for the study of production problems in the new region and with the new and unfamiliar Douglas fir.[20] The principal business interest of these early landlords was speculation in timberland values. In some regions, the value of timberland, virtually worthless in 1900, rose fifty-fold, the increment exceeding comfortably the estimated six per cent cost of taxes, fire protection, and office expense in merely holding the land.[21]

Smaller land owners found themselves controlled by the large holders, or in no position to compete with large owners in the speculative game. If surrounded by railroad or Weyerhaeuser lands, as would most often be the case, the small holder depended upon his rich neighbors for access to outside mills and markets. Also the manufacturing interests, even before Weyerhaeuser himself got into that end of the business, found themselves dependent upon the large owners for their supply of timber. Weyerhaeuser did not take maximum advantage of this particular position of power. George Smith Long sold Weyerhaeuser timber at going market prices to any and all sawmill operators, who, in any case, were by this time accustomed to buying their timber from the railroads.[22]

As large-scale ownership of timberland developed, the milling of Pacific Northwest lumber also expanded. In 1899, only five per cent of the national production of cut lumber was Pacific Coast Douglas fir. By 1911, Douglas fir accounted for 14 per cent. Production of other lumber, spruce, hemlock, and Western pine from the eastern slope of the Cascades, also expanded[23]

The lumber industry was a peculiarly unstable industry in spite of its growth, given to chronic over-production and periodic price crises.[24] In the early 1900s, lumbermen in the Pacific Northwest made the first efforts to organize to combat some of these

---

[20] Hidy, *et al., op. cit.,* pp. 221-222.

[21] U.S. Dept. of Agriculture, Forest Service, Report No. 114, William B. Greeley, *Some Public and Economic Aspects of the Lumber Industry* (Washington, 1917), p. 16.

[22] Bureau of Corporations, *The Lumber Industry,* Vol. I, p. 96; Hidy, *et al., op. cit.,* p. 228.

[23] Bureau of Corporations, *The Lumber Industry,* Vol. III, p. 2.

[24] Greeley, *Some Public and Economic Aspects of the Lumber Industry,* pp. 58-59.

REBELS OF THE WOODS

problems. In 1899, the first loggers' association was organized, the Puget Sound Timbermen's Association. In 1907, it reorganized more carefully as the Washington Log Brokerage Company to avoid breaking the Sherman Anti-Trust Law.[25] In 1900, the South-western Washington Lumber Manufacturers' Association was formed to service primarily the short log industry from Tacoma, Washington, to Portland, Oregon on the Columbia. It published price lists to keep its members informed of the log market and to keep them from being victimized by traveling brokers quoting mis-information about the market. In 1901, the Puget Sound lumbermen organized the Pacific Coast Lumber Manufacturers' Association to publish industry-wide price lists, to establish a system of uniform grades, and to engage in tariff lobbying and other "legislative ac-tion." Also in 1901, the Columbia River and Western Oregon lumbermen organized the Oregon and Washington Lumber Man-ufacturers' Association. In 1911, all these various associations were supplanted by, or subsumed under, the new West Coast Lumber Manufacturers' Association. It set itself the tasks of publishing price lists, lobbying, establishing uniform grades and standards, fighting labor organization. In 1904, 1905, 1909, and 1910 the new associations organized curtailments of production—business-men's strikes, in a sense—to combat price slumps brought on by over-production.[26]

These associations increasingly took on the less-publicized job of combating organized labor. In such an unstable industry, labor had to be supplied as cheaply as possible, and with the least fuss. The last thing any large or small lumber company wanted was to be tied to a labor contract on wage rates, seniority rights, or job security. The ideal labor force was in fact the labor force that ob-tained in the industry before World War I, an army of transients without residential roots that could be hired cheaply when needed and discharged just as easily when not needed, as part-time farmers called "stump ranchers." This working force, made up in large part of "bums," "hoboes," "skid road characters," had one additional advantage: it was disreputable and commanded no feelings of responsibility or paternalism.

It was in this rapidly expanding and changing industry, experi-

---

[25] Bureau of Corporations, *The Lumber Industry*, Vol. III, p. 361.
[26] *Ibid.*, pp. 384-386.

encing its first problems of industry-wide organization, tending toward oligopoly in the ownership of its sources of raw materials, still imbued with an ideology of rugged individualism, that the I.W.W. introduced its troublesome presence. In large part, the I.W.W. objectives and ideology were as romantic and inappropriate as the attitudes of the lumber magnates or their lesser satellites in the region. As a national organization, the I.W.W. cannot be viewed merely as a phenomenon of the Pacific Northwest and its post-frontier industrial revolution. But after a brief look at the founding and refining of the national organization, the reasons for its taking root in the Pacific Northwest should become more apparent.

For over a decade, the Wobblies preached their gospel of the "One Big Union" from corner soap boxes, sang their irreverent songs, badgered law-enforcement officers, and occasionally even fought pitched battles with sheriffs and vigilantes. Although the I.W.W. was formed around the grandiose ambition to organize the entire working class of America, and perhaps even the world, it found its most hospitable reception in the economies of the post-frontier West. From 1909, to the outbreak of World War I it did also threaten to become a force among unskilled, immigrant workers in the East and Midwest. At McKees Rocks, Pennsylvania, in 1909; at Lawrence, Massachusetts, in 1912; at Patterson, New Jersey, in 1913, the I.W.W. conducted brief and famous strikes which, for a few weeks, swelled the membership rolls of the organization. Inability to reconcile practical business unionism with their revolutionary commitment—the essential romanticism of the program—made these strike-born unions short-lived, and they barely survived the particular strikes that had brought them into existence. The I.W.W., as a way of life, caught on only among migratory workers in agriculture, nonferrous mining, and lumbering, that labor force peculiar to a frontier economy in the throes of change from, let us say, a lonely prospector or a new gold rush to the Guggenheim family.

Whatever its practical accomplishments or its spiritual effects upon the American labor movement, the I.W.W. has continued to interest historians, folklorists, and novelists because of its "personality." Zealous, anarchical, and free from middle-class social restraints, Wobblies acted with humor or fanaticism, out of idealis-

9

tic motives or simple malice, but always with dash and spirit. Before the first world war, Wobblies openly advocated sabotage, the term first appearing in their press in 1910.[27] The I.W.W. press thereafter regularly displayed in its cartoons the symbols for sabotage, the wooden shoe or the black cat. When prosecuting attorneys in the many I.W.W. trials presented such cartoons or other editorial incitations as evidence of criminal conspiracy, the I.W.W. defense attorneys explained that everyone misunderstood what the I.W.W. intended by the term sabotage. They explained that the I.W.W. intended nothing more sinister than the withdrawal of the workers' efficiency, nothing more than "ca' canny" or "soldiering" on the job. But the fearful public, perhaps with some justification, continued to think of I.W.W. sabotage as wilful destruction of property and the endangering of human life, setting forest fires, for example, or driving railroad spikes into logs to strip the teeth from saws in lumber mills, or throwing tools into the moving parts of threshing machines. There is a kind of phantom quality to I.W.W. sabotage, more rhetoric than demonstrable deed. Robert Bruère, making a study of the I.W.W. for a New York newspaper during the First World War, could find no hard evidence of Wobbly sabotage. Upon close investigation, it always seemed to be something that had happened to somebody else some other place.[28] In the spate of prosecutions under Criminal Syndicalism laws that followed the first world war, prosecutors never proved a single instance of I.W.W. sabotage.[29] The National Civil Liberties Bureau, later to become the American Civil Liberties Union, claimed that nothing except its egregrious cartoons and editorials could be held against the I.W.W. and that its record for committing acts of sabotage was no worse than that of any militant union in the American Federation of Labor.[30]

The I.W.W. also upon occasion fell back on coercion in its organizing drives, using a tactic called "box car recruiting" that

[27] *Solidarity*, June 4, 1910.

[28] Robert Bruère, "The Industrial Workers of the World," *Harper's* (July 1918), p. 256.

[29] Eldridge Foster Dowell, *A History of Criminal Syndicalism Legislation in the United States* (Baltimore, 1939), p. 36.

[30] National Civil Liberties Bureau, *Memorandum Regarding the Prosecution of the Radical Labor Movement in the United States* (New York, 1919), p. 4.

made the "red card" of membership a necessary ticket for any transient travelling on railroad freight cars in the West. Novices, or "scissorbills," who tried to ride without that evidence of I.W.W. membership, risked being thrown off the trains.[31] The headquarters in Chicago piously frowned on this tactic and insisted it wanted only voluntary members, but it could obviously do little to stop the practice even if it had been determined to do so.

The I.W.W. advertised itself in a raucous press. It published two principal newspapers, *Solidarity* in Chicago and the *Industrial Worker* in the Pacific Northwest. District branches from New York to San Francisco also published smaller, more ephemeral bulletins and news sheets, and during World War I, regional "defense committees" published bulletins and pamphlets to replace suppressed newspapers and to publicize the plight of "class war prisoners." After the war, two monthly periodicals served the organization as journals of opinion, the *One Big Union Monthly* and its successor, the *Industrial Pioneer*. The I.W.W. also supported an extensive foreign-language press, especially during the brief period before the war when it reached out to organize the masses of unskilled and immigrant workers in the East. At one time or another, the I.W.W. published newspapers in Russian, Yiddish, Finnish, Swedish, Italian, Spanish, Polish, and Slovenian. As late as the 1950s, it still published a Finnish newspaper in Duluth, Minnesota, and a Hungarian newspaper in Cleveland, Ohio.[32]

Black headlines in almost every issue of *Solidarity* or the *Industrial Worker* warned of some "frame-up" under way in a bourgeois court. The press appealed almost continually for contributions to all manner of "defense funds," and almost every month the I.W.W. had at least one martyr sitting in prison, appealing to the solidarity of the working class to win freedom for him. The number of such martyrs multiplied so rapidly during the anti-radical campaigns of World War I that the I.W.W. established special committees and published special bulletins to keep track of them all. Besides publicizing the plight of "class war" victims, the I.W.W. press also published its characteristic cartoons, glorifying a sturdy

---

[31] Nels Anderson, *The Hobo: The Sociology of the Homeless Man* (Chicago, 1923), p. 232; Philip Taft, "The I.W.W. in the Grain Belt," *Labor History* (Winter 1960), pp. 53-67.

[32] *Industrial Worker*, July 11, 1952, p. 2; The two newspapers were the *Industrialisti* and the *Bermunkas*.

workman who belabored serpents of capitalism with a formidable club labeled "I.W.W." from behind a shield labeled "organization" or "solidarity," or picturing the archetypical workman striding up a path labeled "solidarity" toward a sunrise labeled "cooperative commonwealth" while the devils of capitalism lurking in the shadows beside the path prevail against him naught. The newspapers also featured a comic strip that pictured the durable stupidity of "Mr. Block," a square-headed worker who tenaciously held to his conviction that he and his employer shared economic interests in spite of his regular disillusionments and the persistent but apparently futile advice of a sophisticated Wobbly.

Out of their rootlessness, the Wobblies invented a startling new way to harass the "master class." The "free speech fight" added martyrs to their hagiography and exasperated the authorities and respectable citizens of a dozen towns and cities of the West. In the free-speech fight, Wobblies flooded into a town to violate an ordinance prohibiting street meetings. When thrown in jail and presumably put *hors de combat*, they continued their agitation. They enraged their jailers by staging noisily-advertised hunger strikes over real or fancied mistreatment, and they "built battleships," making deafening uproars by pounding, rattling, and shouting in protest over their treatment. Although it was not their purpose to be prison reformers, they did on a few occasions publicize unsavory conditions and induce respectable citizens to make changes. The Wobblies defended their free-speech tactic as a practical necessity. The organization had to recruit most of its members on the run, so to speak, and soap-box meetings in cities' skid-road districts accomplished that purpose. Open street meetings, therefore, had to be defended against restrictive ordinances and unfriendly sheriffs and city policemen. But, as revolutionaries, the Wobblies also knew that free-speech fights were provocative of repressive violence by the "master class" and hence eminently educational.

The I.W.W. probably revealed its roguish personality most fully in its songs, for it was famed as a singing organization. The I.W.W. song book—affectionately called "the little red song book" —has gone through numerous editions.[33] Joe Hill, a Wobbly "martyr" convicted of murder and executed by firing squad in Utah, wrote many of the most popular I.W.W. songs, and at least

---

[33] *I.W.W. Songs to Fan the Flames of Discontent* (Chicago, 1945).

one of them, "The Preacher and the Slave," sung to the tune of "In the Sweet Bye and Bye," attained almost universal renown. A phrase from it, "pie in the sky," has become part of the treasury of ordinary American speech.[34]

> Long-haired preachers come out every night,
> Try to tell you what's wrong and what's right,
> But when asked how 'bout something to eat
> They will answer with voices so sweet:
>
> Chorus:
>
> You will eat, bye and bye,
> In that glorious land above the sky;
> Work and pray, live on hay,
> You'll get pie in the sky when you die.
>
> And the Starvation Army they play,
> And they sing and they clap and they pray.
> Till they get all your coin on the drum,
> Then they tell you when you're on the bum:
>
> Chorus:
>
> Workingmen of all countries unite,
> Side by side we for freedom will fight:
> When the world and its wealth we have gained
> To the grafters we'll sing this refrain:
>
> Last Chorus:
>
> You will eat, bye and bye.
> When you've learned how to cook and to fry;
> Chop some wood, 'twill do you good,
> And you'll eat in the sweet bye and bye.

Another of Joe Hill's lyrics, "Casey Jones—The Union Scab," sung to the tune of "Casey Jones," attained some popularity among Wobblies.[35]

> The workers on the S. P. line to strike sent out a call;
> But Casey Jones, the engineer, he wouldn't strike at all;
> His boiler it was leaking, and its drivers on the bum,
> And his engine and its bearings, they were all out of plumb.

---

[34] *Ibid.,* p. 9. [35] *Ibid.,* p. 46.

REBELS OF THE WOODS

Chorus:

Casey Jones kept his junk pile running;
Casey Jones was working double time;
Casey Jones got a wooden medal,
For being good and faithful on the S. P. line.

The remainder of the song tells of the I.W.W.'s sabotage of Casey Jones's engine, his descent into hell, and the ignominous tasks there assigned him because he had "scabbed" during the Southern Pacific strike.

Chorus:

Casey Jones went to Hell a-flying.
"Casey Jones," the devil said, "Oh, fine;
Casey Jones, get busy shoveling sulphur—
That's what you get for scabbing on the S. P. line."

Ralph Chaplin, the Wobbly poet with perhaps the most pretensions to literary quality, wrote one song, "Solidarity," that has rivaled the songs of Joe Hill in popularity. It won recognition outside the I.W.W., and has become the virtual anthem of the labor movement. It is sung to the tune of "John Brown's Body."[36]

When the Union's inspiration through the workers' blood
    shall run,
There can be no power greater anywhere beneath the sun.
Yet what force on earth is weaker than the feeble strength
    of one ?
        But the Union makes us strong!

Chorus:

Solidarity forever!
Solidarity forever!
Solidarity forever!
For the Union makes us strong.

Wobblies sang many of their songs to the tunes of familiar hymns, a practice that undoubtedly increased their horrendous reputation. As transients, they learned most of the common evangelical hymns from their close propinquity to skid-road missions and street-corner evangelists. As street-corner agitators them-

---

[36] *Ibid.,* p. 10.

14

selves, they often had to compete with the Salvation Army or the Volunteers of America for audiences. The song, "Dump the Bosses Off Your Back," sung sweetly to the tune of "Take It to the Lord in Prayer," exemplifies their sacrilegious mimicking of hymns.[37]

> Are you poor, forlorn and hungry?
>   Are there lots of things you lack?
> Is your life made up of misery?
>   Then dump the bosses off your back.
>
> Are your clothes all patched and tattered?
>   Are you living in a shack?
> Would you have your troubles scattered?
>   Then dump the bosses off your back.

Another such Wobbly "hymn," "Christians at War," sung to the tune of "Onward, Christian Soldiers," expressed the anti-militarism of the Left and Wobblies' contempt for the hypocrisy of the "master class."[38]

> Onward, Christian soldiers! Duty's way is plain;
> Slay your Christian neighbors, or by them be slain.
> Pulpiteers are spouting effervescent swill,
> God above is calling you to rob and rape and kill,
> All your acts are sanctified by the Lamb on high;
> If you love the Holy Ghost, go murder, pray and die.
>
> Onward, Christian soldiers, rip and tear and smite!
> Let the gentle Jesus bless your dynamite.
> Splinter skulls with shrapnel, fertilize the sod;
> Folks who do not speak your tongue deserve the curse of God.
> Smash the doors of every house, pretty maidens seize;
> Use your might and sacred right to treat them as you please.
>
> Onward, Christian soldiers! Blighting all you meet,
> Trampling human freedom under pious feet.
> Praise the Lord whose dollar-sign dupes his favored race!
> Make the foreign trash respect your bullion brand of grace.
> Trust in mock salvation, serve as pirates' tools;
> History will say of you: "That pack of G— d— fools."

Many I.W.W. songs sounded an extremely sardonic note. Wobblies viewed "liberal" or "American" ideals with unconcealed

---

[37] *Ibid.,* p. 11.   [38] *Ibid.,* p. 12.

REBELS OF THE WOODS

cynicism because, as hoboes, they encountered the ideals put into practice by jailers, sheriffs, vigilantes, railroad detectives, and self-righteous small town burghers. T-Bone Slim, a popular Wobbly troubadour and journalist, mixed this cynicism with humors in a song called "The Popular Wobbly," sung to the tune of "They Go Wild, Simply Wild Over Me."[39]

> I'm as mild manner'd man as can be
> And I've never done them harm that I can see,
> Still on me they put a ban and they throw me in the can,
> They go wild, simply wild over me.
>
> Oh the jailer, he went wild over me,
> And he locked me up and threw away the key—
> It seems to be the rage so they keep me in a cage,
> They go wild, simply wild over me.
>
> Will the roses grow wild over me
> When I'm gone into the land that is to be?
> When my soul and body part in the stillness of my heart,
> Will the roses grow wild over me?

More than a few I.W.W. songs reveal a sentimentality verging on outright mawkishness, perhaps a characteristic to be expected in extroverted activists when they become "serious." Joe Hill's "The Rebel Girl" is such a sentimental ballad,[40] and Joe Hill in particular could be guilty of such lapses into "tear-jerking."

> There are women of many descriptions
> In this queer world, as everybody knows,
> Some are living in beautiful mansions,
> And are wearing the finest of clothes.
> There are blue-blooded queens and princesses,
> Who have charms made of diamonds and pearl;
> But the only and Thoroughbred Lady
> Is the Rebel Girl.

[39] *Ibid.*, p. 37. This song has been adapted by the Student Nonviolent Coordinating Committee of the Civil Rights Movement for its uses, and in this version may be found in: Guy and Candy Carawan, *We Shall Overcome* (New York, 1963). T-Bone Slim was the pen name of Matt Valentine Huhta. He died in 1942 while on duty as a barge captain on the Hudson River. Joyce L. Kornbluh, editor, *Rebel Voices: An I.W.W. Anthology* (Ann Arbor, Mich., 1964), p. 84.

[40] *I.W.W. Songs . . .*, *op. cit.*, p. 5.

Chorus:

That's the Rebel Girl. That's the Rebel Girl.
To the working class she's a precious pearl.
She brings courage, pride and joy
To the Fighting Rebel Boy.
We've had girls before
But we need some more
In the Industrial Workers of the World,
For it's great to fight for freedom
With a Rebel Girl.

This group of zestful revolutionaries, with their rowdy songs, did not spring into existence overnight but evolved over a period of several years from a more inclusive and representative organization. After the founding of the American Federation of Labor in the 1880s, many American radicals in the labor movement watched its progress with little enthusiasm. Class-conscious socialists wished a more radical program of unionism for the working class, and other radicals believed that industrial unionism could better serve the workers in an industrial society. Some radicals made peace with things as they were, worked within the A.F.L. and strove during its annual conventions to commit it to a more radical program. Their policy of infiltration came to be called "boring from within."[41] Other radicals could not abide such expediency and urged instead a policy of "dual unionism," or the founding of radical unions rival to the existing A.F.L. unions.[42] In 1895, for example, the Socialist Labor Party founded its satellite Socialist Trade and Labor Alliance for socialist workers. It was scarcely a success, recruiting only a few hundred members who were already members of the Socialist Labor Party.[43] Striking miners in Idaho, while in jail, established the Western Federation of Miners, an industrial union that frankly endorsed the socialist "class struggle" doctrine.[44]

[41] Max Hayes, editor of the "Voice of Labor" feature in the *International Socialist Review;* Victor Berger, prominent Milwaukee Socialist leader; William Z. Foster, founder of a little Syndicalist League in 1912 and later head of the American Communist Party, were only a few of the radicals who advocated "boring from within."

[42] Morris Hillquit, *History of Socialism in the United States* (New York, 1906), p. 302.

[43] *Ibid.*

[44] Selig Pearlman and Philip Taft, *American Labor Movements*, Vol. IV of John R. Commons, *et al., History of Labor in the United States* (4 vols.; New York, 1926-1935), pp. 172-173.

For over a decade, it conducted violent strikes throughout the non-ferrous mining region of the Rocky Mountains. In its setting of a frontier economy undergoing large-scale reorganization with Eastern capital, with its propensity to violence, with its literal-minded acceptance of the "class struggle" idea, the Western Federation of Miners is a clear prototype of the I.W.W. Eugene Debs organized his American Railway Union in the 1890s as a militant industrial union, rival to the conservative railroad brotherhoods.[45]

These and other dissident unionists realized that their competing unions could be justified only if they someday supplanted the A.F.L. entirely. Radicals began to discuss the need for a national organization of industrial unions strong enough to replace the A.F.L. William Trautmann, editor of the Brewery Workers' journal, *Brauer Zeitung,* early discussed the need for a national "dual union" in his editorials.[46] The Western Federation of Miners also recognized that it needed a broader base, including nonminers, for successful competition with the A.F.L., and it created its own general federations, the Western Labor Union in 1898 and the American Labor Union in 1902.[47] Neither of these general federations were much more successful than the Socialist Trade and Labor Alliance in the East, an analogous organization.

In January 1905, after years of informal discussion and planning, about thirty union leaders and radicals met in Chicago to lay the foundation for a new national labor organization. Calling themselves the Conference of Industrial Unionists, they published a manifesto, belaboring the A.F.L. and listing the principles for sound, radical industrial unionism. They called upon all like-minded unionists to attend a formal constitutional convention in June.[48]

> Social relations and groupings only reflect mechanical and industrial conditions. The *great facts* of present industry are the displacement of human skill by machines and the increase of capitalist power through concentration . . .

[45] Hillquit, *History of Socialism,* p. 323.

[46] Louis Levine, "The Development of Syndicalism in America," *Political Science Quarterly,* XXVIII (Sept. 1913), p. 461.

[47] *Ibid.,* p. 459.

[48] "Manifesto of the Conference of Industrial Unionists," in Daniel De Leon, "Socialist Reconstruction of Society," *Speeches and Editorials,* Vol. I (New York, n.d.), pp. 59-62.

Because of these facts trade divisions among laborers and competition among capitalists are alike disappearing. Class divisions grow more fixed and class antagonisms more sharp . . .

Universal economic evils afflicting the working class can be eradicated only by a universal working class movement . . .[49]

Two hundred and three delegates answered the call to write the constitution for the new labor union, which they named the Industrial Workers of the World. William D. Haywood of the Western Federation of Miners brought the convention to order by pounding on a table with a piece of wood and announcing, "Fellow workers, this is the Continental Congress of the working class . . ."[50]

Although all the delegates shared a common purpose and agreed upon a few common principles, they differed from each other in temperament and background, and in the radical orthodoxies they embraced. In many ways, it was like any "unity" convention of the Left before or after. Only a hundred of the delegates, slightly less than half, actually represented functioning labor unions, most of them insignificant in the main stream of the American labor movement. Some of the delegates represented only "paper organization" with ambitious programs and radical constitutions but few actual members. A few delegates came from disgruntled Socialist-controlled locals of international unions within the A.F.L. Some came empowered to install their unions in the new I.W.W. immediately; others came inspired only by a general sympathy with the Manifesto of the Conference of Industrial Unionists but without the express power to enter their unions as charter members of the new I.W.W.[51] Sixty of the delegates represented no unions at all but came as invited "individual delegates." They had received invitations because of their prominence in the labor and radical movements. Eugene Debs came as an "individual delegate," as did A. M. Simons, the socialist editor; "Mother" Jones, the almost legendary organizer of the coal miners; and Lucy Parsons, the widow of one of the anarchists executed after the Haymarket Riot of 1886.[52]

---

[49] *Proceedings of the First Annual Convention of the Industrial Workers of the World* (New York, 1905), p. 204.

[50] *Ibid.*, p. 1.

[51] *Ibid.*, p. 54.　　　　[52] *Ibid.*

The two most influential delegations also represented the hetero-geneity of the convention. The Western Federation of Miners sent a delegation of five men to represent its 27,000 members, and two of its delegates, Vincent St. John and William D. Haywood, subse-quently became two of the most widely known national leaders of the I.W.W. The much smaller Socialist Trade and Labor Alliance, claiming only 1,600 members, sent a delegation of fourteen men led by Daniel De Leon, the oracle and prophet of the Socialist Labor Party. Haywood and St. John, miners by occupation and activists by temperament, expressed their radical beliefs in scarcely more than slogans, and needed no more. Haywood's memoirs reveal no theorist or philosopher of revolution but rather a simple man of simple beliefs and a considerable gift for practical leadership.[53] De Leon, on the other hand, was an intellectual, a lawyer by train-ing and a graduate of the University of Leyden, who had lectured on international law at Columbia University before his conversion to Marxism. Inept at the kind of leadership at which St. John or Haywood excelled, he tended to make either bitter foes or worship-ful disciples out of the radicals who worked with him. He pressed his viewpoint with "Talmudic logic," telling sarcasm, and a culti-vated but biting wit. He insisted upon doctrinal purity in the organizations he dominated.[54] Although the simple radicalism of Haywood came to the same practical conclusions as the involuted intellections of De Leon, the temperamental and intellectual gap was enormous.

Enthusiasm for the immediate job at hand and their common belief in a few basic principles welded the delegates together and carried them through the task of constitution-making. The I.W.W. entered the labor movement as a centralized organization of pro-posed industrial unions under an executive board in Chicago. The founders planned thirteen industrial "departments" into which the entire working class could someday be organized, and each of the departments was to include a number of national industrial unions. The elaborate organizational blueprint, however, never really func-tioned during the life of the I.W.W. Most Wobblies belonged to virtually autonomous industrial unions or were simply "members at large." During the *floruit* of the organization only one indus-

---

[53] William D. Haywood, *Bill Haywood's Book* (New York, 1929).
[54] Morris Hillquit, *Loose Leaves from a Busy Life* (New York, 1934), p. 46.

trial union, the Agricultural Workers' Organization, included most of the members, including the lumber workers of our story. But the I.W.W. theorists kept the blueprint and treasured it. Graphically represented in the form of a wheel diagram, it was there and ready for the day when the entire proletariat should flock into the I.W.W.[55]

The wheel diagram was the work of Father Thomas J. Hagerty, editor of the American Labor Union's newspaper and a delegate from that somewhat attenuated body. Although his archbishop had suspended him in 1892 for his support of a miners' strike, Hagerty claimed that he had never been defrocked or excommunicated and that he was still a priest of the church, albeit inactive to say the least. As chairman of the constitution committee of the convention in 1905, Hagerty also drafted the famous preamble to the I.W.W. constitution with its implacable "the working class and the employing class have nothing in common."[56]

From the beginning, the I.W.W. imposed severe restrictions upon its constituent unions to make sure that they would never cast aside revolutionary principles simply to facilitate practical business unionism. Unions could not require high initiation fees nor charge exhorbitant dues, and they had to accept I.W.W. membership cards as interchangeable from union to union. They were forbidden to make time contracts with employers, and they could not elect officials to the same office in consecutive years. Officials got paid only the equivalent of the average wages in their regular occupations.[57]

This new labor union, national and even international in its ambitions, almost immediately began to evolve into that special society of transient workers we shall see in operation in the lumber industry of the Pacific Northwest. In 1906, at the second convention, most of the Socialist Party members and the realistic unionists left the organization after the convention had deposed C. O. Sherman, the Secretary-President, and had abolished the office. The majority,

[55] Samuel Gompers referred to the wheel diagram contemptuously as "Father Hagerty's wheel of fortune." *Seventy Years of Life and Labor: An Autobiography* (New York, 1925), Vol. I, p. 425.

[56] Robert E. Doherty, "Thomas J. Hagerty, The Church, and Socialism," *Labor History* (Winter 1962), p. 53.

[57] Vincent St. John, *The I.W.W.: Its History, Structure and Methods* (Chicago, 1917), pp. 14-15.

calling themselves the "proletarian rabble,"[58] charged Sherman with mismanaging office funds, with corruption in office, and with betraying the revolutionary purpose of the I.W.W. Sherman had spent over seven thousand dollars during his year in office for travel and operating expenses. Wobblies thought that he must have viewed the I.W.W. as some ordinary business union and himself as a typical "labor leader" to have squandered proletarian funds so callously.[59] Sherman and his supporters locked up the I.W.W. headquarters in Chicago and, with the aid of the police, kept the majority faction out. The bourgeois courts decided the dispute in favor of the majority faction, and Sherman took his followers to Joliet, Illinois, where he founded a rival and short-lived I.W.W. of his own.[60] Nobody evinced much dismay at the time that the courts of the "master class" had come to the defense of the "proletarian rabble."

The Western Federation of Miners, the only functioning union within the I.W.W. with a significant membership, supported Sherman in the dispute, and in protest, withdrew from the I.W.W. The arrest of Haywood, a leader of both the W.F.M. and the I.W.W., for the murder of ex-Governor Frank Steunenberg of Idaho, also induced the W.F.M. to cut loose from Haywood and the I.W.W. Harry Orchard, born Albert E. Horsley, confessed to the actual bombing of the front gate of Steunenberg's home in Caldwell, Idaho, but he claimed that an "inner circle" of W.F.M. leaders had put him up to it, a small body of conspirators that included Haywood, Charles Moyer, and George Pettibone. The police arrested the three men on the basis of Harry Orchard's allegations and spirited them from Colorado to Idaho without benefit of extradition proceedings—"kidnapped" them, their defenders charged. Clarence Darrow successfully defended Haywood in a famous trial in 1907. After his acquittal Haywood resigned from the W.F.M., not without sighs of relief from that organization. The miners, in their 1907 convention, then fastidiously severed their connections with the I.W.W. Both the Sherman ouster and the embarrassing

[58] Paul F. Brissenden, *The I.W.W.: A Study of American Syndicalism* (New York, 1919), p. 136.

[59] Rudolph Katz, "With De Leon Since '89," *Daniel De Leon, the Man and His Work: A Symposium* (New York, 1934), p. 122. This biography appeared originally in the *Weekly People* before the First World War.

[60] *Ibid.*, p. 125.

notoriety of Haywood and his new associates, influenced the decision of the W.F.M.[61]

After Sherman and his supporters left, an uneasy coalition of Western transient workers and doctrinaire members of the Socialist Labor Party under De Leon controlled the I.W.W. In 1908, De Leon and his disciples left the I.W.W. The delegates to the 1908 convention barred De Leon on a technicality, claiming that he should have come as a delegate from a printing-workers' union instead of as a delegate from an office-workers' union.[62] The so-called "overalls brigade" from the Pacific Northwest controlled the convention. This delegation of "real" proletarians had assembled in Portland, Oregon, under the leadership of Jack Walsh, a local soap-box orator. The twenty delegates had assumed a kind of uniform of denim overalls and red bandana handkerchiefs and had proceeded to Chicago via box car, making stops in Centralia, Tacoma, Seattle, Missoula, and points east to conduct street meetings to pass the hat and collect money. In Chicago they slept on park benches near Lake Michigan.[63]

These delegates from the Pacific Northwest charged that De Leon wanted to capture the I.W.W. and make it an adjunct to the Socialist Labor Party just as the Socialist Trade and Labor Alliance had been. This issue of political socialism and the I.W.W. at the convention was a real issue, but both sides, De Leon and the anarchical delegates, exaggerated it out of all proportion. The Westerners—the "slummists" or "bummery," as De Leon contemptuously called them—eschewed political action entirely. They advocated only strikes, "direct action," sabotage on the economic front. They believed that carrying on political activity inevitably corrupted revolutionary zeal, that it implied a tacit agreement to carry on the struggle within the forms and according to the rules of the "master class." Their anarchism sprang somewhat from their condition of life as homeless and disfranchised transients and perhaps, by this time, from a second or third-hand knowledge of the ideas of European syndicalism. The De Leon faction, on the other

---

[61] The most recent study of the Steunenberg murder case is: David H. Grover, *Debaters and Dynamiters: The Story of the Haywood Trial* (Corvallis, Ore., 1964).

[62] Katz, *op. cit.*, p. 152.

[63] Daniel De Leon, "The I.W.W. Convention," *Weekly People*, Oct. 3, 1908; *Industrial Union Bulletin*, Sept. 19, 1908.

hand, defended political action as a necessary expedient pending the actual destruction of capitalism and the bourgeois state.[64] But the temperamental differences between the Western delegates and De Leon counted for as much in the dispute as did the actual small kernel of ideological differences. With his Van Dyke beard, his sarcasm, his aristocratic air, De Leon antagonized the cruder, intensely class-conscious delegates from the West.

After expelling De Leon, the Westerners proceeded to amend the constitution of the I.W.W. They thought that certain phrases in the preamble to the constitution had been the loopholes through which De Leon had intended to infiltrate and capture the organization. The Wobblies eliminated the one brief reference to political action from the following part of the preamble: [65]

> Between these two classes a struggle must go on until the toilers come together *on the political,* as well as the industrial field, and take hold of that which they produce by their labor through an organization of the working class . . .

With this relatively minor change in its constitution, a change nevertheless summing up many bitter personal and ideological differences, the I.W.W. emerged as a more homogeneous body of radicals. The group interests of the "overalls brigade," or its allies, thereafter remained dominant, and despite the catholic pretensions of the name, the I.W.W. became more and more typically a society of Western migratory workers.

But this evolution of the I.W.W. into a peculiarly Western movement, with a rawness to match the rawness of the capitalism it was to combat, did not come about simply through a number of changes in its program and wording of its constitution. The changes and the refining schisms accompanied and reflected an evolution in the spirit of the organization, an adaptation to the culture of its most typical members. The constitutional convention of 1905— "composed prevailingly of a body of men socialistically inclined"[66] —had considered industrial unionism the natural expression of the "class struggle" of their socialist ideology. The later hyper-radical-

---

[64] Daniel De Leon, "Socialist Reconstruction of Society," *Speeches and Editorials* (New York, 1934), vol. I, p. 39.

[65] Brissenden, *op. cit.,* Appendix II.

[66] Robert Franklin Hoxie, *Trade Unionism in the United States* (New York, 1919), p. 151.

ism of the I.W.W., with its policy of low initiation fees, inter-changeable membership cards, and "rank-and-file" rule, appealed to only one part of the American working class, a group that, once attracted, came to possess the I.W.W. and to impress its unique culture upon it. The founders had considered their principles sound for the entire working class; in effect, only Western migratory workers adopted the principles enthusiastically.

As the exploitative industries of the West—lumber, mining, agri-culture—lost their makeshift and transitory frontier characteristics, they needed a suddenly expanded supply of wage workers, a labor army recruited in large part from hoboes and migrants. This reservoir of workers, unskilled or semi-skilled, made up of young, homeless men and unattached immigrants, followed seasonal occu-pations, harvesting wheat from Oklahoma to Canada, logging in the "short log" territory east of the Cascades or the "long log" territory west of the Cascades, maintaining the grades of the great transcontinental railroads, or mining silver, lead, or copper in the Rocky Mountain mining states. At the end of the working season—or even off and on during the working season—they accumulated modest "stakes" from their pay and tried to survive till the next job. With as little as thirty dollars in their "stakes,"[67] they drifted into the cities of the upper Midwest and the West, congregating in the "flophouse" districts of Chicago, Minneapolis, Spokane, Seattle, Portland, and San Francisco. They supplemented their savings when necessary with the charity of souplines and skid road missions. Chicago usually played host to forty to sixty thousand every winter. Seattle could expect five to seven thousand, and in some years as many as thirteen thousand.[68]

These transients found the I.W.W. a congenial organization; the low initiation fees and dues did not tax their meager and irregu-lar incomes. Interchangeable membership cards permitted them to remain in the organization even when making their sometimes bewildering changes in jobs. The rejection of political action fitted their condition because they never voted and had no obvious "stake in society." The I.W.W.'s militant and radical philosophy, more-

---

[67] Carleton H. Parker, "The Casual Laborer," in *The Casual Laborer and Other Essays* (New York, 1920), p. 80.

[68] Robert S. Wilson, *Community Planning for Homeless Men and Boys: The Experience of Sixteen Cities in the Winter of 1930-1931* (New York, 1931), pp. 29, 112.

over, gave outlet and meaning to otherwise bitter and abnormal lives. From the I.W.W., they got the comforting assurance that they were the salt of the earth and the favored of history, that out of their anger and their aspirations for a better life, the inevitable cooperative commonwealth would blossom.

Probably most transient workers became Wobblies at one time or another during their careers, either enthusiastically or because of coercive "box-car recruiting." But the dedicated Wobbly, the member remaining loyal even during the periods of calm between free-speech fights or wildcat strikes, was an uncommon creature even among the hoboes. Then as now, the life of the road attracted many people cast off from more respectable society. The ranks of the migratory workers included a disproportionate number of feeble-minded, neurotic runaways from middle-class homes, wife-deserters, unattached aliens, and the variously deracinated. The committed Wobbly in this group was frequently the untutored intellectual who spent as much of his time of idleness in the public library as he did in the bar or brothel. Such Wobblies, on the soap box, interlarded their speeches with citations to Victor Hugo or Herbert Spencer. They displayed formidable memories for statistics on American industries. One University of Wisconsin professor, who lived and worked with Wobblies in the wheat fields for a season, reported a Wobbly who had memorized the entire *Communist Manifesto*, who could quote extensively from other Marxist works, and who showed considerable familiarity with the ideas of Ruskin, Carlyle, Morris, and other Victorian social critics.[69] The I.W.W. halls usually contained libraries of dog-eared copies of Darwin, Spencer, Voltaire, Tom Paine, and assorted government documents.

The I.W.W. halls in the West became something more than mere union halls. They served as social clubs, dormitories, mess halls, and mail drops. The I.W.W. established them in the low-rent districts of Western towns and cities, near the railroad stations, the missions, the brothels and the cheap saloons. On the door of a typical store-front hall, the local officials emblazoned the emblem of the I.W.W., and behind the glass of the large windows, they displayed recent issues of socialist and I.W.W. periodicals and

---

[69] D. D. Lescohier, "With the I.W.W. in the Wheat Lands," *Harper's*, (Aug. 1923), p. 375.

newspapers. Inside the hall, Wobblies arranged their battered furniture, perhaps a piano that had seen previous service in a saloon, a roll-top desk, some tables and chairs, and a few spittoons. Entering a hall in the evening, a visitor might see several shabbily dressed young men crouched over the stove brewing a mulligan stew, its ambiguous odors permeating the hall. While they poked and stirred their supper they might argue heatedly some point in economics or theology. A musical Wobbly played I.W.W. songs on the piano while others unrolled their "bindles," or blanket rolls, on the floor to sleep.[70]

The I.W.W. thus fulfilled more needs of its members than did any ordinary labor union. To the migratory worker—"an invert to half the stimuli of conventional life"[71]—the I.W.W. supplied a home, friendships, and a sense of belonging somewhere. When the Westerners expelled De Leon and drove the Socialists away, when they deposed Sherman, when they tinkered with the constitution to ban all political activity, they acted not simply to purify the program of the I.W.W., but also to possess it and to rid it of elements not sharing their culture.

The founders in 1905 had never considered the possibility that their identification of industrial unionism with revolution might be belied by the facts of the American social environment. For them the only obstacle to the successful winning of the class struggle in America was the conservative craft unionism of the A.F.L. Neither did it occur to the western Wobblies after 1908 that successful industrial unionism might require the same practical, unrevolutionary tactics employed by the disdained A.F.L. Industrial unionism they viewed too simply as the natural expression of the class struggle, and the class struggle was a central tenet not to be questioned. So the I.W.W. worked assiduously for both goals, immediate industrial unionism and revolution, but found itself frustrated in reaching either goal. When they failed to create durable unions, Wobblies did not re-examine their doctrines. They did not decide to scrap their revolutionary goal and organize "business unions," nor conversely did they decide to give up their goal of unionism

---

[70] Photographs or descriptions of I.W.W. halls appear many places in the I.W.W.'s press: *Lumber Workers' Bulletin*, Nov. 1, 1922, p. 2; *Industrial Worker*, June 30, 1917, p. 1; *International Socialist Review*, (Oct. 1912), p. 375; and elsewhere.

[71] Carlton H. Parker, *op. cit.*

to become more purely a revolutionary elite, a kind of American Bolsheviki. Like doctrinaires, they resisted the facts and transformed their inappropriate beliefs into dogma. For a decade, the sheer momentum of their enthusiasm overcame the friction of reality. A special environment, particularly in the West, permitted them an intoxicating notoriety that also shielded them from reality. As opposition grew more and more violent, especially during the first world war, the I.W.W. decayed and retreated into its dogma, making an amazing *volte face* from irrepressible activism to crotchety inaction.

Thus we have set the stage, the changing pioneer society of the Pacific Northwest. We have introduced the characters, new-style entrepreneurs and employers such as Weyerhaeuser and his retainers, the old settlers with their traditional myths, and the Wobblies trying to make sense out of their frustrating lives through an ideology of class conflict and revenge. The history of their conflicts is sometimes difficult to get straight. All the eye-witnesses are, of course, violent partisans, subject at any moment to perjury or wild exaggeration, whether they be I.W.W. pamphlet writers or writers for the Seattle *Times*. Because the violence of word and deed occurred so long ago, the historian is tempted to strike some attitude of amused dispassion, to admit all the claims of all the sides and to compromise by making a safe romance. Another temptation is to slip into belated partisanship, to praise or blame, to egg on the brave Wobblies or, from the other side, to cheer the vigilantes defending the decencies against attacks by the *Lumpen-Proletariat*. Another temptation is to attempt an antiseptic understanding, to make a behavioral analysis of data collected, as it were, with tweezers. But history must somehow reconstruct the emotional tone, the existential immediacy of the past if it is to be true to its *métier*. The assumption—or perhaps presumption—of this work is that from the testimony of angry witnesses, not always conflicting as to matters of brute fact, the actuality may be glimpsed and understanding need not preclude a critical empathy.

28

CHAPTER II

A
TIME
OF
TESTING

The I.W.W. appeared in the Pacific Northwest within a year of its founding, and almost from the beginning the Wobbly displayed there those traits that won for him his horrendous reputation. His contentiousness, activism, and propensity to violence early evoked concern. De Leon certainly had those traits in mind when he derogated the "overalls brigade" as the "bummery." Not De Leon alone, but the radical press also, came to fix a conception of the Western Wobbly as a troublesome anarchist. A commentator in *Solidarity*, calling himself "Sin-Bad," lamented the increasing importance of this typical Wobbly in the organization. Vagrants, he charged, lacked the self-discipline of the revolutionary, and they probably drove away more stable and valuable members of the working class who might object to joining a society of hoboes or frequenting a union hall turned into a hobo "jungle." After all, Sin-Bad argued, even the contemptible "scissorbill," the anti-union worker, justified his attitudes by pointing to his nominal right to change jobs as evidence of his "freedom" under open-shop capitalism. It disgusted Sin-Bad to see Wobblies acting as if they accepted this spurious argument. "The I.W.W. will grow bigger and stronger when the Wobbly learns to stay on the job."[1] Frank Bohn, an intellectual and charter member of the I.W.W., a disciple of De Leon who had deserted De Leon in 1908 in order to stay

[1] *Solidarity*, Jan. 16, 1915, p. 3.

29

in the I.W.W., emphasized also the disputatious nature of the Westerner and charged that he was little more than a "spittoon philosopher." He asked: "Is this chair-warming sect now the leading element in the I.W.W.?"[2] The image of the Wobbly as vagabond troubled some members down into the declining old age of the organization. One indignant Wobbly, Card No. 331378, urged the organization in 1923 to "come alive," give up its self-destructive notion that the migrant worker was the ideal revolutionary. After the 1908 schism in the I.W.W., the commercial press also began to see the Western Wobbly—oftentimes merely the Wobbly without reference to habitat—as an irresponsible rogue, a kind of backwoods bomb-thrower with a "passion for disputation."[3]

Despite this quick rise to notoriety in the region, the I.W.W. grew much more slowly in actual membership. By 1907, the Seattle local had expanded sufficiently to establish several branches in other towns, but even so claimed a membership of only 800.[4] The depression of 1907, affecting all unions, destroyed even this modest beginning, and the Seattle local reorganized the following year with only sixty-eight members.[5] Not till 1912 were Wobblies numerous enough in the lumber industry to satisfy the constitutional requirements for forming their own national union within the I.W.W.[6] This ambitious union, the National Industrial Union of Forest and Lumber Workers, lasted only one year. From 1913 till 1917, when the I.W.W. launched another lumber-workers' union, the Wobbly lumberjacks carried on their revolutionary struggle under the aegis of the Agricultural Workers' Organization of the I.W.W.[7]

Several factors explain the slow, uncertain growth of the I.W.W. in the region, the same factors, by and large, that explain its failure to grow nationally. The confusion in its goals, the conflict between revolution and industrial unionism, limited the appeal of the organization among average working men. To the average

---

[2] *International Socialist Review* (July 1911), p. 44.

[3] John Spargo, "Why the I.W.W. Flourishes," *World's Work* (Jan. 1920), p. 244; *General Office Bulletin*, Sept. 1923, pp. 16-17, 23-24.

[4] Cloice R. Howd, *Industrial Relations in the West Coast Lumber Industry*, U. S. Dept. of Labor, Bureau of Labor Statistics, Bulletin No. 349, (Washington, 1924), p. 64.

[5] *Industrial Worker*, Apr. 6, 1911, p. 4.

[6] *Ibid.*, Nov. 23, 1911, p. 2.

[7] Charlotte Todes, *Labor and Lumber* (New York, 1931), p. 160.

worker, such an act as joining the I.W.W. must have seemed tantamount to becoming a professional revolutionary, not something one did to improve one's economic position. Moreover, the labor movement in the Pacific Northwest had weak roots. Only a small elite of skilled workers—typographers, machinists, and such—possessed any union experience or tradition, and only when extreme crises drew the class lines through society did this elite evince any desire to cooperate, gingerly, with the I.W.W. The I.W.W., for its part, antagonized the weak A.F.L. unions of the region with its obvious "dual unionism" and its intemperate propaganda against the A.F.L. leadership, "misleaders of labor," in the language of the Wobblies. Hence the I.W.W. recruited from that special labor force, the mobile and deracinated, upon which the expanding industries of the region more and more depended. These workers had little to lose. They had no neighbors to chide them for being Wobblies.

Sin-Bad, in his complaint, thus described accurately a kind of Wobbly and a condition relevant to the Pacific Northwest. As the I.W.W. recruited more and more selectively from the ranks of migratory workers—the workers most ready for its militant program—other workers stood aloof. The peculiar fame of the organization had the effect of repelling more of the working class than it attracted. But these few and scattered Wobblies made a considerable impression with only their gestures toward actual unionism.

The I.W.W. made its name a feared household word by adapting its tactics to the facts of life in the region. Out of its Western experience, for example, it evolved its novel "job delegate" system. Any Wobbly could act as a full-time organizer while still pursuing the regular routine of casual labor. Wobblies supplied themselves with membership cards, account notebooks, and a sample of I.W.W. literature, and like *colporteurs* carried their gospel with them on the job. The job delegate recruited members, collected dues, kept rudimentary records, and became, in fact, "an official whose headquarters was where he hung his hat."[8] The I.W.W. hall became only a regional headquarters, a social club, or "propaganda club,"[9] and it lost almost all the business functions of the

---

[8] G. R. Leighton, "Seattle, Washington: The Edge of the Last Frontier," *Harpers* (Mar. 1939), p. 425.

[9] Paul F. Brissenden, *The I.W.W.: A Study of American Syndicalism* (New York, 1919), p. 313.

ordinary union hall or office. The job-delegate system maximized the effectiveness of the I.W.W., spreading its message insistently into camps and work gangs remote from the usual organizational methods, and making the I.W.W. minority an almost ubiquitous irritant with influence out of all proportion to its size.

Another tactic adapted to its Western experience, and one felt more acutely by the general public, was the "free-speech fight." In these actions, the I.W.W. made the best use of its scattered and footloose membership. Wobblies invaded unfriendly towns that prohibited street meetings. They deliberately broke the law and made their speeches. They thus provoked arrest and "almost literally broke into the jails by hundreds."[10] They fought these curious battles with perverse delight but also with high seriousness, explaining them as necessary defenses to protect their right to organize and recruit openly. This particular explanation of the free-speech fights, as the defense of a constitutional right that the organization needed, explains only part of the Wobblies' motivations. They also intended the conflicts to be revolutionary acts, as attacks upon the "master class."

Because the I.W.W. failed to create effective unions, it sought these new ways—such as street oratory and demonstrations—to advertise their movement. More urgently, Wobblies needed outlets for revolutionary zeal. If their unions were only cadres, incapable of conducting real strikes, they could nonetheless use their small, mobile forces in guerrilla skirmishes. Being unattached to family, home, or garden, they could concentrate their members from an entire region upon a limited sector of the class-war front. By relying upon this tactic and similar tactics of harassment, the I.W.W., of course, tacitly admitted its failure to organize the entire working class into the contemplated "One Big Union." Free-speech fights could only heighten the class conflict, convince a few fence-sitters, and serve to release pent-up revolutionary energies. But they served no immediate function within the labor movement. One journalist for the A.F.L. observed:[11]

> While it denounces politics and political action most vehemently, the I.W.W. is itself a quasi-political organization. It differs from other political bodies in the means more than the

[10] *Ibid.*, p. 260.
[11] *Oregon Labor Press,* Sept. 1, 1917, p. 1.

ends. It uses so-called direct action instead of the ballot box. Most of its big fights have been with the political authorities, on the political field, without any economic significance to the working class.

Although Wobblies described their free-speech fights as practical defenses of their right to organize openly, they admitted more privately that the conflicts were also offensive. They piously invoked their First Amendment rights, but they were really uninterested in the purely constitutional issues. They were not, after all, civil libertarians. They invoked their constitutional rights only to educate the unorganized and watching workers in the folly of relying "upon phrases written upon musty pieces of parchment by slave-holding labor skinners of the past."[12] The workers had to learn the hard way that they needed a new proletarian morality and a new mode of justice.[13]

Before 1916, California witnessed the most violent free-speech fights, but the I.W.W. by no means spared the Pacific Northwest. In the fall and winter of 1909, Wobblies fought a protracted free-speech fight with the authorities of Spokane, Washington. This struggle established the characteristic pattern of subsequent free-speech fights: the provocation of arrest in protest over an ordinance regulating or forbidding street meetings, mounting tensions and mass arrests, an increasing obstinacy on the part of both the I.W.W. and the authorities, the involvement of liberal sympathizers outraged by obvious violations of a basic constitutional guarantee, and a settlement, through negotiation or simple exhaustion, usually unfavorable to the I.W.W. But in the Spokane fight, the I.W.W. won an almost complete victory.

The fight began in Spokane as a protest over a real injustice. Employment agencies—or "sharks," as the Wobblies called them— victimized casual laborers all over the Pacific Northwest and in Spokane as well. The agencies supplied workers to the logging camps, the construction sites, the railroad section gangs, and other work sites hiring transient workers. They charged the worker for the service, "a dollar for a job," in many cities. Sometimes the foremen or employers on the jobs entered into corrupt bargains with the agencies, the agency collecting the fees from the workers

---

[12] *Industrial Worker*, Mar. 21, 1912, p. 2.
[13] Joseph Ettor, *Industrial Unionism* (Chicago, 1912), p. 15. "New conceptions of Right and Wrong must generate and permeate the workers."

and then splitting the fees with the employer who fired workers as fast, or almost as fast, as he hired them. Wobblies complained that some jobs had a "perpetual motion" system in operation—one work crew going to the job, another crew briefly on the job, another crew leaving. The Somers Lumber Company, for example, hired 3,000 men during one winter to maintain a crew of fifty men.[14]

Thirty-one of these employment agencies lined Stevens Street in Spokane, most of them primitive in their business practices, the agent keeping his records in one pocket in a dog-eared notebook and his roll of bills in the other pocket.[15] Wobblies began their campaign against these hated "sharks" or "leeches" in 1908, holding protest demonstrations in Stevens Street in front of the offices. The Associated Agencies of Spokane responded to this campaign by getting the city council in December 1908, to pass an ordinance prohibiting street meetings, the law to become effective on January 1, 1909. Mayor N. S. Pratt made no objections. He apparently had no desire to defend the rights of I.W.W. members. Although he was a prominent wholesale lumberman and a pioneer of the industry in the Inland Empire,[16] he probably saw the I.W.W. as more an annoyance from the skid-road nether world than as an economic threat to his industry.

Wobblies at first obeyed the ordinance. On one occasion in January 1909, they even served as peace-makers in an angry demonstration they had not instigated. A noisy mob of several thousand men began to throw chunks of ice and stones through the windows of the Red Cross Employment Agency at 224 Stevens Street. James H. Walsh, the leader of the "overalls brigade" at the I.W.W. convention of the previous year, mounted a chair in the street and shouted down the crowd. He then invited everybody to adjourn to the I.W.W. hall nearby on Front Avenue. In the hall Walsh warned the now pacified rioters about Pinkerton agents in their midst who had been egging them on, preparing them for the inevitable arrests or policemen's clubs.[17]

---

[14] Fred Heslewood, "Barbarous Spokane," *International Socialist Review*, (Feb. 1910), p. 711.

[15] Nels Anderson, *The Hobo: The Sociology of the Homeless Man* (Chicago, 1923), p. 10.

[16] *Timberman*, Nov. 1909, p. 47.

[17] Spokane *Spokesman-Review*, Jan. 18, 1909, p. 1.

In March, after a few months of peaceful compliance with the ordinance, the anger of demonstrators boiled over again. But the police quelled the uprising quickly and arrested forty-eight persons in one episode. Peace lasted through the spring and summer. In August, however, the city council, realizing that they had silenced song birds with their blanket ordinance as well as the Wobbly crows, passed an amendment to the law that permitted the Salva-Army to hold its street meetings. Wobblies, having very sensitive noses for class ideological discrimination, rose to the challenge.[18] They decided to test the constitutionality of both the original law and the new Salvation Army exemption. James J. Thompson violated the ordinance and got himself arrested on October 25, 1909. Other Wobblies did the same. Thompson appealed his city police court conviction to a Superior Court. In this appeal the judge on November 2, 1909, upheld his conviction under the original law but declared the Salvation Army exemption to be unconstitutional.[19] To a degree the I.W.W. was vindicated, but it had by this time decided for massive action against the original prohibition whatever the outcome of the Thompson case. The favoritism to the Salvation Army had rankled, but the real issue was still the original law. On October 28, 1909, the *Industrial Worker* ran a bold headline: "Wanted—Men To Fill the Jails of Spokane."[20]

Thus, in early November, the I.W.W. and the city of Spokane prepared for battle. The I.W.W. called upon all its locals in the region for contingents of free-speech fighters to crowd the Spokane jails. The police chief assured the public that he would enforce the law and that he had accommodations for five hundred prisoners if necessary.[21] The mayor tried belatedly to make a deal, offering to release all the I.W.W. prisoners if the I.W.W. would agree to abide by the afore-mentioned test case of James J. Thompson.[22] The I.W.W. turned down the offer. In a final effort to prevent the conflict, delegates from the A.F.L. unions in Spokane and from

---

[18] *Industrial Worker,* Oct. 28, 1909, p. 1; Spokane *Spokesman-Review,* Nov. 2, 1909, p. 2.

[19] Selig Perlman and Philip Taft, *American Labor Movements,* Vol. IV of John R. Commons, *et al., History of Labor in the United States* (4 vols., New York, 1926-1935), p. 237.

[20] *Industrial Worker,* Oct. 28, 1909, p. 1.

[21] Spokane *Spokesman-Review,* Nov. 2, 1909, p. 1.

[22] *Ibid.,* Nov. 12, 1909, p. 7.

the Socialist Party petitioned the city council to repeal the offending ordinance and to permit use of the streets under minimal and sensible restrictions. The president of the Fidelity National Bank, speaking for the local establishment, testified in support of the prohibition, and his testimony apparently outweighed that of the labor and Socialist witnesses at the hearing. The council did not repeal the ordinance.[23]

As the battle started in November the police raided the I.W.W. hall, arrested four leaders, closed the offices of the *Industrial Worker*, and proclaimed, somewhat prematurely, that they had nipped insurrection and conspiracy in the bud.[24] Volunteer editors put out the next few editions of the *Industrial Worker*. With the December 10 issue, the police returned and confiscated the whole edition. The paper then moved to Seattle. Police arrests mounted in early November, but capturing the obvious leaders at the I.W.W. hall and making the mass arrests did not check the conflict. Wobblies from flop houses and hobo jungles throughout the region flocked to Spokane. Wheat harvesters fresh from the Dakota harvests streamed into the city also. All were determined to force a repeal of the ordinance and to heighten the class struggle in the process. Some of these box-car militants had difficulty getting to Spokane so late in the traveling season and limped into the city on frost-bitten feet. But the cold journeys did not extinguish their revolutionary fire. In November alone, the police arrested over six hundred Wobblies who tried to speak on the streets.[25] Spokane became a battlefield, with the police arresting more and more vagrants, and the I.W.W. from California to Minnesota dispatching more and more replacements.

Some liberals in the city began to raise their voices in defense of the Wobblies. After the arrest of the local I.W.W. leaders, the liberals made plans for a mass protest-meeting against the ordinance, beginning to seem more and more ridiculous, and against the increasingly ugly tactics of the police. Mrs. Z. W. Commerford, chairwoman of the College Women's Equal Suffrage Club, Mrs.

[23] Elizabeth Gurley Flynn, "The Free Speech Fight at Spokane," *International Socialist Review*, (Dec. 1909), p. 487.

[24] Portland *Oregonian*, Nov. 3, 1909, p. 6.

[25] Ralph Chaplin, *Wobbly: The Rough-and-Tumble Story of an American Radical* (Chicago, 1948), p. 150.

Rose B. Moore, chairwoman of the social-economics committee of the Women's Club, several respected clergymen, and many Socialists participated in the plans. At the last minute, however, the trustees of the Masonic Temple, perhaps succumbing to pressure from the authorities, cancelled the use of their hall for the meeting.[26]

Some of the liberal sympathizers became as agitated and angry as the Wobbly participants. Samuel T. Crane, a lawyer, watching the police and deputies rounding up Wobbly street speakers under his window, leaned out and began to berate the police. When he hurried down to the street to deliver his objections in person and at closer quarters, the police arrested him with the Wobblies and charged him with disorderly conduct.[27] He conducted his own defense in police court, and tenaciously cross-examined the police chief testifying against him. He pressed the chief with leading questions and innuendoes. "How much had you been drinking on the day you arrested me?" The judge had to clear the court to silence the spectators, who laughed as if at a vaudeville show. The following day, the spectators found that carpenters the previous evening had partitioned the court to make it into a small room with space for very few onlookers.[28]

The struggle continued into the early winter, each side growing apparently more and more unyielding. The authorities put their overflow of prisoners into the unused Franklin school building, and the Wobblies there and in the prison carried on the struggle even though off the firing lines. They refused to work. The equally determined authorities put them on a bread and water diet till they did work for their keep. The prisoners thereupon went on a complete hunger strike. The authorities retaliated with various kinds of brutality. According to the I.W.W. accounts, the guards at the city jail forced prisoners into a small cell, six by eight feet, and "sweated" them by turning up the heat. Prisoners fainted during this treatment, and only the pressure from closely packed bodies kept them from falling to the floor. After the sweating, the guards returned the prisoners to their underheated cells.[29] Three Wobblies

26 Portland *Oregonian*, Nov. 4, 1909, p. 6.

27 Spokane *Spokesman-Review*, Nov. 6, 1909, p. 1.

28 Elizabeth Gurley Flynn, "The Shame of Spokane," *International Socialist Review* (Jan. 1910), p. 613.

29 Flynn, "The Free Speech Fight at Spokane," *op. cit.*, p. 486.

died in the completely unheated Franklin School building, presumably as a consequence of their self-imposed hunger strike, their refusal to cut their own firewood, and the resulting illnesses from cold and hunger.[30]

Three times a week, the police shuttled the prisoners in the Franklin School building, about eight at a time, to the city jail for baths. Sympathizers sometimes threw food into the police wagon from the side of the street, but Bill Shannon, a particularly disagreeable guard, took a "fiendish delight" in kicking it away from the hungry men.[31] The press snickered somewhat insensitively at the hobo prisoners for objecting so vociferously to the baths. Hoboes, of course, were not noted for their fastidiousness.[32] But the I.W.W. accounts of the baths indicated why men even more habituated to soap might object to them. Guards stripped the shrinking prisoners, pushed them under scalding sprays, then into an icy rinse, and then transported them back to the unheated quarters in the school building.[33]

On November 31, the police arrested the second cadre of I.W.W. leaders, among them a young girl, a black-haired firebrand named Elizabeth Gurley Flynn. She resisted arrest as she delivered her street oration by chaining herself to a lamp post. Her trial, and the trial of those arrested with her, began in February 1910, but the prosecution dropped the charges in March and released all the defendants as a result of the peace settlement that ended the free-speech fight. Elizabeth Flynn, during her long imprisonment, complained loudly about her treatment and the treatment meted out to the other prisoners in the jail. In the December 1910, issue of the *Industrial Worker*, the last issue published in Spokane, she exposed an unsavory police racket in the jail. The jailers ran a kind of illicit municipal brothel in the women's section of the jail, acting as unlikely "madams," procurers, and sometimes as nonpaying customers.[34]

The mayor replied to her insistent charges and to the *Industrial Worker's* exposure by making some highly uncomplimentary re-

[30] Chaplin, *Wobbly, op. cit.,* p. 150.
[31] Flynn, "The Shame of Spokane," p. 612.
[32] Portland *Oregonian,* Nov. 14, 1909, p. 4.
[33] Flynn, "The Shame of Spokane," *op. cit.,* p. 611.
[34] *Industrial Worker,* Dec. 10, 1909, p. 1.

marks about her, whereupon Miss Flynn's defense attorney brought forward an ultimatum: the mayor should either bring suit for slander or apologize. When he did neither, the defense attorney entered a suit against him for defamation of character, asking damages of ten thousand dollars. By March, the city of Spokane and individual officials had law suits pending against them in excess of one hundred thousand dollars.[35] Thus the I.W.W. attacked the master class on a bewildering number of flanks, on the job, on the city streets, in jail, even in court.

Out of weariness—or possibly even fear of the damage suits—the city authorities made peace with the I.W.W. in March 1910. The Wobblies had made preparations for continuing the struggle into the spring and summer. The city agreed to the following terms: Street speaking would be permitted. All I.W.W. prisoners would be released. The I.W.W. would be allowed to reopen its hall. The *Industrial Worker* could return to Spokane. All I.W.W. damage suits against the city would be dropped. The I.W.W. would refrain from speaking on the streets until the offending ordinance could be officially repealed. The city council, by unanimous vote, repealed the law on March 9, 1910.[36]

The liberal sympathizers, of course, did not see the free-speech fight as an episode in some implacable class struggle nor as the testing of revolutionary tactics, but they did try to make sense out of it within their own philosophy of reform and civil liberties. They exerted pressure to ameliorate the conditions that, in their view, had brought on the troubles. The I.W.W. had publicized their grievance against fraudulent employment agencies in Spokane. The liberals agreed that these "sharks," more than anyone else, had precipitated the fight. Under lobbying pressure from local reformers, the city council revoked the licenses of nineteen of the thirty-one agencies and promised to repay some of the losses suffered by defrauded workers.[37] Later, the Washington state legislature acted upon this problem first publicized by the Wobblies and passed a law regulating agencies in the state.[38] The Women's Club

[35] Elizabeth Gurley Flynn, "Latest News from Spokane," *International Socialist Review* (Mar. 1910), p. 831.

[36] *International Socialist Review* (Apr. 1910), pp. 947-948; *Industrial Worker*, Mar. 12, 1910, p. 1.

[37] Flynn, "Latest News from Spokane," p. 828.

[38] *Session Laws of the State of Washington, 1915*, chap. I, secs. 1, 2.

—presumably its "social-economics committee" that had helped to plan the abortive protest meeting—petitioned the council for a jail matron to remedy some of the outlandish conditions publicized by Elizabeth Gurley Flynn. The council passed a resolution authorizing such a matron for the jail, but the finance committee tabled it, fiscal responsibility apparently taking precedent over sexual morality. Two prison guards, particularly disliked by the Wobblies, lost their jobs.[39]

Although the liberals who had defended the Wobbly free-speech fighters won these few tangible reforms, the I.W.W. victory, from the perspective of the revolution, was a dubious victory in an ambiguous conflict. Wobblies won no important tactical advantage in the class struggle, nor did they bring the general strike appreciably closer. But they had advertised themselves and their movement, had experienced the exhilarations of combat, had at least disconcerted the class enemy. The city authorities—as often happens with inept conservatives—cooperated inadvertently with the Wobblies by responding to provocation in a way best fitted to reinforce Wobbly beliefs and, moreover, to activate the nonrevolutionary reformers.

The I.W.W. fought a less spectacular free-speech fight in Aberdeen, Washington, two years later. The conflict began in the same pattern as the Spokane conflict with the local business community banding together against the I.W.W. invasion. In Aberdeen, however, the city authorities and the business leaders —sometimes the same persons—prevented a Wobbly victory by responding to the invasion with more efficient tactics of their own. They deported the Wobblies rather than jailing them, thus sparing themselves the expense and trouble of boarding dozens of disagreeable prisoners.

As in Spokane, Wobblies disrupted traffic and outraged opinion in the streets of downtown Aberdeen with their singing and forensics. The city council passed an ordinance restricting the use of the streets. However genuine the motives were to regulate traffic, the councilmen probably felt no great remorse that their traffic regulation cut short the Wobbly orations. Delegates from the Socialist Party in Aberdeen, appearing before the council, expressed their

---

[39] Flynn, "Latest News from Spokane," p. 828.

satisfaction that the law was honestly intended.[40] In October 1911, however, the mayor received a telegram from the Chicago head-quarters of the I.W.W., telling him that the I.W.W. considered the law a personal affront and warning him that Wobblies intended to force its repeal or "make grass grow in the streets."[41] The telegram, of course, antagonized the city authorities and stiffened their resolve to enforce the law. "Aberdeen is the best little city on the map," the newspaper editor commented belligerently. The I.W.W. had certainly not built Aberdeen, but even it was welcome in the city if it agreed to behave, if its members acted like "decent citizens."[42]

At its height, the free-speech fight in Aberdeen lasted only a few days. Wobblies persisted in trying to speak on the streets after the ordinance had gone into effect. They began their major offensive late in November 1911. Police arrested five speakers on the evening of November 22. A crowd of I.W.W. sympathizers followed the police and their prisoners to the jail. Outside the jail, the crowd shouted, sang, threatened, demanded the release of the prisoners. The police dispersed the crowd with the icy spray of a fire hose.[43] Aberdeen girded itself for another of the I.W.W.'s free-speech fights. Frightening rumors spread through the town that five hun-dred Wobblies had left British Columbia for Aberdeen and that the I.W.W. had called upon all Wobblies in California to join the invading forces.[44]

These fears, together with a knowledge of Spokane's ordeal of two years earlier, inspired the citizens of Aberdeen to invent a more efficient means of dealing with the I.W.W. The day after the riot in front of the jail, five hundred of the city's "most prominent business and professional men" formed a battalion of special police. The Chamber of Commerce called the meeting and sponsored the organization. The mayor, J. W. Parks, deputized the five hundred immediately. These special police closed the saloons that day at six o'clock, patrolled the streets and the roads leading into the city. They detained every suspicious person they encountered.[45] After the night's patrol, the deputized citizens collected their bag of

---

[40] Aberdeen *Daily World*, Nov. 24, 1911, p. 4.
[41] *Industrial Worker*, Nov. 23, 1911, p. 2.
[42] Aberdeen *Daily World*, Nov. 25, 1911, p. 4.
[43] Portland *Oregonian*, Nov. 24, 1911, p. 1.
[44] Aberdeen *Daily World*, Nov. 23, 1911, p. 1.
[45] *Ibid.*, Nov. 24, 1911, p. 1.

prisoners, took them to the jail, questioned them, and then escorted them out of the city, giving each prisoner two loaves of bread for the road and a stern warning not to return.[46]

Wobblies complained that new tactics were being used against them, "to club our members to death." The I.W.W. advised caution. "We must be prepared to meet these new tactics and we must not meet them with axe handles because we have a queer faculty of knowing that there is no such things as EQUALITY BEFORE THE LAW."[47] The I.W.W. erred in considering police violence and vigilante action the peculiarly "new tactic" being used. There was nothing particularly new about that. The citizens of Aberdeen made their only innovation in the strategy of countering free-speech fights by keeping Wobblies out of the city and by deporting those they did bother to capture. But they took no pains to conceal their readiness for violence. "The citizens' police have armed themselves with wagon spokes and axe handles for use as clubs, and these weapons have proved most effective."[48]

In Aberdeen, the I.W.W. attracted feeble liberal support. Wobblies and their sympathizers made only one joint protest, an attempt to hold a mass meeting in the Empire Theater. They rented the theater after the riot at the jail, but the police and deputized citizens easily suppressed the meeting by roping off the street and arresting all persons approaching the theater. W. J. Patterson, president of the Hayes and Hayes Bank, and Dudley G. Allen, secretary of the Chamber of Commerce, cooperated in making the first arrest.[49]

Mayor Parks traveled to Montesano on November 25, to help organize a countywide vigilante force. In Montesano, the Wobblies invited him to their hall, received him cordially, apologized for the disorder in front of the jail on the first night of the troubles, and asked for a peace settlement on the basis of the *status quo ante bellum*. The mayor did not make the decision himself but invited several Wobblies to accompany him to Aberdeen to present their peace offer to a mass meeting of citizens. He assured them a safe conduct both ways. Many Aberdeen citizens and the special police

---

[46] *Industrial Worker,* Dec. 14, 1911, p. 1.

[47] *Ibid.,* Nov. 23, 1911, p. 1.

[48] Portland *Oregonian,* Nov. 25, 1911, p. 2.

[49] Aberdeen *Daily World,* Nov. 24, 1911, p. 6.

force assembled hurriedly at two o'clock in the afternoon. After hearing the Wobblies' offer, they bluntly turned it down. There was not much to negotiate. The city had won. E. E. Miller, president of the Chamber of Commerce, told the Wobblies of the decision and sent them on their way.[50]

For some reason, the I.W.W. chose not to make Aberdeen a major battleground. Their reluctance to invade Aberdeen in great numbers and their surprising cordiality toward the mayor on his trip to the county seat of Montesano revealed the organization in an unusually passive mood, almost affable, and in strong contrast to the ferocious rhetoric in its press. Perhaps Wobblies of the Grays Harbor region could not generate real enthusiasm for a conflict in large part provoked by a telegram from the Chicago headquarters. Perhaps the Wobblies were set back and confused by the new defensive tactics that kept them out of the town and the jail.

The I.W.W. almost institutionalized the free-speech fight along the Pacific Coast. It became for that era in the annals of protest what the "sit down" strike of the 1930s became, or the "sit in" of the civil rights movement of the 1960s. But Wobblies also improvised other tactics, sharing with the free-speech fight the objective of harrassing the "master class" and of provoking conflicts that would "educate" the working class. These other improvisations were also, in part, adaptations to its failure as a labor union. If a handful of zealots could not conduct a general strike without the cooperation of all workers, they could still make considerable noise and generate gratifyingly confused struggles. Oftentimes the more routine, improvized agitations—parades, soap-box speeches, proselytizing on the job, or pamphleteering—set off whole series of conflicts during which it was difficult to determine what the particular motives of the Wobblies were and whether or not they were more sinned against than sinners.

Without experiencing anything as climatic as a free-speech fight, Seattle still lived with a chronic "I.W.W. problem" that began with the first appearance of the Wobblies in the city and lasted into the 1920s. Since the 1890s, the Puget Sound area had witnessed a progression of strange radicalisms, from a free-love anarchist community to the more ordinary Populist movement. The Seattle area also supported a strong Socialist Party and a radi-

---

[50] Portland *Oregonian*, Nov. 28, 1911, p. 4.

calized labor movement which reached its climax in the famous General Strike of early 1919. In Seattle, therefore, the I.W.W. was only one ingredient in a long-simmering radical stew.

In 1912 and 1913, the I.W.W. got caught up in Seattle's flamboyant local politics, more as a kind of whipping boy, or even as an innocent bystander, than as an instigator or agitator of trouble. From the days of the railroad boom of the 1880s and the Yukon gold rush of the following decade, Seattle had grown prodigiously and in the course of its spectacular growth had become one of the "sin towns"—to slip into the terminology of Sunday Supplement feature writers—of the Pacific Coast. The "open town" versus "closed town" issue insinuated itself into all local politics. In 1912, indignant reforming citizens succeeded in recalling Mayor Hiram Gill from office. Gill had presided over a particularly blatant "open town" administration. George F. Cotterill replaced Gill in the mayor's office, and he tried to close the brothels and administer a "closed town."[51] He won the bitter enmity of Colonel Alden J. Blethen, the owner of the Seattle *Times*, a power in Seattle who had backed the Gill administration. Although Blethen was charged himself with complicity in the corruption of the Gill regime, it is unlikely that he was personally involved. He was, rather, one of those self-styled "realistic" conservatives who thought regulated brothels not only helped business but also assured the virtue of all decent citizens' wives and daughters. Colonel Blethen—his dubious colonelcy dating from brief service on the militia staff of the Governor of Minnesota before his move to Seattle—worshipped the military with a school boy's simplicity. The flag and all hackneyed Fourth of July patriotism stirred him to the depths. He flew Old Glory over the *Times* building and raised and lowered it every day with military ceremony. A printed flag in color also fluttered from the masthead of the newspaper.

Blethen lashed out at Mayor Cotterill first over the Leonard Olsson affair. Olsson, a Tacoma Wobbly, lost his citizenship in a

---

[51] Murray Morgan, *Skid Road: An Informal Portrait of Seattle* (New York, 1951), p. 187. This popular history of the city of Seattle includes an entertaining section on the complicated local political struggles in Seattle before the First World War. Lowell S. Hawley and Ralph Bushnell Potts, *Counsel for the Damned: A Biography of George Francis Vanderveer* (Philadelphia, 1953), also tells the political story in a concise and entertaining manner.

federal court on the grounds that he had been guilty of fraud in his naturalization. No I.W.W. member, obviously, could be sincere in swearing his allegiance to the United States Constitution. In a Circuit Court of Appeals case in February 1913, Olsson got his citizenship restored.[52] But he won his appeal only after several months of angry charges and counter-charges among the local politicians, I.W.W. demonstrations in Seattle, an investigation by a special subcommittee of the House of Representatives Judiciary Committee, a new trial won for him by the Attorney-General of the United States, and the resignation of C. H. Hanford, the original trial judge in the denaturalization proceedings. Blethen, stretching connections to the breaking point, launched his attack on Cotterill for not suppressing the I.W.W. sympathy demonstrations for Olsson. In particular, Blethen blamed the mayor for permitting a May Day parade in Seattle in 1912. In the parade, the Wobblies proudly bore the red flag next to the Stars and Stripes. Patriotic onlookers had objected, and the whole parade had dissolved in a brawl between marchers and bystanders. Cotterill defended himself against Blethen's abuse by citing the First Amendment's guarantee of free speech and assembly, and by explaining that he had told the Wobbly marchers they could display the red flag only if they also carried the Stars and Stripes. His defense, however, sounded a little plaintive against the thunder from the *Times*.[53]

But the troubles between the mayor's office, the newspaper, and the radical dissenters reached a peak of confused violence in the summer of 1913. Blethen struck out against his anarchist-coddling enemies during the Potlatch Days celebration in Seattle. The business leaders of the city had planned this summer festival as a stimulant to business. Secretary of the Navy Josephus Daniels came to the city for the occasion to review a parade of sailors and soldiers and to address the city fathers at a supper meeting in the exclusive Rainier Club. Elements of the Pacific Fleet were despatched to the Seattle harbor for the occasion, and the sailors, joined by soldiers from a nearby camp, were given leave after their duty in the afternoon parade.

M. M. Mattison, a political writer for Colonel Blethen's *Times*, wrote a masterpiece of tortuous reportage on the Daniels' speech.

---

[52] Hawley and Potts, *Counsel for the Damned*, pp. 142-145; United States v. Olsson, 196 Fed. 562; Olsson v. United States, 201 Fed. 1022.

[53] Hawley and Potts, *op. cit.*, p. 144.

He reported the Secretary's routine remarks on patriotism, a pre-digested speech that the Secretary had been giving all over the country, as if it had been a specific assault on Mayor Cotterill for molly-coddling the red-flag anarchists. Also, in the same issue of the *Times*, Blethen's writers reported a minor skirmish in the streets of Seattle between the servicemen and a street orator, identified loosely as one of the radicals, and left the unmistakable impression that the incident was an example of the kind of dereliction of duty about which the Secretary of the Navy had been speaking. The *Times* somehow connected everything, the weirdly distorted version of Daniels' remarks, the exaggerated story of the violence in the streets, and the radical threat of the I.W.W. It ended by "quoting" many presumably overheard comments that "real patriots" should rise up in wrath and do the mayor's work for him by "cleaning out" the "reds."[54] The speaker who had precipitated the incident with the soldiers and sailors was Mrs. Annie Miller, a pacifist and no Wobbly. She had been heckled by the listening servicemen, pulled off her stand, and handled roughly when she had tried to return to it. At this point a well-dressed onlooker—obviously no Wobbly—came to her defense and hit an offending serviceman.[55]

The following evening, July 18, a considerable body of sailors and soldiers coursed through the skid-road district of Seattle, cheered on by a light-hearted, carnival crowd of Potlatch Days celebrants. The mob demolished the headquarters of the Socialist Party and piled the wrecked furniture in the street. The servicemen similarly raided the I.W.W. hall. They also invaded a Salvation Army mission in their tipsy zeal and had well begun their patriotic demolition when a sailor noticed a "God Is Love" sign. He shouted in dismay, "Boys, we're in the wrong place!"[56]

Mayor Cotterill acted with decisiveness. He sent twenty-five policemen to the *Times* building and closed down the newspaper to prevent it, he charged, from further incitation to riot. He ordered that the next issues of the newspaper would have to pass his censorship before being released for distribution. He also ordered the saloons closed, thus putting a sobering lid on the Potlatch Days festivities.[57]

[54] Seattle *Daily Times,* July 17, 1913, p. 1.
[55] Seattle *Sun,* July 20, 1913, p. 1.
[56] Seattle *Post-Intelligencer,* July 19, 1913, pp. 1, 2.
[57] *Ibid.,* July 20, 1913, pp. 1, 2.

Blethen responded just as quickly and in a fiery rage. He called a compliant judge from his bed in the middle of the night to get a restraining order to counter the mayor's actions against his newspaper. On the next day, July 20, he had an uncensored issue of the *Times* on the streets with a front-page editorial lambasting Cotterill unmercifully and announcing a lawsuit against the mayor. But by this time the conflict was rapidly becoming anti-climatic. The previous night, the night after the mob action against the I.W.W. and Socialist Party headquarters, shore police from the fleet and military police from the army camp had patrolled the city and kept the peace.

The mayor presented a bill for damages to the headquarters to the city council, and the council, as might have been expected, denied the city's liability. Colonel Blethen raged again at the gall of the mayor in supporting the "reds." The Seattle *Daily Sun*—an independent newspaper with a brief two-year history in the city—published the mayor's side in a long and detailed exposition. The mayor reviewed in depth the history of his conflict with Blethen and explained his unexceptionable position on free speech. He blamed Blethen and his irresponsible journalism for the riots. Blethen was the anarchist, the inciter to riot. Moreover, if he could be "blown down by a putrid blast" from Blethen, he did not deserve his public office.[58]

Bruce Rogers, a joint delegate of both the I.W.W. and the Socialist Party, went to Washington, D.C., in an effort to collect an indemnity from the United States government. The I.W.W. alone claimed $1,650.[59] Representative J. W. Bryan, a supporter of Cotterill, took up the matter in the House of Representatives and entered a resolution calling for an investigation by the Navy Department and for indemnification. The House declared his resolution out of order on a technicality, because he could not ask for an appropriation as a resolution.[60] Bryan also defended on the floor of the House his and Cotterill's faction in Washington's Democratic politics. He introduced the whole story of the conflict, the stories from the *Times*, the mayor's defense in the *Daily Sun*, the whole Olsson-Judge Hanford squabble, and even an account of a speech

---

[58] Seattle *Sun*, July 20, 1913, p. 1.
[59] *Industrial Worker*, Sept. 4, 1913, p. 4.
[60] *Congressional Record*, 63rd Cong., 1st Sess. (1913), L, Pt. 5, 4400.

he had made to his constituents at a mass meeting in Seattle.[61]

While this political whirlpool swirled around them, the Wobblies made their own propaganda, even though they seemed to be relegated to the role of pawns or victims. The attack on their hall supplied them with material for a hundred speeches. For days after the Potlatch Days riots Wobbly orators drew crowds at regular evening meetings on Fourth Avenue between Pike and Pine Streets. On July 21, the day after Cotterill and Blethen had locked horns, the police had to disperse a crowd of over two thousand at the I.W.W. meeting in the street.[62] The court grated an injunction to complaining storekeepers on Fourth Avenue that enjoined the I.W.W. from holding any more meetings.[63] For a few days, the Wobblies persisted in the face of the injunction and threatened another major free-speech fight. The police continued to disperse the crowds and to arrest the speakers. The conflict subsided, however, without producing another battle as in Spokane in 1909.

In other cities and towns, I.W.W. agitation and the outrage and impatience of authorities and citizens set off chaotic conflicts that did not have the classic simplicity or the dramatic unities of a free-speech fight. In Florence, Oregon, in November 1913, the mere presence of Wobblies in town and their renting an office aroused the citizenry to action. With firm, but unusually gentle force, the citizens of Florence took seven Wobblies from their newly-rented office and escorted them to the mouth of the Siuslaw River and warned them not to return.[64] The vigilantes even refunded the rent on the office that the I.W.W. had paid in advance, and also paid their prisoners a nominal sum—about twenty dollars—for the furniture they had been forced to leave behind.[65] Governor Oswald West of Oregon, a liberal, was perturbed by this apparent illegal deportation and confiscation of property, and sent Captain Harry K. Metcalf of the Cottage Grove militia company to Florence to

---

[61] Representative J. W. Bryan, from an anti-Gill point of view, sketches the whole history in his remarks before the House. He includes the news stories from the *Sun*, the *Daily Times*, his own speech in Seattle, and everything else he can think of. *Congressional Record*, 63rd Cong., 1st Sess. (1913), L, Pt. 3, 2900-2905, 440; Pt. 6, 5980-5983.

[62] Portland *Oregonian*, July 26, 1913, p. 4.

[63] *Ibid.*, July 27, 1913, p. 10.

[64] *Ibid.*, Nov. 15, 1913, p. 1.

[65] Florence *The West*, Nov. 21, 1913, p. 1.

investigate. West even considered martial law for Florence if the investigation revealed its need. He intended to protect the rights of all citizens, he declared, against "mob law."[66] Metcalf reported that Florence citizens, eager for a railroad connection and other economic improvements, had feared the effect of the I.W.W. on the city's reputation.[67] The editor of the Florence newspaper responded to Governor West's intervention in critical and defensive tones, citing the obnoxiousness of I.W.W. propaganda, and the fact that many Wobblies were foreigners, and demanding that the United States Congress save everybody from the I.W.W. scourge by passing an immigration-restriction law.[68]

In Portland, Oregon, the I.W.W. troubles almost approached Seattle's in duration and confusion. Wobblies made their first appearance in the city in 1907 as participants in a protest parade over the trial of William D. Haywood for plotting the murder of ex-Governor Steunenberg. Forty of the sixty local unions in the city, five Socialist Party locals, and the two I.W.W. locals joined in the parade of over three thousand marchers. The I.W.W. was new to the city. Police and marchers exchanged jocular remarks, and there was no hint of violence.[69]

By 1911, however, the Wobblies in Portland had begun rowdy street meetings and had begun to stir up the usual angry response. The usual "decent citizens" began to complain of the abusive, profane language of Wobbly speakers.[70] In the spring of 1912, Wobblies made themselves unpopular by heckling a speech by Robert Baden-Powell, the founder of the Boy Scouts.[71] Also in the spring of 1912, Wobbly construction workers on a track-laying job for the Portland Railway, Light and Power Company went out on a brief strike—more a protest demonstration than a strike—against a five-dollar "job fee" collected from all workers by the contractor. Five hundred workers joined in the protest over this extortion, reminiscent of the employment agencies' racket in Spokane. The contractors fired and rehired workers rapidly, the Wobblies

[66] *Ibid.,* Nov. 28, 1913, p. 2; Portland *Oregonian,* Nov. 16, 1913, p. 1.
[67] Florence *The West,* Nov. 28, 1913, p. 2.
[68] *Ibid.,* Nov. 21, 1913, p. 2.
[69] Portland *Oregonian,* Feb. 24, 1907, p. 38.
[70] *Ibid.,* Dec. 1, 1911, p. 11.
[71] Portland *Oregonian,* May 3, 1912, p. 15.

charged, in order to collect the "job fees" over and over again.[72]

In the summer of 1913, Wobblies contested a ruling of the Portland mayor prohibiting their use of the streets for meetings. A few nights of rioting ensued. Spanish-American War veterans, acting as special deputies, arrested over a score of demonstrators on the night of July 17.[73] The veterans had earlier taken an intense dislike toward the I.W.W. because Wobbly speakers had been in the habit of using a Spanish-American War memorial in Lownsdale Park as a speakers' platform. The veterans considered this a kind of desecration.[74] Following the arrests, Wobblies and Socialists left free rioted in front of the court house and demanded the release of one of the prisoners, George Reece, whose arrest they thought was particularly unjust.[75] The Portland city council considered a new and tougher ordinance to prohibit all street speaking, but tabled it as the trouble subsided. On one occasion, the police saved a group of Wobblies from attack by another group of Wobblies when they prevented a group of Wobblies from the De Leon faction from fighting it out with a group of Chicago-based Wobblies over possession of a choice speaking platform.[76]

In their routine agitations in the Pacific Northwest, the Wobblies invented tactics of annoyance and harassment that revealed a certain elfin humor mixed with the grim class-war fanaticism. During the winter of 1913-1914, Wobblies in Portland decided there were easier ways of eating than by begging at back doors or by singing for their suppers in skid-road missions. On December 21, 1913, forty disheveled Wobblies marched into the Meves Restaurant at Sixth and Washington and demanded food.

"Mayor Albee will pay for it," they explained gravely.

Twenty policeman ejected them from the restaurant as a crowd of five hundred spectators gathered on the sidewalk to watch the show. The restaurant manager explained somewhat solemnly to the reporters that he doubted Mr. Albee's intention of paying. On the same day, fourteen other Wobblies entered the Peerless Cafeteria but fled when the policemen appeared.[77] The next day, seven

---

[72] *Industrial Worker*, May 30, 1912, p. 4.
[73] Portland *Oregonian*, July 18, 1913, pp. 1, 5.
[74] *Ibid.*, Jan. 30, 1912, p. 12.
[75] *Ibid.*, July 19, 1913, p. 1.
[76] *Ibid.*, July 28, 1913, p. 7.   [77] *Ibid.*, Dec. 22, 1913, p. 10.

men ordered expensive steaks at another restaurant, wolfed down
the food with evident relish, and then leaned back in their chairs
and calmly told their waiter to summon the police. While they
waited they lounged at their ease, "placidly picking their teeth."[78]
The court sentenced ten men for trying this particular restaurant
trick.[79]

Being individualists, unwilling at times to cooperate even with
their own national headquarters, Wobblies in the Pacific Northwest tended to shun close ties with other radicals or liberals. They
preferred to initiate and carry out their own policies. Circumstances, however, often forced them into working alliances with
Socialists, as in Seattle and Portland. Being so small a minority,
they also found themselves agitating within groups they had not
initiated. In both Seattle and Portland, during the unemployment
crisis of the winter of 1913-1914, Wobblies joined various groups
of the unemployed. In January 1914, an army of the unemployed—
called the "idle army" by the press—formed in Portland and began
a trek up the Willamette River Valley in quest of jobs and to
publicize their plight. Although Mr. and Mrs. E. W. Rimer, the
nominal commanders of the army, disclaimed any I.W.W. connections or sympathies, the newspapers and the public came to suspect,
with some justification, that the march was largely another Wobbly stunt. Two-thirds of the recruits in the "army" were under
twenty-five years of age; the majority were single and foreign-
born; many could scarcely speak English. They were the Wobbly
type.[80]

In Oregon City, the mayor furnished the army of one hundred
and twenty-five marchers with supper and breakfast and the use
of the city armory.[81] In Woodburn, the mayor, less hospitable,
organized a hasty committee of citizens as large as the invading
army to escort it right through and out of town.[82] When the army
got to Salem, the state capital, it camped across the street from the
home of Governor West. The Governor tried unsuccessfully to
get an emergency grant of $50,000 from the state budget to start
road-work projects for the men. The Salem churches took up
collections for the men and even found some temporary work

---

[78] *Ibid.*, Dec. 23, 1913, p. 13.   [81] *Ibid.*, Jan. 9, 1914, p. 5.
[79] *Ibid.*   [82] *Ibid.*, Jan. 11, 1914, p. 10.
[80] *Ibid.*, Jan. 12, 1914, p. 9.

for many.[83] But public sympathy played out rather quickly. All but four of the men who had been put to work quit in protest over the arrest of twenty-one of their number who tried the restaurant-begging trick. Within two days the army—including the arrested twenty-one beggars—had been firmly escorted out of the state capital.[84] In Albany, the mayor called out the Fire Department to threaten the army with fire hoses and to hurry it out of town.[85] The army held together as far as Eugene, being shuttled from town to town by citizens sometimes anxious to be charitable and sometimes just anxious. At each town the bedraggled army held public meetings, singing songs, making speeches, and distributing literature.[86]

Wobblies also joined forces with the unemployed who organized and stayed in Portland. Forming themselves into an informal corporation, they petitioned the city council for food and shelter. The council gave them permission to occupy the unused Gypsy Smith Tabernacle, a barn-like structure that had been erected to house the revival meetings of the famous evangelist.[87] The council also appropriated five hundred dollars for blankets. The Oregon Civic League helped the men solicit food from groceries, restaurants, and individual donors. In exchange for these favors, the authorities asked the men to keep their own order. In one group that drifted in and out of the Tabernacle, only fourteen out of over three hundred questioned admitted affiliation with the I.W.W. Perhaps more unadmitted Wobblies were present also; one did not unnecessarily antagonize a questioner at the very moment one was getting a handout. Among the early leaders of the group, Wobblies were more numerous. By the time the group disbanded in April 1914, however, most conspicuous Wobblies had been removed from leadership.[88]

In 1914, during the same crisis of unemployment, Wobblies helped to found the Seattle Unemployed League. Within a short time, they had registered over four thousand members, and had

---

[83] Portland *Daily Journal*, Jan. 13, 1914, p. 1.
[84] *Ibid.*, Jan. 14, 1914, p. 9.
[85] Portland *Oregonian*, Jan. 17, 1914, p. 1.
[86] *Ibid.*, Jan. 16, 1914, p. 1.
[87] *Ibid.*, Jan. 22, 1914, p. 7.
[88] Arthur Evans Wood, *A Study of the Unemployed in Portland, Oregon*, Reed College Social Service Bulletin, No. 3, 1914, pp. 5, 21.

begun to publish a little news sheet to solicit contributions. As the radical influence within the organization became more recognizable—especially with the first four issues of the news sheet put out by a Wobbly editor—gifts began to dry up, and the membership ceased to grow. At a mass meeting in the Seattle Redman Hall, held under the auspices of the Open Forum, the leaders of the Unemployed League, Joyce Schiffman and Marquerite Titus, made their radical orientation unmistakable. They turned a blistering attack upon Mayor Gill. One of the participants claimed that Gill had callously advised two hundred and fifty unemployed men to send their families to the county poor farm and to take themselves to the public stockade for the part-time leaf-raking jobs that the city had created for the unemployed. Gill called Walker C. Smith, one of his Wobbly accusers, a liar. Immediately a man in the audience leaped to his feet to substantiate Smith's charges.[89] The meeting somehow progressed to a more or less orderly conclusion, but it hardly generated the wide popular interest in the problems of the unemployed that its organizers had hoped for. As the depression lifted during the war-order boom of 1915, the Seattle Unemployed League, merely an I.W.W. rump at the end, disappeared.

Upon these free-speech conflicts and similar agitations in the towns of the region, the I.W.W. built its fearsome reputation. Although it turned to these heckling tactics only because of its failure as a labor union, it still remained at least a nominal labor union. Whenever Wobblies found themselves numerous enough on a job they called a strike and demanded higher wages or, more typically, the improvement of some particular working condition. Even these economic actions of the I.W.W., however, smacked of the quasi-political agitation of the soap box. They began their little strikes as much to disconcert the bosses as to alleviate the oppression of the working class. Because they eschewed time contracts with employers on principle and because they viewed routine collective bargaining as a subtle form of entrapment by the master class, they had to conduct their strikes to force immediate concessions over particular grievances. Such a philosophy of unionism, based on an absolute mistrust of the employer, doomed almost all strikes this side of the apocalyptic "general strike," to failure or minor vic-

---

[89] *Solidarity*, Jan. 23, 1915, p. 1.

tories. I.W.W. philosophy made strikes into guerrilla skirmishes difficult to distinguish from political agitation and harassment.

The first strike of the I.W.W. in the Pacific Northwest, in the lumber mills of Portland, in the spring of 1907, proved to be not only the most important strike conducted by the I.W.W. before the first world war but also the most conventional. Only two years old and still including many heterogeneous radical elements, the I.W.W. conducted the Portland strike in a peaceful and almost conservative manner. Except for the occasional references to the class struggle—references that were not unknown even in some A.F.L. strikes in those days—the strike might very well have been an ordinary A.F.L. walk-out. The I.W.W. maintained impeccable order, even enjoining its pickets from shouting "scab."[90] It kept its eye fixed upon the immediate demands, and did not seem for a moment to confuse the strike with the revolution.

Eleven chutemen at the Eastern and Western mill—not even Wobblies—began the general walk-out on March 1, 1907. They called the strike for higher wages and a shorter work day. The pay at the time was $2.75 for a twelve-hour day.[91] The strike spread rapidly. Workers at the large Inman-Poulsen mill left their jobs two days later, and by March 4, the growing I.W.W. local announced that it intended to close every mill in Portland. I.W.W. delegates went to every mill at closing time and badgered and persuaded the workers to join the strike. By March 8, the I.W.W. objective had been largely reached. W. Y. Yarrow, the I.W.W. organizer, claimed that the I.W.W. had signed up 1,600 men and that almost all the mills had been closed.[92]

The logging camps in the Columbia Valley closed down as their market in Portland disappeared. After two weeks of the strike, logging operators met in Portland to commiserate with the mill owners and to form the Columbia River Loggers' Association, an organization intended partly to stiffen the resistance of the Portland mill owners and the whole local lumber industry against the threat of unionism.[93] The logging companies agreed to close down their operations and to endorse the open shop stand of the Portland mill owners.

[90] Portland *Oregonian*, Mar. 12, 1907, p. 10.
[91] *Ibid.*, Mar. 4, 1907, p. 6.
[92] *Ibid.*, Mar. 6, 1907, p. 10; Mar. 8, 1907, p. 1.
[93] *Ibid.*, Mar. 14, 1907, p. 1.

After three weeks of the strike, during which time the I.W.W. leaders negotiated peacefully but futilely with the mill owners,[94] many of the two thousand strikers began to drift back to work. The industry probably welcomed the strike. It gave mill owners an excuse to shut down and not to fill long-period contracts at a depressed period in the lumber market.[95] Yarrow tried to force concessions by bluster, but the mill owners were hardly frightened. He threatened to extend the strike from Mexico to British Columbia and to strike logging operations as well.[96] About a thousand workers kept the picket lines to the end, but most workers returned to work or, if transients, left Portland for other jobs.[97] As the strike deteriorated, Wobblies turned their wrath on the A.F.L., branding C. H. Gram, president of the Oregon Federation of Labor, a "liar" and a "labor faker,"[98] and charging the A.F.L. with supplying "scabs" to break the strike.[99]

The I.W.W. exaggerated somewhat. At the beginning of the strike the Federated Council of Portland promised to lend support to the unorganized strikers if they would join the skeletal lumber workers' unions of the A.F.L.[100] When the strikers turned instead to the I.W.W. for leadership, the Federated Council withdrew its provisional support. But even after withdrawing support, the A.F.L. leaders advised members to respect the I.W.W. picket lines.[101] The weary and defeated strikers who returned to work and broke the strike were new members of the I.W.W. if they were members of any labor union. The workers in lumber mills who had any connection with A.F.L. unions—the "aristocracy of labor" in Portland as elsewhere—were too few to break a strike of two thousand workers.

After the schism of 1908 and as the I.W.W. developed its distinctive personality, its strikes tended to diminish in size and importance and to grow in fire-eating militancy. The agitation accompanying the smaller strikes after 1908 made them hard to

---

94 *Ibid.,* Mar. 9, 1907, p. 10.
95 *Ibid.*
96 *Ibid.,* Mar. 12, 1907, p. 10.
97 *Ibid.,* Mar. 24, 1907, p. 34.
98 *Ibid.,* Mar. 15, 1907, p. 14.
99 James Rowan, *The I.W.W. in the Lumber Industry* (Seattle, n.d.), p. 22.
100 Portland *Oregonian,* Mar. 4, 1907, p. 6.
101 *Ibid.,* Mar. 9, 1907, p. 10.

distinguish from the general nonunion hell-raising of the I.W.W. The strikes led to riots on the picket lines, subsidiary free-speech fights and street demonstrations, pamphleteering and propaganda barrages. They produced hardly any material benefits in the form of higher wages or durable changes in working conditions.

A strike in the Seattle tailor shops revealed most of the features of a typical I.W.W. strike, small in scope, the threat of violence, police intervention, and failure. The I.W.W. tailors' union differed from most I.W.W. unions in one respect; in Seattle, it had job control in many of the city's tailor shops and, therefore, within its limited jurisdiction, was an unusually strong and successful union.[102] Although a news story remarked, aptly, that the causes of the strike were "obscure"[103]—an attribute of most I.W.W. strikes of the period—the I.W.W. claimed discriminatory hiring practices as the cause. Early in the strike the employers secured an anti-picketing injunction, and the Wobblies treated the injunction as cavalierly as they were wont to treat anti-street-speaking laws or injunctions. They continued to picket. Police arrested over a hundred Wobblies and charged them with contempt of court. In sympathy with the I.W.W., tailor-shop employees in all the Seattle establishments joined the strike.[104] The Wobblies made demonstrations of their picket lines. In front of one shop they massed thirty pickets, two of them women. These woman pickets, carried away by their enthusiasm to discourage "scabs," slapped and scratched some women trying to break through the thirty pickets to go to work. A riot squad of Seattle policemen was called to separate the angry women and to disperse the interested bystanders.[105] The A.F.L. tailors' union supported the I.W.W. in the initial stages of the strike, but returned to work long before the I.W.W. had conceded that it was over. After the strike, the Wobblies forgot their quarrel with the employers for a moment and engaged in the usual quarrel with their A.F.L. rivals. A few Wobblies even blamed their own leaders for ending the strike prema-

---

[102] Report of J. M. Foss, *Stenographic Report of the Eighth Annual Convention of the Industrial Workers of the World* (Cleveland, Ohio, 1913), p. 38.

[103] Portland *Oregonian*, May 15, 1912, p. 1.

[104] Report of J. M. Foss, p. 38.

[105] Portland *Oregonian*, May 15, 1912, p. 1.

turely, claiming that the committee that had settled with the employers had been only a "self-constituted" committee.[106]

Only a few months after the defeat of the Aberdeen free-speech fight, Wobblies capitalized on an unorganized strike of mill workers in nearby Hoquiam to revive their fight with the master class in the Grays Harbor area. On March 14, 1912, two hundred Wobblies swarmed into a Hoquiam mill yard and persuaded most of the workers there to leave their jobs. The mob then marched *en masse* to another nearby mill and persuaded those workers to join the strike, shouting their pleas and commands over a twelve-foot fence. They represented, according to the employers, the "lowest class of laborers." In the morning, as a mob they had been frightening, but later they seemed only distasteful.[107]

After this initial walkout, Dr. Herman Titus, an I.W.W. sympathizer and the founder of the Seattle Open Forum, appeared on the scene and held a mass meeting for the strikers in Hoquiam. After the mass meeting—a typical I.W.W. revival with parodies of hymns and impassioned speeches—many of the strikers joined the I.W.W.[108] But the strike never progressed very far beyond the gains of the first day. Even the mills affected by the first walkout remained in operation, working with incomplete work crews. Other mills lost even fewer workers to the strike. The employers imported no strike breakers, and because of market conditions they seemed not to care whether they operated their mills at full capacity or not.[109]

But the I.W.W. used the abortive strike as a means of getting back into Aberdeen, from which it had been barred and deported only a few months earlier. Wobblies drifted into Aberdeen at night, strolling in singly or in small groups so as to escape notice.[110] In Aberdeen, the citizens' battalion quickly revived. Resolved to uphold a kind of rough-and-ready due process and to act fairly if not legally, the citizens' committee invited I.W.W. organizers to present their case before both sides committed themselves to resuming the free-speech fight. In the discussions, Aberdeen businessmen

[106] Report of J. M. Foss, p. 39.
[107] Aberdeen *Daily World*, Mar. 14, 1912, p. 6.
[108] Portland *Oregonian*, Mar. 15, 1912, p. 1.
[109] Aberdeen *Daily World*, Mar. 19, 1912, p. 8; Portland *Oregonian*, March 19, 1912, p. 1.
[110] Portland *Oregonian*, Mar. 16, 1912, pp. 1, 7.

proposed a free, public employment agency financed by assessments levied on the mill owners. The I.W.W. considered the proposal no real solution to the class war, especially when its proponents decided that it would hire no aliens and would maintain the principle of the open shop.[111] Employers blamed the Hoquiam strike on the susceptibility of the foreign-born workers to Wobbly agitation. The I.W.W. considered the proposal to hire only "Americans" as only a trick to dupe the "scissorbills."[112]

The surprising show of moderation by the Aberdeen committee and the I.W.W. during the negotiations proved to be only the lull before the usual storm. Both sides soon fell back into violence. Wobblies rioted in front of the Northwest Lumber Company mill in Hoquiam. The manager of the Coates mill came to the gate and threatened pickets with a revolver when they massed too close. The municipal court sentenced scores of Wobblies on misdemeanor charges arising out of the picketing. Because the municipal judge denied the Wobblies jury trials—a regular demand of Wobblies hauled before police judges—the Wobblies boycotted his business. In Aberdeen, Wobblies rioted in front of the Anderson Middleton mill. Freely swinging night sticks, police separated Wobblies from "scabs" and made wholesale arrests. Those Wobblies not arrested followed the police and the prisoners to the jail, hurling insults and demanding the release of the prisoners.[113]

By the time of the Anderson Middleton mill riot the strike had virtually ended. Many employees had approached former employers and asked for their jobs back.[114] G. A. Biscay and W. A. Thorne, the two principal I.W.W. organizers in Aberdeen and Hoquiam, packed their bags and prepared to leave their hotel in Aberdeen. A group of masked citizens captured them at the hotel and led them, struggling and shouting, through the downtown streets of Aberdeen to a waiting automobile. Over a hundred spectators watched the reluctant parade but made no effort to interfere with it. Outside the city, the masked vigilantes beat Biscay and Thorne and sent them on their way. The sheriff and city attorney made no effort to prosecute the kidnappers even though many

---

111 Aberdeen *Daily World*, Mar. 18, 1912, p. 1; Mar. 23, 1912, p. 1.
112 *Industrial Worker*, Mar. 28, 1912, p. 1.
113 Portland *Oregonian*, Mar. 26, 1912, p. 5.
114 *Ibid.*, Mar. 22, 1912, p. 8.

working men in the town demanded investigation and action.[115]

In December 1912, Wobbly construction workers on the grade of an interurban railway outside Eugene, Oregon, walked off their jobs. Their little strike repeated the usual pattern. They gave no notice and made no demands at the beginning. The following day they issued a statement from the I.W.W. hall in Eugene, demanding a nine-hour day, reinstatement on the job for all who had walked off, and an end to bullying and mistreatment by foremen.[116] The strikers and hangers-on at the I.W.W. hall tried to induce all the workers on the project to join the strike. They met the work car as it left the city in the morning and as it returned in the evening and, amid scenes of near riot, tried to persuade the workers on the car to join the strike.[117] Every evening, forty or fifty Wobblies paraded down Willamette Street, the main street of Eugene, carrying placards, singing songs, and shouting their grievances. They also picketed the Quick Lunch on lower Willamette Street because the restaurant owner catered to "scabs" and because he even furnished free eggs and vegetables to the spectators who wished to pelt the nightly paraders.[118]

James Morgan, one of the leaders of the little strike, assaulted a worker on the work car, a back-sliding Wobbly caught trying to return to the job on the grade. Morgan chose to go to jail rather than pay the modest fine. From jail, Morgan wrote a letter to the editor of one of the local newspapers and presented his case to the public. He insisted that the strike was only temporarily ended, that the I.W.W. would return in force in the spring. He did not feel guilty about assaulting the "scab." Such workers, he commented, were "feeble-minded," and the particular worker he had attacked was "just walking around to save funeral expenses."[119]

A local strike of loggers in the Coos Bay region of the Oregon coast reveals again the typical I.W.W. strike. Wobblies in logging camps walked off the job in May 1913, to protest the laying-off of several of their fellow Wobblies. Afterwards, almost as if for good measure, they formulated a number of demands, higher wages and better living conditions in the camps.[120] By June, the strike had

[115] *Ibid.,* May 3, 1912, p. 7.
[116] Eugene *Guard,* Dec. 2, 1912, pp. 1, 8.
[117] *Ibid.,* Dec. 3, 1912, p. 6. [119] *Ibid.,* Dec. 13, 1912, p. 8.
[118] *Ibid.,* Dec. 11, 1912, p. 8. [120] Coos Bay *News,* May 13, 1913, p. 4.

died but the citizens of the area had been stimulated to radical action against the few Wobblies who remained behind. A group of Marshfield citizens—six hundred in all—deported Secretary W. J. Edgworth of the local I.W.W. hall by marching him out of town and giving him a boat ride eight miles down the coast. The citizens, however, let two Wobblies escape during the raid on the hall, and while most of the town was busy deporting Edgworth, the two Wobblies, with characteristic effrontery, mounted soap boxes in downtown Marshfield to harangue the few lethargic citizens still in town. The returning vigilantes soon discovered them and deported them on a second boat, first marching them through the streets and forcing them periodically to kneel and kiss an American flag.[121]

Thus, in the period between its founding and the first world war, the I.W.W. in the Pacific Northwest developed its tactical weapons and grew into its distinctive personality. Incapable of functioning as a real labor union, it practiced its philosophy in curious quasi-political agitation designed to annoy the authorities and the presumed class enemy. Wobblies casually sowed prodigious dragons' teeth, and they lived to suffer the terrible armed men.

Why did the I.W.W., though a failure in its main purpose, succeed in evoking so much hostility, even from the more sober elements of organized labor? Obviously they provoked much violence against themselves deliberately as a means of justifying their own doctrine to themselves. But, more important, they entered an American garden as outsiders and outcasts, invited in to be the hired gardeners, to be sure, but on the tacit understanding that they would not complain that the garden grew tares and nettles. Their very existence as hoboes and aliens, as well as the rude and heathenish doctrine of class division they shouted so loudly, made them a rebuke to and a denial of the cherished myth. That Jeffersonian myth at the heart of this post-frontier society was actually threatened much more by the railroad boom and the beginning of large-scale capitalist exploitation of the region's resources than by the I.W.W. rhetoric. But the I.W.W. appeared, almost providentially it would seem, as scapegoats.

The pattern of using Wobblies as scapegoats revealed itself most clearly during the hysterical war months of 1917 and 1918 when

[121] Portland *Oregonian*, June 26, 1913, p. 4.

the threat to the myth hid itself behind an anti-I.W.W. frenzy. But from 1907 to 1916 the sacrifice was being prepared. Mayors, city councilmen, sheriffs, presidents of banks and Chambers of Commerce, lumber-mill owners and main-street merchants all joined forces to preserve the myth by making war on the I.W.W. The I.W.W. unwittingly made itself terribly available for all the fury that soon descended upon it.

CHAPTER III

A
HARVES
OF
VIOLENCE

In the free-speech fight at Everett, Washington, in late 1916, the I.W.W. reaped a bitter harvest from its first decade of sowing revolution. Emboldened perhaps by their own fearsome reputation, Wobblies descended upon Everett to speak on the downtown streets, their determination increasing with each arrest and beating they suffered at the hands of Snohomish County deputies. The intransigence of both Wobblies and authorities reached its furious climax at the city dock with a gun battle that left at least seven men killed and many more wounded. The conflict in Everett repeated in the main pattern of earlier free-speech fights along the Pacific Coast, but its crescendo of violence, its terrible dramatic unity, marked it a culmination to all harassment of Wobblies before the first world war. It summed up in a few moments of history—illumined as if by a flash of lightning—all the I.W.W.'s exhortations, all its rowdy hymn singing under the street lights of small Western towns, all its picaresque militancy, all its "martyrdoms," and also all the righteous indignation and violence of authorities and respectable burghers.

The I.W.W. did not bring class conflict into Everett; rather, the almost feudal organization of the community made it inevitable. Everett was a new city of about 30,000 people thirty miles north of Seattle on Puget Sound. Two agents of John D. Rockefeller, scouting for profitable ways to invest their employer's millions, had founded the city as a promotion in the early 1890s.[1] By 1900, the new settlement boasted a population of 8,000 and a growing complex of lumber and shingle mills. It had also become a station on the Great Northern Railroad.[2] In 1902, the Weyerhaeuser Timber Company purchased the dilapidated Bell-Nelson Mill Company property in Everett and began thus its manufacturing career in the Pacific Northwest lumber industry. It remained the only mill of the Weyerhaeuser Timber Company in the whole Pacific Northwest—a "barometer mill"[3]—until 1915, when the company built its Everett Mill B.

The residents of Everett proudly called their city the "City of Smokestacks."[4] The large, permanent mills obtained their raw materials of spruce, fir, and cedar from the log booms floated to the Everett harbor from all around the shores of Puget Sound.[5] The city's shingle mills alone accounted for a good share of the shingle production of the whole region, and by 1912 almost four-fifths of all shingles cut in the United States came from the Pacific Northwest.[6] A perfume of cedar hung permanently over the city, an industrial by-product considerably more poetic than the usual smelly effluvia of industrial towns. Everett had other differences. It had no obvious slums, no "I.W.W. problem," no blatant poverty, and hardly any transients among its settled, home-body labor force.[7]

The life of the city, of course, depended almost totally upon its lumber and shingle mills, and lumbermen, as might be expected, controlled the economic resources of the community, its retail stores, its banks, most of its real estate.[8] Lumbermen also comprised the local aristocracy and dominated the social and political life of the city. Fred K. Baker of the F. K. Baker Lumber Company served

---

[1] Ralph W. Hidy, Frank Ernest Hill, and Allan Nevins, *Timber and Men: The Weyerhaeuser Story* (New York, 1963), p. 221.

[2] *Ibid.*

[3] *Ibid.* p. 228.

[4] Lowell S. Hawley and Ralph Bushnell Potts, *Counsel for the Damned: A Biography of George Francis Vanderveer* (Philadelphia, 1953), p. 171.

[5] *Ibid.*

[6] Wilson Compton, *The Organization of the Lumber Industry* (Chicago, 1916), p. 45.

[7] Hawley and Potts, *op. cit.*, p. 172.

[8] G. R. Leighton, "Seattle, Washington: The Edge of the Last Frontier," *Harper's*, (Mar., 1939), p. 428.

as president of the Everett Commercial Club.[9] David M. Clough, a former Governor of Minnesota and head of the Clough-Hartley Lumber Company, was a leading citizen. His son-in-law and business partner, Roland Hartley, later became Governor of Washington.[10]

Even before the first appearance of the I.W.W. in Everett, the local community leaders concerned themselves with that potential threat. The news of the I.W.W. troubles in Seattle in 1912 and 1913 and of Colonel Blethen's crusade against "red flag anarchism" found sympathetic readers in Everett. The International Union of Shingle Weavers, a militant affiliate of the A.F.L. with strong representation in Everett, had also thoroughly aroused the passions of workers and local aristocracy before the first Wobbly appeared.

The shingle weavers had organized an independent union as early as 1890. In January 1903, the union affiliated with the A.F.L. under the name International Shingle Weavers of America. For several years, from 1913 to 1915, the A.F.L. granted complete jurisdiction over all regional timber workers to the International Shingle Weavers. The I.W.W. looked covetously toward the union, and from 1908 on tried persistently but unsuccessfully to woo the Shingle Weavers away from the A.F.L., even introducing a resolution to that effect which was unanimously voted down in the convention of the union in 1912.[11] In the notoriously "open shop" lumber industry the relative success of the International Shingle Weavers, and even the elan which allowed the union to resist the blandishments of the I.W.W., can be explained by the pride of craft that most workers possessed. Shingle weaving was a dangerous trade. Workers manipulated blocks of cedar wood through open saws by hand, somewhat like a butcher slicing bologna. Most veteran shingle weavers could be easily identified by their variously mutilated hands—or even handless arms.[12]

In 1915, the Shingle Weavers in Everett and in their other locals had gone out on strike protesting a twenty per cent cut in wages.[13]

---

[9] *American Lumberman*, Nov. 11, 1916, p. 28.

[10] Leighton, *op. cit.*, p. 428.

[11] *Industrial Worker*, Apr. 12, 1913, p. 1.

[12] Cloice R. Howd, *Industrial Relations in the West Coast Lumber Industry*, U.S. Dept. of Labor, Bureau of Labor Statistics, Bulletin No. 349 (Washington, 1924), pp. 36-37.

[13] Seattle *Union Record*, Apr. 15, 1916, p. 3; Apr. 22, 1916, p. 1.

The strike failed, but the strikers extracted a promise from the mill
owners that as soon as the market improved the old wage scale
would be restored. When in the spring of 1916 lumber prices again
reached the 1914 level, the Shingle Weavers demanded the honor-
ing of the promise.[14] Most shingle mills in the region granted the
raise in wages to the old 1914 level, but the Everett mill owners, the
most influential in the industry, refused or delayed. On May 1,
1916, over four hundred shingle weavers in Everett left their jobs,
beginning a long and bitter strike.[15]

For a time, their strike seemed to be succeeding. The Clough-
Hartley mill, with an ostentatious disregard for the strike, planned
to resume full operations on June 1, with a new open-shop policy.
But on June 1, no one showed up for work.[16] As the weeks passed,
however, the Shingle Weavers union began to show signs of dis-
organization. On August 18, only eighteen pickets appeared for
duty on the picket line, and strike breakers spirited these few
militants away to a railroad trestle and beat them severely.[17]

The I.W.W. appeared in Everett in August, as the Shingle
Weavers' strike seemed to be entering its last bitter stages of defeat.
Everett businessmen, determinedly "open shop" in their principles,
hostile toward the Shingle Weavers and opposed to the I.W.W. on
abstract principle, accused the defeated Shingle Weavers of inviting
the Wobbly agitators into Everett as a spiteful act of revenge.[18]
But Wobblies had needed no formal invitation. They had planned
a membership drive for 1916, and the troubled waters of Everett
seemed to them an ideal place to angle for new members and an
appropriate place to churn up more educative class conflict. On
July 31, the headquarters at Chicago sent James Rowan, a black-
haired volatile Irishman, to Everett to scout the sentiment for
industrial unionism and revolution.[19]

The conflict began almost quietly, with a face-to-face disagree-

[14] *Ibid.*, Apr. 15, 1916, p. 3.
[15] Cloice R. Howd, *op. cit.*, p. 61.
[16] Seattle *Union Record*, June 3, 1916, p. 1.
[17] *Ibid.*, Aug. 26, 1916, p. 8.
[18] *American Lumberman*, Nov. 11, 1916, p. 28.
[19] Walker C. Smith, *The Everett Massacre* (Chicago, n.d.) p. 35. This little
book is one of the better I.W.W. pamphlets, tendentious and biased, of
course, but argued with an impressive marshalling of facts. Interestingly
enough, the "facts" do not seem to be much in dispute among all the pro- or
anti-I.W.W. writers, only the "interpretation."

ment between two men and a routine arrest. But even this insignificant event revealed the seeds of obstinacy and anger that eventually flowered into open warfare between battalions of armed men. Rowan began his campaign in Everett by conducting a small street meeting on the night of his arrival. He discussed the exploitative nature of the lumber industry and distributed pamphlets that described the Bureau of Corporations' investigations of the "lumber trust."[20] In the course of his harangue he repeated the I.W.W.'s stock criticism of the A.F.L.; its craft organization and its predilection for making deals with employers encouraged workers in different craft to "scab" on each other. It was more rightfully the "American Separation of Labor." Jake Michel, an official of the Everett Labor Council, shouted indignantly from the sidewalk audience that Rowan was a liar. Sheriff Donald McRae of Snohomish County, expectantly waiting for trouble in a nearby parked car, offered to arrest Rowan. But Michel, probably a little taken aback by the sheriff's eagerness, demurred and explained that Rowan had not said anything to warrant arresting him. Nevertheless, McRae pulled Rowan down from his soap box and took him to the county jail. There the sheriff blustered and threatened and, after an hour of this lecturing, released the presumably cowed Rowan. But, unintimidated, Rowan rushed back to the corner and resumed his speech at the point where Michel and the sheriff had interrupted him. An Everett city policeman then arrested him and locked him up in the city jail. The next morning, the judge of the municipal court sentenced him to thirty days in jail for peddling his pamphlets without a license but offered him the alternative sentence of banishment. With the tenacity typical of Wobblies even in defeat, Rowan demanded to be represented by counsel and was refused by the court, demanded a jury trial and was refused, demanded a postponement and was refused. Finally, with no further harassments to draw from his bag of tricks, Rowan chose the alternative sentence of leaving town. He left to get a job in the woods and to familiarize himself with working conditions in the lumber industry.[21]

The Chicago headquarters of the I.W.W. responded to this first

---

[20] U.S. Dept. of Commerce and Labor; Bureau of Corporations, *The Lumber Industry*, 2 vols.; 4 parts (Washington, 1913-1914).

[21] Smith, *op. cit.*, p. 35.

defeat by sending Levi Remick to Everett. Remick talked to sympathetic Shingle Weavers and sold them some I.W.W. pamphlets on the street before the police ordered him also to stop peddling without a license. The city officials quoted him such an exorbitant fee for a license that he left for Seattle to raise funds to open a hall in Everett where he could distribute his literature free from the city licensing regulations. He returned to Everett a few days later and opened an I.W.W. hall on Hewitt Avenue.[22] Through most of August, the police and the sheriff allowed the hall to function unmolested, but the brief calm marked only a breathing spell in the conflict that had already well begun. Both Wobblies and authorities had squared off and were circling each other cautiously.

In the latter part of August, the resolve of both sides produced more open conflict. The I.W.W. decided to sponsor a speech by James P. Thompson, one of its better known organizers and a leader of the Spokane free-speech fight of seven years earlier. Various I.W.W. sympathizers, mostly from the Shingle Weavers, had petitioned the Seattle I.W.W. office for such a major speaker. The I.W.W. scheduled Thompson's speech for August 22. When they found they could not rent a hall in Everett for the meeting, they decided reluctantly to hold it on the street. On the day before the speech, Sheriff McRae and several city policemen stormed into the hall, tore all the advertisements for the meeting from the walls, and warned Remick with colorful expletives that they intended to suppress the meeting. Remick locked the hall and hurried to Seattle for advice.[23]

Shortly after Remick had locked the hall and left for Seattle, Rowan returned to Everett from a job in the woods. Finding the hall locked, he pried his way in and reopened it for business. McRae and a policeman rushed back to the hall within an hour of its reopening and ordered Rowan to leave town immediately or serve his thirty-day jail sentence. Rowan left town. In Seattle, the report made by Remick, and, a few hours later, the corroborative report of Rowan, made the Wobblies even more determined to hold the meeting in Everett.[24]

According to schedule, Thompson arrived in Everett and began to conduct his meeting, speaking to a large crowd of sympathizers, hecklers, and mere curiosity seekers. He spoke for an uninterrupted

[22] *Ibid.*, pp. 35-36.   [23] *Ibid.*, p. 37.   [24] *Ibid.*, p. 38

half hour before fifteen policemen pushed through the crowd and arrested him. Rowan, back in town for the meeting, took Thompson's place and began to lead the crowd in singing the "Red Flag." The police dragged him away. A woman then rushed to replace Rowan and to take up the singing again. She too was arrested. Another woman rushed forward and began to recite the Declaration of Independence, and she too was quickly silenced. Jake Michel, suddenly changing sides from his first position in the conflict, began to speak in protest over the arrests, and he also was arrested.[25] Exasperated by all these eager replacements rushing forward to the soap box after each arrest, the police devised a system whereby they could capture all the disturbers of the peace at once and thus end the troubles quickly. They joined hands and formed a circle around the speakers and their immediate audience, allowing the innocent bystanders to slip out of the cordon and holding in the suspected Wobblies.[26] Then they marched their prisoners through the streets *en masse* to the city jail. Rowan somehow escaped this police-escorted parade. He rushed back to the corner and resumed the meeting, speaking for almost half an hour before being arrested again.[27]

The following morning, the police marched the prisoners to the city dock and put them on a passenger boat bound for Seattle, appropriating the thirteen dollars needed to pay the fares from the pocket of one of the more affluent deportees. Upon arriving in Seattle the Wobblies—those who were indeed Wobblies—conferred with the Seattle members at a specially-called meeting in the I.W.W. hall. They formed a Free Speech Committee, and volunteers began immediately to conduct street meetings in Seattle to raise funds for the struggle. At the same time, in Everett, the A.F.L. Labor Council passed a stinging resolution condemning Sheriff McRae and the city official for suppressing free speech.[28]

In all the I.W.W. literature Sheriff McRae is identified as a hireling of the "lumber trust," as a "lackey of the lumber barons," or with some such ideologically charged names. But McRae had been a member of the International Shingle Weavers' union before his elevation to the sheriff's office, and he had even contributed to the strike fund of his union. Although he gave much trouble to the

---

[25] *Ibid.*, Seattle *Union Record*, Aug. 16, 1916, p. 8.
[26] *Ibid.*   [27] Smith, *op. cit.*, p. 38   [28] *Ibid.*, p. 41.

I.W.W. in Everett, the Wobblies—or someone—gave him tit for tat. He received annoying telephone calls. His property was decorated with I.W.W. propaganda stickers. He received anonymous and threatening mail. He also lost two valuable hunting dogs to poisoners, and this particular sabotage led him to an entirely sincere feeling of outrage against the I.W.W. Perhaps he did not need to be "bought out" by the "lumber trust."[29]

In spite of the rising tempers of Seattle Wobblies and ample evidence of an increasing toughness on the part of officials in Everett, the conflict subsided. Several militant Wobblies, fired by the meeting at Seattle, did return to Everett the next day. A squad of Sheriff McRae's deputies met them at the interurban railroad station and sent them back to Seattle. Several days later, however, F. W. Stead, an organizer from Seattle, returned to Everett without meeting any deputies. He reopened the hall and for several weeks kept it open without incident. Rowan, after serving eight days in jail for his part in the Thompson meeting, conducted street meetings for several consecutive evenings without even seeing a deputy or policeman. Somewhat prematurely, the I.W.W. celebrated an easy victory. "Everett Fight an Easy Victory," the I.W.W. press announced.[30] Subsequent I.W.W. histories, however, explained the strange lull with less self-congratulation. Federal mediators had come to Everett to investigate the labor troubles in the shingle mills, and the Everett authorities during their visit had concealed their real intentions and had behaved with moderation toward the I.W.W. only to make a good impression. During the truce, however, the authorities and the business leaders of the Commercial Club organized their forces and quietly built a formidable army of volunteer deputies, organized into specialized squadrons with such functions as guarding the ingresses to the city or patrolling hobo jungles.[31]

On September 9, after the mediators had left, the conflict erupted again into violence. Some Wobblies assembled at Mukilteo, a small town about four miles from Everett, and boarded a launch they had rented, the *Wanderer*. They hoped to smuggle themselves into Everett by avoiding the carefully watched common carriers. As

---

29 Hawley and Potts, *op. cit.*, p. 181.
30 *Industrial Worker*, Sept. 2, 1916, p. 1.
31 Smith, *op. cit.*, p. 41.

they approached the city dock of Everett, another launch carrying armed deputies pulled abreast of them. The deputies opened fire on the *Wanderer*, overtook it, and boarded it. After cuffing and manhandling the captured Wobblies to impress a lesson upon them, the deputies took them ashore and locked them up in the county jail. For over a week, the prisoners waited in jail without a hearing and without charges being preferred against them. McRae eventually released them after his deputies had gone over them again to emphasize the lesson that they were unwelcome.[32]

Two days after the unsuccessful invasion of the *Wanderer*, the few Wobblies still in Everett renewed the conflict by trying once again to hold street meetings. The first attempt produced a small riot. Deputies pulled the first speaker, Harry Feinberg, from the stand and dragged him to the county jail. Instead of booking him and locking him up for trial, they proceeded to beat him up on the steps of the jail. When he broke away and fled down the street, they wildly fired their pistols after him. A second speaker, only a few minutes later, suffered the same fate. John Ovist, the third speaker, took his beating on the street corner without the unnecessary formality of being arrested and taken to the jail. During the fracas at the street corner, which continued after the first few arrests, the deputies put white handkerchiefs around their necks to identify themselves and to avoid hitting each other. The device, however, did not help them to distinguish bystanders from Wobblies, and a number of Everett citizens, in no way connected to the I.W.W., suffered welts and bruises along with the Wobblies.[33]

As tension increased in Everett, citizens began to choose sides more actively. The I.W.W. even muted its revolutionary message somewhat and began to emphasize the constitutional issues involved, and to point out the decay of law and order, the attack on persons such as Jake Michel, the lack of discrimination by hastily-organized deputies. The force of deputies, of course, did not lack for volunteers, but, as in all previous free-speech fights, the I.W.W. won considerable public support and sympathy. One angry citizen, injured by the nondiscriminating deputies at the riot on Hewitt and Wetmore Streets, telephoned the Chief of Police the following

---

[32] *Industrial Worker*, Sept. 16, 1916, p. 1; Portland *Oregonian*, Mar. 28, 1917, p. 6.
[33] Smith, *op. cit.*, pp. 51-58.

morning and lodged a bitter complaint. The chief was—or claimed to be—shocked at the report. But he refused to accept responsibility for the acts of Sheriff McRae's deputies, insisting that the sheriff's office and the Commercial Club had bypassed him and had taken over the control of the city.[34] Merchants in Everett began to display signs in their windows notifying customers that they did *not* belong to the Commercial Club.[35]

Public support for the Wobblies—or at the very least, citizens' opposition to the sheriff's office—began to organize in September. Two thousand persons gathered at the Everett Labor Temple and planned a mass meeting for all citizens of Everett. About a third of the town—ten thousand people—attended the mass meeting in the city park. McRae and city officials answered complaints and defended their actions. Because of such public pressure, McRae promised to allow the I.W.W. to return to Everett.[36] Not trusting McRae's contrition but quite willing to test his promise, Wobblies reopened their hall, but several days later McRae and a contingent of deputies pushed their way into the hall and deported the new organizer as peremptorily as his predecessors. The I.W.W. did not for several weeks try again to open the hall.[37]

In October, the struggle settled into a dogged and vigilant stalemate, the Wobblies making persistent efforts to infiltrate the city, the deputies guarding the ingresses turning back the Wobblies with fists and clubs. During the month, the deputies deported between three and four hundred real or suspected Wobblies. They also enlisted the aid of railroad detectives, who became unusually severe with transients who had previously ridden in empty freight cars with little interference.[38]

On October 30, the I.W.W. made a major effort to break the blockade. Forty-one Wobblies, many just off the harvest fields of the Pacific Northwest, boarded a passenger boat in Seattle to try to break into Everett in force. The contingent was at least twice as big as any earlier one. Deputies with their identifying white handkerchiefs around their necks met the boat at the city dock. They sifted the forty-one Wobblies from among the other pas-

---

[34] *Ibid.*, p. 61; Seattle *Union Record*, Apr. 7, 1917, p. 4.
[35] Seattle *Union Record*, Nov. 11, 1916, p. 5.
[36] *Industrial Worker*, Sept. 23, 1916, p. 1.
[37] Smith, *op. cit.*, p. 63.
[38] *Ibid.*, pp. 72-75.

sengers and then proceeded to beat them mercilessly with clubs and revolver butts. In the excitement, as horrified passengers scurried to get away, the deputies clouted Wobblies, some of the passengers, and even some of themselves, as they flailed wildly and drunkenly on the congested dock. One deputy, Joe Schofield, opened the scalp of another deputy as he swung his revolver butt enthusiastically but with uncertain aim among the crowd.[39]

The deputies loaded their battered prisoners into waiting trucks and automobiles and drove them through the gathering dusk to Beverly Park, a lonely wooded area outside Everett and on the railroad tracks leading to Seattle. There the deputies deployed themselves into two lines facing each other and forced the Wobblies, one by one, to run the gauntlet. In a cold, penetrating rain they beat the Wobblies with clubs, blackjacks, and revolver butts, and fired after them if they broke through the lines and tried to escape.[40] After the night's work was done, when the bruised and bleeding Wobblies assembled on the interurban train for Seattle, the startled passengers wondered if there had just been a train wreck in the vicinity.

The following morning, and for the next few days, Everett seethed with curiosity and indignation. Deputies, patrolling their beats, stopped citizens on the street to deny gratuitously any part in the affair at Beverly Park. A committee of Everett clergymen and other citizens assembled to discuss the affair and to appoint a team of investigators to go out to Beverly Park to inspect the grounds.[41] The committee also discussed the urgent need to get the affairs of the city back into the hands of responsible officials. It proposed another mass meeting in the city park. One clergyman left for Seattle to get the support of the I.W.W. in the proposed mass meeting. The committee decided such a meeting was necessary because the Everett press had carried no reports of the I.W.W. troubles nor of the Beverly Park beatings.[42]

The I.W.W. needed no urging by the visiting clergyman to take

---

[39] *Industrial Worker*, Nov. 4, 1916, p. 1.

[40] *Ibid.*; Portland *Oregon Daily Journal*, Nov. 6, 1916, p. 13; Portland *Oregonian*, Mar. 13, 1917, p. 6.

[41] Seattle *Union Record*, Apr. 21, 1917, p. 5.

[42] Anna Louise Strong, "The Verdict at Everett," *Survey* (May 19, 1917), p. 161. The local Everett newspaper is indeed a worthless source on the I.W.W. troubles.

part in the proposed meeting. In fact, the Seattle I.W.W. promptly usurped the planning for the meeting. The I.W.W. decided to hold the meeting on the following Sunday afternoon, November 5, in the city park of Everett.[43] It notified all I.W.W. branches and locals in the region of the plans and began publishing handbills and circulars for distribution in Everett. It also notified the authorities in Everett of its plan, in none too diplomatic terms, and it invited reporters from the Seattle daily newspapers to accompany the Wobbly army. Organizers began to sign up recruits in the Seattle hall for the excursion.[44]

Sheriff McRae and the Commercial Club made their preparations also for the threatened invasion. On November 4, the day before the scheduled mass meeting, McRae stormed into the I.W.W. hall and arrested all the Wobblies he found there. He boasted to Chester Micklin, the Wobbly in charge, that the meeting the next day would not be held. He offered Micklin a bet of a hundred dollars that it would not be held.[45] In the evening, three hundred deputies met in the Commercial Club to form the Everett Open Shop League, a name that made no pretense, obviously, of concealing the alliance of economic interest and law and order. Leigh H. Irvine, director of the Employers' Association of Washington, a violently anti-union body, exhorted the meeting of deputies,[46] and after his speech, the deputies received their arms and their instructions to assemble the next day on the call of the mill whistles.[47]

At almost the last minute, the I.W.W. leaders in Seattle decided to transport their army to Everett by boat. The interurban railroad could not supply enough extra coaches, and the I.W.W. could not assemble enough automobiles or trucks. On Sunday morning, November 5, three hundred singing Wobblies, marching four abreast, paraded through the streets of Seattle to the waterfront. About two hundred and fifty filed aboard the *Verona*, a regular passenger boat, at the Colman Dock. Thirty-eight other Wobblies had to

[43] Smith, *op. cit.*, pp. 79-80.
[44] Charles Ashleigh, "Defense Fires Opening Guns," *International Socialist Review* (May 1917), p. 673.
[45] Smith, *op. cit.*, p. 82.
[46] *American Lumberman*, Nov. 11, 1916, p. 28.
[47] Seattle *Union Record*, Apr. 28, 1917, p. 4.

REBELS OF THE WOODS

wait half an hour to board the *Calista*, the next scheduled passenger boat for Everett.[48]

At about one o'clock in the afternoon, the mill whistles in Everett summoned the deputies to the Commercial Club. The Seattle police had telegraphed officials in Everett that the Wobbly army had left by boat. Although the I.W.W. had certainly not concealed its departure or its aim, news of the embarkation reached Everett in garbled form. Relayed through two or three officials, the news reached the assembled deputies in a frightening form. They heard that a boatload of Wobblies, armed to the teeth, had left Seattle determined to avenge the Beverly Park beatings.[49] The deputies then apparently fortified themselves with liquor and marched to the city dock to await the *Verona*. Hundreds of Everett citizens, familiar with the plans for the forthcoming meeting in the city park, also came to the city dock to wait for the Wobblies. Roped away from the dock itself, they found vantage points on adjacent docks and on the low hill overlooking the harbor. The deputies took up defensive positions inside the warehouse at the end of the dock and Sheriff McRae and two deputies took up a position out in the open on the dock. It was hardly a military deployment. McRae and the two deputies were in the line of fire from the concealed deputies behind them. A tugboat in the harbor, filled with deputies, also directed its fire toward the men on the dock and in the warehouse.[50]

As the *Verona* neared the dock, the two hundred and fifty Wobbly passengers crowded the main deck. A few had climbed up onto the cabin and one Wobbly, Hugo Gerlot, had scaled the mast and was waving at the crowd of spectators on the hill as the boat cut through the harbor. He and the other Wobblies on the main deck were singing the English Transport Workers' song, "Hold the Fort":

> We meet today in Freedom's cause,
>   And raise our voices high,
> We'll join our hands in union strong,
>   To battle or to die.

---

[48] Portland *Oregon Daily Journal*, Nov. 6, 1916, p. 13.
[49] Smith, *op. cit.*, p. 85; Portland *Oregon Daily Journal*, Nov. 6, 1916, p. 13.
[50] Smith, *op. cit.*, pp. 85-87.

74

Hold the fort for we are coming,
   Union men be strong.
Side by side we battle onward,
   Victory will come.

The bowline of the *Verona* had been made fast before McRae, standing on the dock, raised his hand to silence the singing and shouting.

"Who is your leader?" he shouted.

"We're all leaders!" the men on the deck chorused.

"You can't land here," McRae announced.

"The hell we can't!" the Wobblies shouted as they crowded the deck around the gangplank, ready to leave the boat.[51]

At that instant a shot split the tense momentary silence. Immediately, whole volleys cracked through the air. Many of the crowded Wobblies on the deck crumpled under the fire. The rest rushed frantically toward the sheltered side of the cabin, starting a panic rush that threatened to capsize the boat.[52] Some Wobblies tried to slide across the deck to unfasten the bowline but were driven back by the heavy fire. Ernest Shellgren, the engineer of the *Verona*, backed the boat away from the dock at full power, snapping the bowline. After almost ten minutes of gun fire, the *Verona* churned out into the harbor and out of range. On its melancholy return to Seattle the defeated *Verona* met the *Calista*, and the battered and wounded Wobblies warned their comrades not to proceed.[53]

The unwounded Wobblies gave crude first-aid to the thirty-one wounded men aboard, three of whom had been ordinary passengers of the *Verona*. They carried their dead to the cabin, Hugo Gerlot, John Looney, Gustav Johnson, and Abraham Rabinowitz. One of the wounded, Felix Baron, was to die later in Seattle. The I.W.W. claimed subsequently that at least half a dozen other Wobblies, unidentified free-speech fighters, had been killed and had fallen into the harbor from the boat. Rumors later circulated that residents of Everett had found bodies washed up on the shore.[54] Back on the Everett dock, the deputies counted their dead and wounded.

[51] *Ibid.*, p. 88.
[52] Seattle *Post-Intelligencer*, Apr. 14, 1917, p. 5.
[53] Walker C. Smith, "The Voyage of the Verona," *International Socialist Review*, (Dec. 1916), p. 342.
[54] Seattle *Union Record*, Dec. 9, 1916, p. 1.

Lieutenant C. O. Curtis and Deputy Jefferson Beard were dead. Nineteen others were wounded. Sheriff McRae, one of the nineteen, had gunshot wounds in his left leg and heel. The battle had been confused. During its height one frightened deputy had fled from the warehouse at the end of the dock, wounded slightly in the ear. He took refuge among the bystanders on an adjacent dock, shouting hysterically, "They're crazy in there, firing in all directions!"[55]

When the *Verona* reached Seattle, scores of policemen swarmed aboard to take the dead to the morgue, separate the wounded for medical care, and arrest all the other Wobblies. At the jail, police proceeded to sift out the most culpable conspirators from the crowd of over two hundred prisoners. A private detective, for many weeks a paid violence-advocating *agent provocateur* among the Wobblies, from a darkened cell picked out seventy-four ringleaders as the crowd of prisoners filed past.[56] The state charged these men with murder, for "having assisted, counselled, aided and abetted and encouraged some unknown person to kill Jefferson Beard on the fifth of November, 1916."[57] The initial, informal charge to the press had mentioned both of the dead deputies, Curtis as well as Beard, but the District Attorney requested that the killing of C. O. Curtis be dropped from the formal charge. The prosecution thereafter never referred to Curtis. The I.W.W. requested a new coroner's inquest, claimed that the state had dropped the name of Curtis from the charge because Curtis had been killed by a rifle bullet and only the deputies had been using rifles.[58] The I.W.W. also claimed that it could produce several witnesses to testify that Curtis on his death bed had actually identified the fellow deputy who had shot him.[59] If the prosecution in the face of these facts tacitly admitted the innocence of the I.W.W. in the death of Curtis, the I.W.W. asked, could not Beard have met his death in the same way?

After the firing had ceased on November 5, and after the *Verona* had disappeared from the harbor, a stunned quiet descended upon Everett. The temper of some of the people, seething since the

---

55 Portland *Oregonian*, Apr. 20, 1917, p. 6.
56 Seattle *Union Record*, Apr. 28, 1917, p. 4.
57 Hawley and Potts, *op. cit.*, p. 193.
58 Seattle *Union Record*, Nov. 11, 1916, p. 5; Smith, *op. cit.*, p. 141.
59 *Solidarity*, Jan. 13, 1917, p. 1.

episode at Beverly Park, now boiled over into angry condemnation of McRae's regime. The deputies had gone much too far.[60] Some citizens growled openly to their neighbors that the I.W.W. should come back again in force and clean up the town. The I.W.W., perhaps with a certain amount of romantic wishful thinking, reported the mayor to be suffering from deep remorse. He had visited the International Shingle Weavers picket line, a rifle tucked under his arm, and had urged the pickets to separate as a precaution against possible sniping from the deputies. He also publicly donned a hair shirt by speaking on the corner of Hewitt and Wetmore to a street meeting, disclaiming any responsibility for the bloodshed at the city dock and attacking the Commercial Club as the culprit.[61] But apparently his disclaimer, even in these perhaps less-than-trustworthy I.W.W. reports, did not represent real contrition. Two hours after the battle at the dock, three Everett Wobblies came out from their hiding and with typical bravado or itch for martyrdom, delivered speeches from the corner of Hewitt and Wetmore Streets. Deputies arrested them immediately. The I.W.W. account claims that the mayor visited the three prisoners in the jail that same evening and personally inflicted a cruel "third degree" upon one of them, crushing the prisoner's fingers under the legs of the cot and beating his head against the cement floor.[62]

Within a few days after the climactic fury at the dock, Wobblies organized to defend their comrades in jail and to make telling propaganda out of their "martyrdoms." A defense committee in Seattle solicited funds for the legal defense, and Herb Mahler, the chairman of the committee, sent urgent appeals to most of the liberal and radical periodicals all over the nation. Charles Ashleigh, an English hobo-intellectual and poet, appropriately enough made the appeal to the radical and bohemian *Masses* magazine of Max Eastman in Greenwich Village.[63] In Seattle and Everett, the committee sponsored numerous "mass meetings" to arouse popular indignation and to stiffen the morale of all radical supporters. In

---

[60] Seattle *Union Record*, Nov. 11, 1916, p. 5.

[61] Smith, *op. cit.*, p. 99; letter from Mayor D. O. Merrill to Herbert Mahler, Aug. 28, 1916, Labor History Archives, Wayne State Univ. Library, Accession No. 130, Series 7, Box 3.

[62] Seattle *Union Record*, Nov. 18, 1916, p. 1.

[63] Charles Ashleigh, "Everett's Bloody Sunday," *The Masses* (Feb. 1917), pp. 18-19.

Seattle, the I.W.W. committee leased the giant Dreamland Rink for a series of protest meetings. Elizabeth Gurley Flynn led one of the enthusiastic meetings there in January 1917, before the trial began.[64]

The I.W.W. also accepted material and moral support from unexpected sources it did not have to cultivate with mass meetings and revivalistic speeches. Mayor Gill of Seattle, back in office at the head of a "reform" administration, infuriated conservatives and surprised even the Wobblies by making a public statement exonerating the Wobbly prisoners and condemning the Everett officials:

> In the final analysis it will be found that these cowards in Everett who, without right or justification, shot into the crowd on the boat, were murderers and not the I.W.W.'s ... McRae and his deputies had no legal right to tell the I.W.W.'s or any one else that they could not land there. When the sheriff put his hand on the butt of his gun and told them they could not land, he fired the first shot, in the eyes of the law, and the I.W.W.'s can claim that they shot in self-defense ... If I were one of the party of forty I.W.W.'s who was almost beaten to death by 300 citizens of Everett without being able to defend myself, I probably would have armed myself if I intended to visit Everett again . . .[65]

Gill also sent a supply of tobacco to the Wobblies in the Seattle jail and ordered three hundred blankets distributed to them. His political enemies, preparing another indictment of him and his administration as in 1912, took this shameless defense of the hapless Wobblies as just another evidence of his depravity. In the popular amalgam, corrupt politics, vice, and skid road and its denizens were all mixed up together, as to a degree they were.

The Seattle Central Labor Council volunteered practical aid to the defense by setting aside a hundred dollars for the I.W.W. defense committee and even forming its own *ad hoc* defense committee to help the prisoners;[66] the A.F.L. in Seattle was considerably more to the left than the organization in most other cities of the nation.

The authorities at Seattle eventually returned the seventy-four

64 *Industrial Worker*, Jan. 27, 1917, p. 1.
65 Seattle *Daily Times*, Nov. 8, 1916, p. 1.
66 Seattle *Union Record*, Nov. 11, 1916, p. 1.

Wobblies to the Snohomish County jail in Everett, where they remained throughout the trial. The chief defense attorney, Fred H. Moore of Los Angeles, a famous and colorful defender of Wobblies and radicals on other occasions, secured a change of venue to King County in Seattle. George F. Vanderveer, a Seattle lawyer and former prosecuting attorney of King County, joined the defense and helped secure the change of venue. The two attorneys agreed to a division of labor. Moore, much the more famous of the two at this time, would handle the "class war" or propaganda side of the defense, the part of the trial dearest to the heart of the Wobblies themselves. In fact, to facilitate this part of the defense, the I.W.W. actually forwarded I.W.W. literature anonymously to the prosecution attorneys to make sure it would be introduced into the case. Vanderveer would handle the cross-examination of prosecution witnesses and the more prosaic job of trying to find and present evidence to prove their client innocent.[67]

On March 5, 1917, the state brought Thomas Tracy, the first of the seventy-four Wobblies, to trial before Superior Court Judge J. T. Ronald. Two months later, when public interest in the case had been dissipated by the increased international tensions and the American declaration of war, the jury returned a verdict of not guilty. The weary prosecution thereupon released the other seventy-three prisoners awaiting trial in the jail in Everett. Tracy's trial alone had cost the state over twenty thousand dollars, and the cases against the other Wobblies were weaker than the case against Tracy.[68] For a brief period, after the acquittal but before the release of the seventy-three prisoners, the I.W.W. worried. Perhaps, Wobblies feared, the state intended to go through with the separate trials, relentlessly draining the I.W.W. of funds and destroying the organization by a kind of adaptation of the free-speech tactic of attrition.[69]

The state presented two somewhat disparate cases to the jury, one against the I.W.W. as an organization of criminal conspirators, the other against the individual defendant, Tracy. The division of labor in the defense between Moore and Vanderveer more or less matched the divided case presented by the prosecution. Moore

---

[67] Hawley and Potts, *op. cit.*, pp. 191-192.
[68] Strong, *op. cit.*, p. 38.
[69] Hawley and Potts, *op. cit.*, pp. 211-212.

defended the I.W.W.; Vanderveer defended Tracy. Perhaps to suggest the homicidal intent of the defendant, the state presented voluminous evidence to show that the I.W.W. was a society of conspirators advocating violence and sabotage. The jury heard many samples of I.W.W. propaganda from organizational newspapers and pamphlets.[70] In August 1916, for example, the *Industrial Worker* had published the following ambiguous but ominous threat: "Everett needs a lesson. Its mayor needs a lesson, and the chief of police will be educated. . . . The working class must win and through the use of tactics that will be extremely unpleasant to the city of Everett and enjoyable to the I.W.W., the fight can be won quickly."[71]

A cartoon on the front page of the *Industrial Worker*, also presented to the jury for its consideration, pictured a crouched cat, the symbol for sabotage. The text underneath the picture read: "Sabotage is the weapon of the disinherited. It is a shield of defense and protection against the usuries and vexations of the bosses." Over the picture was a further suggestion: "A good hint; use it!"[72] A few weeks later, the *Industrial Worker* published another cartoon with similar message. The cartoon pictured a wasps' nest with a stream of wasps issuing from it and pursuing a man labeled "Everett." The explanation read: "New tactics have been used and are being used as the workers have realized that saying, 'Here is my head, hit it,' can no longer win fights for the movement."[73]

Even while the trial was in progress, the prosecution could have used more current examples of I.W.W. incitation to sabotage. The Chicago I.W.W. newspaper, *Solidarity*, printed a threatening cartoon that pictured a group of black cats intently watching a mouse hole labeled "Everett trial."[74]

In its indictment of the I.W.W. as a criminal organization, the state examined witnesses who testified that Wobbly street-corner agitators had advocated sabotage and violence; others, including

[70] Portland *Oregonian*, Mar. 16, 1917, p. 6. Because the trial ended in an acquittal and was, of course, not appealed, the official court records are very rudimentary, including nothing more than the subpoena lists and the venue list.
[71] *Industrial Worker*, Aug. 26, 1916, p. 1.
[72] *Ibid.*, Sept. 23, 1916, p. 1.
[73] *Ibid.*, Oct. 7, 1916, p. 1.
[74] *Solidarity*, Mar. 10, 1917, p. 1.

the mayor, who testified to an increase in the number of suspected cases of arson in Everett during the free-speech fight; and still others, who testified that the Wobblies on board the *Verona* had been heavily armed and grimly determined to pay back the brutality of police and deputies. Conservative publicists outside the court room also presented a similar case against the I.W.W. in newspapers and magazines. Wobbly orators had been "crude, vulgar, often foul-mouthed but always effective." These "insolently grinning, defiant agitators" had deliberately provoked the violence by insisting upon speaking at the proscribed street corner when they had "twenty square miles upon which to indulge in free speech without let or hindrance."[75] Wobblies, of course, had been permitted to use the city park without interference during the meeting of Everett citizens that had questioned Sheriff McRae and other officials. But the Wobblies' intransigence angered the Everett businessmen, already furious from the International Shingle Weavers' strike, and they had justifiably "drifted into a dangerous state of mind."[76]

Vanderveer cross-examined the early prosecution witnesses vigorously. After Owen Clay, a special deputy and prosecution witness, had been led through his story, Vanderveer asked him only two simple questions on cross-examination:

"Who shot Jeff Beard?"

"I don't know."

"Did *you* do it?"

"I don't know," the witness replied in an agonized whisper.

Dramatically, Vanderveer had impressed upon the jurors all the confusion, the drunken cross-fire, the irresponsibility on the city dock as the *Verona* tied up.[77]

After Mayor D. D. Merrill had testified to the spate of mysterious fires in Everett during the troubles, implying a campaign of I.W.W. arson, Vanderveer got him to admit that the record for fire losses in the city was, if anything, lower than for any other year in the city's history and that only two fires could possibly

[75] W. V. Woehlke, "The I.W.W. and the Golden Rule," *Sunset* (Feb. 1917), pp. 17-18. This article is perhaps the best non-I.W.W. account of the Everett troubles, an account that admits most of what can be found in Walker C. Smith's I.W.W. pamphlet but tries to explain and to justify the violence against the Wobblies.

[76] *Ibid.*, p. 67.

[77] Hawley and Potts, p. 196.

be suspected as instances of arson. Vanderveer also managed to leave the impression with the jurors, in spite of prosecution objections, that even those two cases of possible arson were acts committed by the *agents provocateur* planted inside the I.W.W. by its enemies. Repeatedly, Vanderveer queried prosecution witnesses about the position of the *Verona* while it was tied to the bollard on the dock, getting into the record the prosecution's consensus on the precise position of the boat. The *Verona* apparently had been nosing the dock with its stern drifting vertically into the harbor.[78] This testimony on the position of the ship, together with other testimony as to Tracy's position on the ship, persuaded the jury of Tracy's innocence.

Although the prosecution's case against the I.W.W. as a criminal organization bore little relevancy to the question of Thomas Tracy's guilt or innocence, the defense, when its time came, devoted a great deal of time in an effort to refute it. Fred Moore, of course, put a brighter interpretation on many matters introduced by the prosecution with innuendo or outrage. Defense witnesses testified in rebuttal that Everett had not experienced any unusual numbers of fires. They testified to the moderation of I.W.W. speakers and pointed to their passive acquiescence to arrest.[79] Indeed, the undisputed exhortations to violence had come from the Pinkerton spy, and Wobblies had quickly pulled him off the soap box themselves.[80] The defense also pointed to the open and unconspiratorial preparations in Seattle for the voyage of November 5, and also to the shock and panic on the deck of the *Verona* when the firing began, as evidence of the peaceful intentions of the invading Wobblies. As to the question of sabotage, the defense brought I.W.W. "experts" to the stand to lecture the jury on the theory and practice of sabotage or "direct action." The secret wrecker with bomb and faggot portrayed by the prosecution was a bogey, these witnesses explained. Sabotage meant only the withdrawal of efficiency on the job or other innocent pranks to disconcert the boss. [81]

In this aggressive defense of the I.W.W. as an organization, Moore presented a parade of Wobbly witnesses beginning with

---

[78] *Ibid.*, p. 199.
[79] Seattle *Union Record*, May 7, 1917, p. 4.
[80] Seattle *Post-Intelligencer*, May 6, 1917, p. 7.
[81] Smith, p. 179.

Herbert Mahler, the secretary of the Seattle branch. Mahler, James Thompson, and others read the I.W.W. preamble to the jury and explained it. They lectured the court on the sectarian distinctions between De Leon and themselves or between Socialists and themselves. Then defense witnesses testified more specifically to the role of the Commercial Club in organizing the army of special deputies.[82] The defense dwelt at length on the Beverly Park beatings, implicating both Sheriff McRae and the Commercial Club. The defense also tried to associate the prosecution at the trial with the guilty plutocracy of Everett. Vanderveer tried to question H. D. Cooley, one of the associate prosecution attorneys, asking him in an insinuating tone who had retained his services. The court sustained an objection to the question just as Vanderveer had anticipated, Actually, Attorney Cooley had been retained by Snohomish County in a quite ordinary way, but the question and the objection left the impression that the "lumber trust" had hired him.[83]

The prosecution tried vigorous cross-examination of the defense witnesses, aware that Vanderveer had scored most of his points for the defense with his implacable questioning of prosecution witnesses. On one occasion, the tactic backfired. Pressing a defense witness hard to get him to admit that in Seattle, while walking the decks of the *Verona*, he had found shells and cartridges, the witness finally blurted out to the horror of the court, "An eye! I found a human eye."[84]

Neither the portrait of the Wobbly delineated by the prosecution nor that presented by the defense seemed entirely real. The real Wobbly resembled neither the cunning villain of the prosecution nor the lovable Huck Finn of the defense. Those delineations of character, however, consumed time and public money without having much bearing on the question of the defendant's guilt or innocence. The prosecution examined many witnesses, Sheriff McRae among them, who positively identified Tracy as the Wobbly who had fired the first shot from the cabin window of the *Verona*. The defense had little difficulty in demolishing this testimony, the crux of the case against Tracy. The court adjourned to the city dock of Everett and witnessed a reenactment of the battle of No-

---

[82] Portland *Oregonian*, Mar. 11, 1917, p. 8.
[83] Seattle *Post-Intelligencer*, Apr. 21, 1917, p. 2; Hawley and Potts, p. 204.
[84] Hawley and Potts, p. 205.

vember 5. Vanderveer then demonstrated that, given the position of the *Verona* at the dock as described by almost all the prosecution witnesses, it was impossible for the witnesses to have seen Tracy or anyone else in the cabin window.[85] Vanderveer's persistent cross-examination on this point undoubtedly won Tracy his freedom.

Reports of the trial soon found their way into the back pages of the newspapers, even in the papers of the Pacific Northwest. Unfortunately for the I.W.W. propaganda aims, the defense began to present its case on April 2, 1917, the same day that President Woodrow Wilson went before a joint session of Congress to ask for a declaration of war. Hence, in spite of the regular mass meetings in Seattle, in spite of the propaganda of the conscientious defense committee, the long trial sank into anticlimax. As the defense and prosecution attorneys delineated their respective villains for the jury, the ruthless plutocrat and the furtive bomber and arsonist, the attention of the public wandered. But later, after it had assimilated the shock of war and had committed itself with crusading ardor to the war effort, the public returned to the Wobbly portrait drawn by the prosecution at the trial of Thomas Tracy and by many other like-minded artists. The conflict at Everett thus summed up a decade of agitation by the I.W.W. and helped to fix the image of an internal enemy within our embattled society.

Perhaps the more realistic picture emerging from the "massacre" and the trial is of a town torn between its dominating business establishment and its polar antagonists, the Wobbly outsiders. The townspeople, in between turned angrily against one side and then the other, really liking neither side, finding both sides threatening to their mythic "way of life," but caught between "lumber barons" and a *jacquerie*. In the coming months, this "middle" would vacillate less and would fall in behind a violent crusade for "Americanism" against the I.W.W.

---

[85] Seattle *Union Record*, Apr. 21, 1917, p. 5.

A
TASTE
OF
POWER

After a decade of dogged agitation that had never done much more than exasperate the "master class," a decade climaxed by the bloody skirmish at Everett, the I.W.W. suddenly and surprisingly grasped power. Wobblies found themselves leading a major strike in the summer of 1917, a strike that paralyzed the lumber industry of the Pacific Northwest and brought the United States government hurrying anxiously to the scene. Years of earnest preaching among submerged migratory workers suddenly and, unexpectedly, returned dividends. Unfortunately for the I.W.W., however, its new power coincided with the nation's entry into the first world war, and the fears and hysteria of the war stimulated vigilantes, local governments, and the United States government to check the Wobblies' first brief exercise of power and then to smash the organization once and for all.

The lumber strike of 1917, still recalled fondly by surviving Wobblies as the high-water mark of the I.W.W.'s influence, raced like a contagion through the camps and mills of the region. Propaganda and agitation alone did not bring on the strike, but as the liberals of the era tried to explain to an intemperate public, agitation *and* intolerable conditions had produced the strike. Conditions in the lumber industry had induced a sullen resignation or a bitter rage in most workers for many years, and the conditions in 1917 were sufficiently bad to have produced labor troubles even if the I.W.W. had not been on hand to make capital out of them.

The nub of the trouble undoubtedly lay in the intransigent atti-tudes of most employers in the industry. Most of them espoused a primitive philosophy of economic individualism and adhered relig-iously to their convenient versions of laissez-faire liberalism, a constellation of beliefs that made them antagonistic to even the most conservative forms of trade unionism. Many employers had themselves risen from the bottom rungs of the economic ladder, from "stump rancher" or sawmill worker, and many shared more of a common culture with their employees than either they or the employees recognized. But the very similarity in culture and tem-perament proved sometimes the most difficult barrier to under-standing. Although the "boss" himself might at one time have worked at the "green chain" in a lumber mill or with a "bucking" crew in the woods, and although he could "speak the same lan-guage" as his employees, he tended to sanctify his own hard struggle as the obligatory route for everyone. As one Westerner expressed the attitude: "I have lived in the woods, worked in the lumber mills, slept on the ground, eaten rough fare, blistered my hands, worked sixteen hours a day—and worked out of it into some-thing better. Why should any husky man make such a 'holler' about working conditions?"[1]

Sustained by such sanctimony, self-made employers could even afford to feel a certain camaraderie with the men in the mills or camps and at the same time little or no responsibility for depressing or degrading working conditions. Such conditions were merely a part of the game and the inevitable products of the sacrosanct free market. Efforts by workers to improve conditions through collec-tive effort were impertinent tamperings with economic law and the prerogatives of property ownership.

A few employers recognized some responsibility toward their employees and even tried to warn their colleagues of an impending storm of labor troubes. J. D. Young, manager of the Inman-Poulsen Logging Company of Kelso, Washington, chastised his fellow lum-bermen at an early convention of the National Lumber Manufac--turers' Association. He scolded them for paying more heed to their

---

[1] Requoted from: Elsie Eaton Newton, "The Ant and the Grasshopper," *Survey* (Sept. 15, 1917), p. 522; for a similar characterization of the "typical" lumberman: Brice P. Disque, "How We Found a Cure for Strikes in the Lumber Industry of the Pacific Northwest," *System* (Sept. 1919), pp. 379-384.

machines and equipment than to the needs of their men. "It is use-
less," he said in commenting on the threat of the I.W.W., "to offer
blind and unreasoning opposition, which will prove unavailing."
Rather, the industry should try to adjust reasonable grievances and
get at the causes of discontent. He looked forward to a bright day
when all logging companies would invite the YMCA into their
camps to bolster morale and improve living conditions.[2] But even
the few employers who acknowledged such a principle of *noblesse
oblige* opposed unionism and the idea of regularized collective bargaining as firmly as did the majority of employers who preached
a more frank and consistent social Darwinism.

Regardless of the social ideology of the lumbermen, the instability of the industry seemed to preclude such luxuries as collective
bargaining in labor-management relations. The open-shop individualism of the operators of camps and mills, in other words, came
about in part as an understandable rationalization of necessity
within an anarchical industry. The lumber industry has been called
the most "American" of our industries, slow to develop "intensive,
exact" managerial practices and skills; in a word, slow to organize
industry-wide oligopolistic controls.[3] The volume of production,
reflecting the lack of control, fluctuated violently, varying as much
as fifty per cent from year to year. In 1922, for example, the production in the Pacific Northwest increased 59 per cent over 1921.[4]
Dependence upon the even more unstable construction industry
accounts for some of the variation. But variation in price perhaps
reflects the instability of the industry more accurately than varia-
tions in production from year to year, because mill owners oftentimes continued production even in the face of rapidly declining
markets and their bookkeepers' red ink. Their investments in speculative timberlands, or logging and milling equipment that deteriorated quickly in disuse, compelled them to maintain production
even at a loss.[5]

2 "The I.W.W. Plague," *Timberman* (Jan. 1913), p. 25.

3 U. S. Dept. of Agriculture; Forest Service, Report No. 114; William B.
Greeley, *Some Public and Economic Aspects of the Lumber Industry* (Washington, 1917), p. 60.

4 *Four L News Letter*, Jan. 15, 1923.

5 Cloice R. Howd, *Industrial Relations in the West Coast Lumber Industry*,
U. S. Dept. of Labor, Bureau of Labor Statistics, Bulletin No. 349, (Washington, 1924), p. 18.

Profits in lumber manufacturing never reached great heights. The biggest "killings," as we have seen, came through the speculative engrossing of timberlands. In the years from 1919 to 1922, the biggest company in the Pacific Northwest produced only 180,000,-000 board feet per year, and three-fourths of the region's sawmills brought in yearly gross receipts of less than $50,000.[6] Timber ownership had become "big business," but lumber manufacturing was still typically "small business." In such an industry it sometimes became the best practice—or seemingly the necessary practice—to "exploit" labor. A rapid turnover of the most casual kind of labor—similar perhaps to the present-day use of casual labor in large-scale commercial agriculture—became the most profitable labor policy.[7]

The labor movement never exerted much pressure in the lumber industry before World War I. In 1903, as we have seen, the A.F.L. chartered the Shingle Weavers union, which had formed independently in the 1890s. In 1905, the A.F.L. granted jurisdiction over all loggers and sawmill workers to a new organization called the International Brotherhood of Woodsmen and Sawmill Workers, but this ambitiously named union at its peak claimed only twelve hundred members, most in western Montana. By 1911 it had dwindled to barely six hundred members, and the A.F.L. disbanded it for the nonpayment of its per capita assessment.[8] In 1906 an independent union on Puget Sound, the Royal Loggers, briefly appeared on the scene with several thousands members. But it collapsed after its promoter ran away with the treasury.[9]

In 1913, the Shingle Weavers union became the International Union of Shingle Weavers, Sawmill Workers, and Woodsmen, assuming the jurisdiction of the defunct International Brotherhood. In 1914, it became simply the International Union of Timber Workers. This union was essentially the Shingle Weavers union expanded to include all lumber workers. It failed to achieve the eight-hour day in a series of strikes and negotiations through 1915, and thereupon the shingle weavers separated themselves to go their

[6] U. S. Dept. of Commerce and Labor; Bureau of Corporations, *The Lumber Industry*, Vol. I, p. 38; Howd, *op. cit.*, p. 26.
[7] Paul H. Douglas, "The Problem of Labor Turnover," *American Economic Review*, VIII (June 1918), pp. 308-316. Howd, *op. cit.*, pp. 38-40.
[8] Howd, *op. cit.*, p. 57.
[9] *Ibid.; Industrial Worker*, Nov. 23, 1911, p. 4.

own way again as the International Shingle Weavers' Union of America.[10] The abandoned loggers and sawmill workers kept their few scattered locals intact and in 1916 became the International Union of Timber Workers, without jurisdiction over the shingle weavers. This confusing history of A.F.L. unions in the industry indicates, if nothing else, that the labor movement was almost as unstable as the industry itself. Moreover, these waxing and waning A.F.L. unions represented only a small percentage of the workers in the industry, most of the locals being situated in the Puget Sound and Grays Harbor region where "home guard" workers were most numerous.[11]

Although the strikers in 1917 made the eight-hour day the very symbol of their discontent, they had previously made little concerted protest over the universal ten-hour day that prevailed in the industry. Workers had always objected, however, to working longer than ten hours—sometimes as many hours as sixteen a day— when the extra work brought no extra pay. Workers also protested their wage scales, particularly if wages for the same work fluctuated widely from job to job or if the wages were suddenly reduced.[12] But, in large, part, working conditions produced the most durable source of labor unrest in the industry, and set off the 1917 strike.

Logging operations had to move their source of supply into the virgin Douglas fir forests of Western Washington and Oregon, into the pine wildernesses of Idaho and Montana. In a region of the United States only a short while removed from the frontier, the life in logging camps was primitive indeed. The typical camp lay at the end of a railroad spur or dirt road leading down through desolate cut-over lands to a small town in the valley. In Idaho and Montana, the camp might not even boast a road or a railroad connecting it to civilization, but rely instead upon a wild mountain river down which the logs were floated and up which the camp's supplies came. A half-dozen or more rough shacks served as bunk houses for the working crews. Outside the huddled ring of shacks stood the foreman's office, the camp store, the "cookie's" shack with its garbage piles and swarms of flies, and the latrines. About two dozen men—oftentimes more—slept in each bunkhouse in fetid conges-

---

[10] Howd, *op. cit.*, p. 60.
[11] "Home guard" was I.W.W. argot for a settled, nonmigratory worker.
[12] Howd, *op. cit.*, p. 40.

REBELS OF THE WOODS

tion.[13] Because logging camps of necessity were impermanent establishments, having to move every year or two with the progress of the cut, they constituted an overhead burden which companies wished to keep to a minimum. Plumbing, windows, landscaping, even adequate sleeping space became luxuries the companies could hardly afford.

Loggers worked in all kinds of weather and frequently returned to camp in wet and muddy clothes. Most camps had no facilities for bathing or for drying clothes,[14] and the men ate their leaden supper of cheap starches and greases while sitting in their wet clothes. After supper the men gathered in the yard in sullen groups to wait for darkness to drift up from the valley below before they squeezed into the crowded bunkhouses. Inside these shacks, as one investigator discovered, "the sweaty steamy odors ... would asphyxiate the uninitiated." As the odors thickened from pipes, tobacco juice, sweat, and drying clothes, the men relaxed as best they could and exchanged gossip about recent binges and favorite prostitutes in the nearest town, or aired their grievances against the foreman. It was not uncommon for an I.W.W. "walking delegate" in their midst to steer the conversation to the class struggle. "It is in these discussions that the opinions of the loggers are formed, and here nearly everything combines to make them radical."[15]

In one camp investigated in 1917, eighty men crammed into one crude barrack built to accommodate fewer than half that number. The building had no windows, and the doors at either end furnished the only ventilation. When the men pressed into their bunks for the night, they closed the doors against the cold, stoked up the stoves, and went to sleep "under groundhog conditions."[16] In another study of logging camps made during the winter of 1917-1918, the investigators discovered that half the camps had only crude wooden bunks, half had no bathing facilities, and half were infested with bedbugs.[17]

---

[13] Rexford G. Tugwell, "The Casual of the Woods," *Survey* (July 3, 1920), p. 473. I.W.W. publications also furnish numerous descriptions of unsavory logging camps.

[14] William F. Ogburn, "Causes and Remedies of the Labor Unrest in the Lumber Industry," University of Washington Forest Club *Annual*, (Seattle, 1918), pp. 11-14.

[15] Tugwell, *op. cit.*, p. 473.

[16] *West Coast Lumberman*, Nov. 1, 1917, p. 39.

[17] Howd. *op. cit.*, p. 42.

Employers passed much of the blame for bad conditions in the camp back to the men. The loggers dirtied clean camps and made no efforts to keep even the worst camps as clean as they could.[18] Moreover, the employers pointed out that they had not brought the lice and the bedbugs to the camps; the loggers carried those pests with them in their oftentimes indescribable "bindles," or bed rolls. Wobblies countered that the loggers would gladly burn their blankets if the employer furnished decent bunks and bedding. Probably employers and workers shared some responsibility for the worst conditions, but it is incontrovertible that improvements came only after agitation and pressure by the workers. As the government's investigators commented during the 1917 strike, "The rigors of nature have been reinforced by the neglects of men."[19] It is doubtful that any YMCA secretary, fully supplied with volleyballs and boxing gloves, could have salvaged morale in the worst camps.

For over a decade, the Wobblies had moved among the homeless men of the logging camps, preaching their bitter gospel in bunkhouses and in the dreary towns where loggers congregated. Perhaps a majority of loggers joined the I.W.W. at one time or another in their careers, although few remained loyal members, paying dues regularly. Most workers sympathized to a degree with the I.W.W. and assimilated at least that simple hostility toward the boss of the I.W.W. ideology. By 1917, therefore, the I.W.W. had formed a considerable reservoir of sympathizers and had attracted enough dues-paying members to embark upon strike action rather than merely street-corner oratory.

The origins of the 1917 strike support the liberals' contention that "conditions"—not I.W.W. agitation alone—set off the widespread labor troubles. In 1917, only a few scattered locals of the National Union of Forest and Lumber Workers, I.W.W. remained; most Wobblies in the lumber industry belonged to the Agricultural Workers' Organization. In 1916, the Agricultural Workers' Organization, meeting in convention in Minneapolis, Minnesota, urged the lumber workers to form their own union. The annual convention of the I.W.W. in the same year passed a

---

[18] *Ibid.*, pp. 42-43.

[19] *Report of the President's Mediation Commission* (Washington, 1918), p. 13.

similar resolution.[20] In March 1917, thirteen Wobbly lumber workers, claiming to represent ten thousand other lumber workers, met in Spokane and launched the Lumber Workers Industrial Union No. 500, I.W.W. At this constituent convention the delegates made somewhat general plans to strike during the coming summer. On June 1, the Spokane branch of the new union set the strike date for July 1.[21]

Before the scheduled time, however, loggers had left their jobs throughout the entire "short-log"[22] region in a number of small, spontaneous strikes. As early as April, the river runners in the mountains east of Spokane left their jobs. The epidemic of small strikes really began in the middle of June near Sand Point, Idaho. There several hundred loggers, unaffiliated at the time with the I.W.W., walked off their jobs as a "sort of instinctive protest"[23] over abominable living conditions. This unscheduled and unplanned strike, like a spark to a string of firecrackers, set off similar protests all over the region. The Wobblies quickly scuttled their formal plans for a July 1 strike, issued a new strike call for June 20, and began to grab for the reins of the unorganized and runaway strikes.[24] Because I.W.W. "delegates" were often the natural leaders in their groups and because, for better or worse, the I.W.W. was the only instrument available the strikers accepted its proffered leadership.

Within two weeks, the strikers had closed virtually all logging operations east of the Cascades. Pickets patrolled the camps and either intimidated or converted would-be workers. Employers closed down the more remote camps either to avoid trouble or because working crews disappeared. Because the strikers were scattered, conducting what were really separate little strikes, they presented many separate lists of demands and grievances, but all of them resembled the original demands proposed by the constituent convention of the Lumber Workers Industrial Union in March.[25]

---

[20] James Rowan, *The I.W.W. in the Lumber Industry* (Seattle, n.d.), p. 69.

[21] *Ibid.*, p. 31.

[22] The "short log" region was the lumbering area east of the Cascades where pine logs were cut shorter than the "long logs" of forty feet or more in the Douglas fir region on the western slope of the Cascades.

[23] State of Washington; Bureau of Labor, *Eleventh Biennial Report, 1917-1918*, p. 66.

[24] Rowan, *op. cit.*, pp. 31-32.

[25] *Ibid.*, p. 30.

One demand common to all the lengthy *cahiers* was the demand for the eight-hour day, a demand that soon became the key issue between strikers and stubborn employers. Wobblies were as willing to fight on this issue as on any of the others, but they did air many other grievances. They demanded sixty dollars a month minimum wages, to be paid on two regular paydays every month. They demanded springs, mattresses, and bedding in all logging camps, showers and laundry rooms, hiring through union halls rather than through employment "sharks," free transportation to the job, abolition of compulsory hospital deductions for illusory services, and the end of discriminations against Wobblies.[26]

Until the middle of July, the I.W.W. showed no interest in extending the strike into western Washington, where most of the important lumber mills were to be found. Wobblies remained aloof as the new A.F.L. union, the International Union of Timber Workers, laid its plans for a strike in all the lumber mills of Washington. The I.W.W. suspected a trap by the A.F.L. to lure the I.W.W. out on a supportive strike at an unpropitious time.[27] On July 9, Wobblies passed the word along to their mill workers: "Don't fall for the bunk." As they surveyed the situation, however, and came to recognize the enthusiasm for a strike among mill workers, they quickly reversed their plans. The Timber Workers had scheduled their strike for July 16. On July 14, Wobbly delegates in the mills and logging camps of western Washington passed on revised instructions to their comrades: "The strike's on."[28] When the Timber Workers joined the walkout two days later, as co-belligerents if not actual allies of the I.W.W., the two unions closed down ninety per cent of the logging and milling operations in western Washington. The Wobblies' demands did not coincide exactly with the Timber Workers' demands, but all the strikers agreed on the eight-hour day.[29]

Even without the support of the A.F.L., during the first two days of its hasty strike in western Washington, the I.W.W. attracted a phenomenal following compared to the paltry following it had attracted during its days of soapbox agitation. In the Ho-

[26] *Industrial Worker*, July 14, 1917, p. 1.
[27] *Defense Bulletin of the Seattle District*, Aug. 7, 1918, p. 3.
[28] Howd, *op. cit.*, p. 71.
[29] Rowan, *op. cit.*, p. 41.

REBELS OF THE WOODS

quiam region alone, an estimated three thousand lumber workers answered the Wobblies' strike call.[30] Even the shipyard workers in Grays Harbor County called a sympathy strike.[31]

Oregon, a secondary lumber-producing area at this time, suffered only briefly from the strike. Probably Oregon lumbermen even benefited from the strike, for they inherited some orders that the larger Washington companies could no longer fill. Neither the Timber Workers nor the I.W.W. claimed many members in Oregon, and both organizations concentrated their main efforts in Washington. The I.W.W., in particular, had only "slight hopes" of success in Oregon.[32] In August, however, Wobblies made the gesture of extending the strike. They hampered logging operations for a time along the Columbia River and for two weeks closed most of the mills in Astoria and Portland. John A. Foss from the General Executive Board in Chicago visited Portland in early August as the strike in Oregon began. After studying the conditions in the industry and the extent of I.W.W. organization, he advised the Portland Wobblies to return to work. [33]

E. E. Weiland, President of the Timber Workers, also visited Portland during the strike and with the assistance of two Washington organizers tried to establish locals of the union in Oregon.[34] A few sawmill workers from Portland assembled at the Eagles' Hall one evening to form the first Oregon local of the Timber Workers.[35] The A.F.L., however, made even less progress than the I.W.W. and, like the I.W.W., continued to view Oregon as a secondary theater of operations.

However surprised and gladdened Wobblies may have been by their graduation from street-corner, soapbox operations, they were not to enjoy the pride of power for long. As the lumber industry creaked to a dead stop, state and local authorities and the government of the United States acted with vigor, making patriotic appeals to the strikers to return to work, trying to get stubborn operators to make just concessions, and launching a forceful campaign, careless of due process and civil liberties, to suppress the I.W.W.

---

[30] Portland *Oregonian*, July 15, 1917, p. 1.

[31] *Industrial Worker*, July 21, 1917, p. 1.

[32] Rowan, *op. cit.*, p. 44.

[33] Portland *Oregonian*, Aug. 15, 1917, p. 11.

[34] Portland *Oregon Labor Press*, Aug. 18, 1917, p. 1.

[35] *Ibid.*, Aug. 25, 1917, p. 1.

A Taste of Power

The governors of Washington and Idaho took an early interest in the strike, an interest not purely patriotic. The nation urgently needed lumber for the building of army cantonments, railroad freight cars, and cargo ships. The War Department's ambitious plan to build thousand of military aircraft required thousands of board feet of Sitka spruce, a splinter-resistant wood ideally suited for the aircraft of that period. Only the Pacific Northwest and the obviously inaccessible Baltic region could supply Sitka spruce in any quantity. Because of this assured, expanding market for lumber products of all kinds, the strike severely frustrated lumbermen and politicians. The governors groaned to see wealth in the form of lucrative war contracts deflected to other states because of the strike. They watched the United States government, of necessity, deal increasingly with the rival lumber interests of the "Southern Pine" region.[36]

In this setting of strike and crisis, Governor Ernest Lister of Washington evolved a strategy in July and August for ending the strike, a policy made up equally of support for the legitimate demands of the strikers and of forceful suppression of the I.W.W. Early in August, the Washington State Council of Defense, a special wartime body, met in conference with twenty-one prominent lumbermen. Governor Lister pleaded with them to grant an industry-wide eight-hour day, and he showed them communications from Secretary of War Newton D. Baker that made the same request. But the lumbermen held out, claiming that the eight-hour day would put them at a competitive disadvantage with the Southern Pine producers.[37] Carleton H. Parker, an I.W.W. "expert" and professor of economics who had been working for the War Department's Cantonments Adjustment Commission in California before joining the Washington State Council of Defense, authored this strategy of Governor Lister to undercut the I.W.W. by making intelligent concessions that would put lumber workers back to work.[38] Lister also publicly expressed his sympathy with the principle of the eight-hour day and urged the employers to give in to

---

[36] Portland *Oregonian*, Sept. 25, 1917, p. 1.

[37] Seattle *Post-Intelligencer*, Aug. 8, 1917, p. 1.

[38] Harold M. Hyman, *Soldiers and Spruce: Origins of the Loyal Legion of Loggers and Lumbermen* (Los Angeles, 1963), pp. 60-61; Carleton H. Parker, *The Casual Laborer and Other Essays* (New York, 1920).

the demand.[39] "I am convinced that peace and efficiency cannot come to the industrial life of the State of Washington until the principle of the eight-hour day is established, and with this principle I am in full accord."[40] He even defended the motives, if not the actions, of the I.W.W. in a speech before a Methodist conference in Tacoma. Only ten per cent of the Wobblies, he stated, were hopelessly "bad men," and the unrest in the lumber industry that they exploited was not their creation.[41] Again, this seeming tenderness toward the individual Wobbly derived from the thought of Carleton H. Parker, who had argued cogently in strategy meetings of the Council of Defense that Wobblies were still needed to produce lumber. The hard line of ruthless suppression and extirpation of the "I.W.W. element," of course, ignored this obvious consideration.[42]

The State Council of Defense, responsible to Governor Lister, initiated its own talks between lumbermen and Timber Workers. Dr. Henry Suzzallo, president of the University of Washington and chairman of the Council, began the conferences by requesting peace terms from both sides. The lumbermen continued to refuse the eight-hour day until all government contracts had been filled and would then only consider it after a referendum. The Timber Workers rejected this proposal, and the lumbermen, in their turn, rejected the union's demand for an immediate eight-hour day with nine hours' pay and the union's solemn promise to maintain production at the level of the ten-hour day.[43] The I.W.W., considered an "outlaw" organization and under general attack, did not share in the futile negotiations.

Nobody chose to negotiate with the I.W.W., neither the lumbermen, the Washington State Council of Defense, Governor Lister, nor the various agencies of the United States government. The authorities, state and federal, considered the I.W.W. strike not so much a simple protest for redress of economic grievances as a revolutionary uprising against the nation's war effort. Consequently the authorities set out to smash the I.W.W., not to try to make deals

---

[39] Spokane *Spokesman-Review*, Aug. 16, 1917, p. 1.

[40] State of Washington; Bureau of Labor, *Eleventh Bienniel Report, 1917-1918*, p. 67.

[41] *Industrial Worker*, Sept. 19, 1917, p. 3.

[42] Hyman, *op. cit., pp.* 69-70.

[43] Spokane *Spokesman-Review*, Aug. 9, 1917, p. 1.

with it. The mauled and battered I.W.W. in August 1917, made its last real protest against the wholesale jailing of its leaders and members, calling a "general strike" for August 20. But the protest was more futile gesture than deed. The "general strike" was abortive.

With its key leaders imprisoned, its "general strike" a failure, and its lumber strike a stalemate, the I.W.W. suddenly ordered retreat. The I.W.W. press announced that it would "take the strike to the job."[44] In subsequent issues of the *Industrial Worker*, the I.W.W. explained how to carry out this tactic and then reported its unbelievable success.[45] The I.W.W. insisted that the new tactic did not mean the defeat of the lumber strike, but only a more telling way of striking. Wobblies returned to work, thus abruptly ending the formal strike, but they continued to snipe at their employers and to restrict lumber production with ingenious kinds of slow-down and sabotage. Camp-hardened "bindle-stiffs" suddenly behaved on the job like inexperienced farm-boy novices, or "hoosiers," following their foremen's instructions to ludicrous, literal-minded extremes, or standing idle and waiting for directions when minor decisions were required not covered by explicit foremen's instructions. Some Wobblies behaved as if the demand for the eight-hour day had been granted, and they quit work every day after eight hours had elapsed. Exasperated foremen, who, correctly enough, considered the ten-hour day still in effect, discharged the Wobblies for walking off the job early. Unconcerned, the migratory Wobblies merely moved to other jobs and repeated the tactic. Other Wobblies stayed on the job for the full ten hours but saw to it that they "worked" only eight hours. The I.W.W. claimed many advantages for these tactics over the formal strike. Authorities could no longer arrest strikers and pickets, because every worker had ostensibly returned to work. The I.W.W. no longer had to devise ways of dealing with "scabs" 'because even the strikers "worked." The I.W.W. also rid itself of a considerable financial burden. As the I.W.W.'s chronicler said, "Much against their will the companies were forced to run the commissary of the strike."[46] Considering the imp of the perverse in the temperament of the

---

[44] Portland *Oregonian*, Sept. 17, 1917, p. 6; *Industrial Worker*, Sept. 19, 1917, p. 1.
[45] *Industrial Worker*, Sept. 26, 1917; Oct. 13, 1917.
[46] Rowan, *op. cit.*, pp. 50-52.

typical Wobbly, the new tactics must also have been satisfying to the soul. With relative impunity Wobblies could attack the "master class" in ways more personal and concrete than by simply striking. They could actually watch the "boss"—in the person of the foreman—grow apoplectic with rage and frustration.

For several months, the I.W.W. persisted in its new tactic of sabotage and obstruction on the job, and it succeeded in crippling lumber production almost as effectively as it had during the summer strike. But however effective the new tactics were in curtailing production, the I.W.W.'s reliance upon them nonetheless signified defeat in its first and last effort to conduct a major strike in the Pacific Northwest. Such random obstructionism meant that the Wobblies had relinquished their first real leadership over a majority of workers in the lumber industry and had resumed the guerrilla methods of the previous decade. The "strike on the job" was, after all, only the attack and provocation of the free-speech fight transferred from the corner soapbox to the job.

The failure of the government's efforts at mediation and the stubbornness of employers also brought an end to the strike of the A.F.L. Timber Workers. As the summer wore on, the Timber Workers found it increasingly difficult to keep even its oldest members loyal to the strike. Family men, less independent than the Wobbly "bindle-stiff," returned to their jobs in order to feed their wives and children. E. E. Weiland finally recognized the trend and announced that the union would not hinder strikers who found it necessary to return to work. He insisted, however, that the strike still continued formally. But by the end of September even this vestigial strike had ended. Mills that had closed during the first summer walkout reopened with nearly full crews and with the ten-hour day.[47]

The federal government, vitally concerned with maintaining peace in the industry as in all industries with war contracts, adopted policies of conciliation and attack similar to those of Governor Lister. Federal officials cooperated in the attack upon the I.W.W. and tried, even more vigorously than the state officials, to end the strike by mediation and negotiation. National Guard troops in the federal service helped the county sheriffs in the massive roundups of Wobblies in the summer of 1917. Federal District Attorneys

---

[47] Portland *Oregonian*, Sept. 9, 1917, p. 1.

exhaustively questioned the Wobbly prisoners for possible violations of federal laws, holding them for as long as they possibly
could as deportable aliens, for possible indictment for draft evasion,
for violation of the Espionage Act. At the same time, agencies of
the executive branch tried desperately to negotiate peace in the
industry. The War Department, for example, probably helped
convince Governor Lister of the essential justice of the eight-hour
day. Secretary of War Baker had wired Lister in August urging
him to work for the adoption of the eight-hour day as a means of
restoring peace.[48] Governor Lister and the Washington State
Council of Defense undoubtedly felt other less publicized pressures
from the federal government to adopt conciliatory policies toward
the non-Wobbly lumber worker.

Late in the fall of 1917, the President's Mediation Commission
visited the Pacific Northwest. President Wilson had created this
special committee in the summer, before the establishment of the
War Labor Board, to investigate and mediate the epidemic labor
conflicts in the West.[49] The Commission conducted hearings and
listened to witnesses from the A.F.L., the Washington State Council
of Defense, and the employers, but it did not succeed in ending the
labor unrest in the lumber industry. Its published report was so eminently fair and dispassionate in discussing the I.W.W. and its role
in the industry that the I.W.W. subsequently used the pamphlet for
its own propaganda purposes and even presented it in court as evidence for its defense during the trials of the following year.[50]

The War Labor Board, as well as other special agencies within
the War Department, also tried to bring peace to the industry.
Carleton H. Parker, the War Department's mediator working with
the Washington State Council of Defense, held conferences in
Spokane with representatives of the Western Pine Manufacturers'
Association. Early in December, he announced that the lumbermen
had accepted the principle of the eight-hour day and that the
shorter day would become effective on January 1, 1918. In the
course of these negotiations, Parker also persuaded the Association

---

[48] State of Washington; Bureau of Labor, *Eleventh Biennial Report, 1917-1918*, p. 67.

[49] John A. Fitch, "A Report on Industrial Unrest: Summary of the Findings of the President's Commission," *Survey* (Feb. 16, 1919), p. 545.

[50] Alexander M. Bing, *War-Time Strikes and Their Adjustment* (New
York, 1921), p. 57.

to form a special committee to be called the Association for Labor Efficiency. This committee selected sixteen lumbermen to go to the University of Washington for a short course in labor relations.[51] The more intractable lumbermen of western Washington, however, cast jaundiced eyes upon this apostacy of their colleagues in the Inland Empire, and they reaffirmed their opposition to the eight-hour day. On December 28, four days before the new policy was to go into effect, the Western Pine Manufacturers' Association withdrew its plan to begin the eight-hour day with the new year.

In performing this futile role as mediator, the federal government encountered two main obstacles: the absence of any representative labor union with which employers could be persuaded to negotiate and the stubborn "open shop" individualism of the employers. The Timber Workers' Union represented only a diminishing minority of mill workers with little influence at all among loggers, and the government could not deal with the somewhat more representative I.W.W., an "outlaw" union it had committed itself to destroy. But even had the Timber Workers' Union been as representative as it was respectable, the government mediators would have had trouble in getting lumbermen to negotiate with it. The "tenacity of old habits of individualism" had prevented the growth of moderate unions, and the old habits made peaceful solutions to labor conflicts difficult if not impossible. "The I.W.W. is filling the vacuum created by the operators," the President's mediators commented.[52]

As the strikers came to place more and more emphasis upon their demand for the eight-hour day, the lumbermen organized to resist. One hundred fifty leading lumbermen and shingle manufacturers gathered secretly at the Seattle Chamber of Commerce and formed the Lumbermen's Protective League. The group set out at once to raise a half million dollars to combat the strike. The lumbermen complained that the eight-hour day would give their keenest rivals in the Southern Pine region, operating on a ten-hour day, a tremendous competitive advantage.[53] The Protective League also resented the apparent pro-labor attitude of the government's medi-

---

[51] Portland *Oregonian*, Dec. 10, 1917, p. 3; Dec. 29, 1917, p. 3.

[52] *Report of the President's Mediation Commission to the President of the United States* (1918), p. 14.

[53] Portland *Oregonian*, July 10, 1917, p. 14.

ators. One of the League members described a government mediator—obviously Parker or Suzzallo—as a naive "college man"
unfamiliar with the hard facts of competition in the lumber industry.[54] The League and most lumbermen also refused to make any
distinction between the A.F.L. and the I.W.W., a distinction of
crucial importance to the mediators who were eager to negotiate
collective agreements and to restore production. The *American
Lumberman*, for example, claimed that the A.F.L. egged on the
I.W.W., that it even financed the I.W.W. strike, and then piously
disclaimed any connection and posed fraudulently as a body of
loyal, patriotic Americans.[55] Vainly did the A.F.L. insist that the
I.W.W. strike and its own were separate efforts, that the eight-
hour day, whoever demanded it, was just, and that, unlike the
revolutionary I.W.W., it was willing to sign a time contract with
lumber operators.[56]

Neither the collapse of the Timber Workers' strike nor the
termination of the I.W.W.'s formal strike brought peace to the
industry. The Wobblies' "strike on the job" continued to hamper
production, and, with less self-advertisement, disgruntled A.F.L.
workers in the mills also restricted their production. The problems
confronting mediators persisted even when the formal strike had,
in a sense, gone underground. To stimulate production, the government obviously had to find some formula to improve the morale
of workers in the industry. In the absence of any labor organization
with which the operators would negotiate, the government found
itself creating its own labor organization.

In October 1917, Colonel Brice P. Disque came to the Pacific
Northwest to investigate the inadequate procurement of spruce
for the Division of Military Aeronautics of the War Department.
He came into the lumber industry as the newest of the government's "trouble shooters" from a background as a professional
officer in the regular Army. In late 1916, Disque had resigned his
commission to accept a position in Michigan as a prison warden,
but he had kept his ties to the Army intact and apparently had
taken the civilian position with every intention of returning to
service when needed. In 1917, while still a prison warden, Disque
read widely on the problems of the lumber industry under the

[54] Fred W. Vincent, "Wing-Bones of Victory," *Sunset* (June 1918), p. 32.
[55] *American Lumberman*, Aug. 4, 1917, p. 53.
[56] Portland *Oregonian*, Aug. 18, 1917, p. 6.

tutelage of James A. B. Scherer, a California college president who was working with the War Department. In October 1917, Disque resigned his civilian job in Michigan and returned to the Army, expecting to be sent to France. Secretary of War Baker, perhaps upon Scherer's advice, asked him to forego service in France and to accept instead a different job in the Army's spruce-production program. Disque agreed to the change in his plans, and left for his first tour of the Pacific Northwest.[57]

At the height of the strike in the summer, spruce shipments had diminished to the vanishing point, and in September, after the I.W.W.'s nominal return to work, shipments had risen to only 2,600,000 feet of the 10,000,000 feet required.[58] Colonel Disque discovered chaos during his two-week inspection and briefing tour. The War Department's procurement officer in Portland operated futilely in the confusion with only one office assistant. Many mill owners did not know the government's specifications, and a large part of the little spruce they did ship was unusable. Over the administrative confusion lay the pall of the bitter labor troubles.[59]

In Seattle, upon his arrival, Disque met with Parker and Suzzallo and discussed the problems of the industry, and Disque imbibed much of Parker's "environmentalist" analysis of the I.W.W. problem. But at this stage he had few definite ideas of his own, no commitment to a particular course of action. After a ten-day tour in the company of Parker, Disque did begin to evolve the general contours of a plan. First, he decided to organize a special division of troops to use where necessary in the logging camps, and to proceed with this plan as directly as possible, bypassing as many bureaucrats, suspicious lumbermen, and A.F.L. leaders as possible. The next step was to get leaders of the industry behind his plan. To accomplish this latter purpose he invited a select group of lumbermen to a meeting in the Benson Hotel in Portland where he presented his idea for military intervention. On November 2, he returned to Washington, D.C. to get Secretary of War Baker's approval and to set the machinery in motion.[60]

---

[57] Hyman, op. cit., pp. 98-100.

[58] History of the Spruce Production Division (Portland, Ore., 1920) pp. 15-16, 55.

[59] Samuel H. Clay, "The Man Who Heads the 'Spruce Drive'," Review of Reviews, LVII (June, 1918), p. 634.

[60] Hyman, op. cit., pp. 112-129.

The actual organizing of what developed into the Loyal Legion of Loggers and Lumbermen—or the "Four L's"—proceeded simply and quickly. The first local of the organization was established in Wheeler, Oregon, on November 30, 1917.[61] For several months the Loyal Legion's principal task was recruiting members; and it fulfilled few functions of a labor union and made few changes in working conditions. The War Department allotted one hundred officers to Disque and the project, and these officers, under First Lieutenant Maurice E. Crumpacker of the Signal Corps, toured the camps and mills of Washington and Oregon administering a loyalty pledge to workers and employers, a simple act which constituted "joining up" in a new organization that was not much more than a name.[62] The pledge read:

I, the undersigned, in consideration of my being a member of the Loyal Legion of Loggers and Lumbermen, do hereby solemnly pledge my efforts during the war to the United States of America, and will support and defend this country against enemies both foreign and domestic.

I further swear, by these presents, to faithfully perform my duty toward this company by directing my best efforts, in every way possible, to the production of logs and lumber for the construction of Army airplanes and ships to be used against our common enemies. That I will stamp out any sedition or acts of hostility against the United States Government which may come within my knowledge, and I will do every act and thing which will in general aid in carrying this war to a successful conclusion.[63]

Besides the one hundred officer-organizers, the War Department supplied the special division of troops requested by Disque, the Spruce Production Division. These soldiers—twenty-five thou-

[61] Clay, *op. cit.*, p. 634. The most recent summary history of the Loyal Legion of Loggers and Lumbermen is R. L. Tyler, "The United States Government as Union Organizer: The Loyal Legion of Loggers and Lumbermen," *Mississippi Valley Historical Review*, XLVII (Dec. 1960), pp. 434-451. The best study of the origins of the organization, based on exhaustive research into hitherto unavailable manuscript and archival materials, is Hyman, *Soldiers and Spruce* (above, note 38).

[62] *History of the Spruce Production Division, op. cit.*, p. 20.

[63] Quoted in Howd, *op. cit.*, p. 78.

REBELS OF THE WOODS

sand of them before the effort was concluded—worked where needed in logging camps and mills, receiving civilian pay when working but living under military discipline.[64] Vancouver Barracks in Washington became the headquarters of the division.

Once pledged to the amorphous Loyal Legion of Loggers and Lumbermen, perhaps after experiencing a certain amount of "hard sell" pressure from the officer-organizers, the new civilian members formed a local. The locals later elected grievance committees, but in the early months, the only real function of the local was to meet production quotas, perhaps manage a suggestion box, and be a display counter of pledged patriots. In fact, at its inception, Disque had not envisioned the Loyal Legion as any kind of labor union, whether genuine or "company." The Army and Disque continued for a time to rely chiefly on their Spruce Production Division of soldier-workers, and only somewhat later did they recognize that in the Loyal Legion they had hit upon a device to accomplish the purposes of a labor union: to get a reasonably willing body of workers once again producing lumber products.[65]

In its infancy in late 1917, the organization of the Loyal Legion was loose and improvised, with Disque making most of the policy decisions in his Headquarters Council, and considering the whole Loyal Legion only an adjunct to the Spruce Production Division. Seven districts were established initially, and others were added later in Idaho and eastern Washington. The district supervisors, selected by Disque from among his corps of officers, distributed literature, passed down his directives, pressed the recruitment of new members in every camp and mill, and kept the records of membership and finances.[66] Not until the late summer of 1918 did a general council of the district representatives convene in Portland to create a formal constitution, or rather to ratify a constitution the essential features of which had already been determined by Disque and his advisers. This first constitution provided for a representative polity. Each local elected delegates to the district boards; the district boards chose both employee and employer delegates for the Headquarters Council over which Disque presided. In Article V of the Constitution, the duties of the conference

---

64 *Industrial Worker*, Jan. 3, 1918, p. 3; Portland *Oregonian*, Dec. 4, 1917, p. 1.
65 Hyman, *op. cit.*, pp. 131-134.
66 Howd, *op. cit.*, p. 81.

committee in each local were described, and Article V came to be viewed as the peculiar contribution of the Loyal Legion in alleviating the "class war." It stipulated that each local elect a conference committee charged with carrying grievances to and negotiating with the employer. If such local conflicts could not be settled amicably by these committees they could be appealed to the district boards, then to the Headquarters Council, and finally to Disque himself. The chairman of the three-man conference committee in each local also served as the employee's delegate to the district council meetings, where policy of a higher level was decided.[67]

With the new organization enrolling thousands of members, with the voice of the I.W.W. drowned out and its agitators seeking cover, and with some of the power and all of the prestige of the War Department at his disposal, in January and February 1918, Disque still hesitated in instituting reforms in the lumber industry. Still foremost in all discussions of reform was the eight-hour day, the issue on which the federal government and the state governors had long since made their recommendations and engaged in their futile negotiations. The labor policy-makers in the federal government, of course, had not given up the objective. Suzzallo and Parker, who had worked closely with Disque from the beginning, continued their maneuvering for the eight-hour day. In January 1918, Parker suggested to the War Department that the Spruce Production Division might be designated the principal contractor in the lumber industry, in which event the War Department could order the eight-hour day as a standard on all its war contracts.[68] Parker, Secretary of War Baker, and others negotiated seriously to accomplish this end. The eight-hour day, in fact, seemed so imminent early in 1918 that an eager War Department underling let out the news prematurely to a Portland A.F.L. organizer who in turn released the news to the press. Disque responded with anger to this news leak and to the presumed evidence it offered him of an eight-hour day conspiracy going on behind his back. He feared that some clique of A.F.L. leaders, War Department bureaucrats, and Parker had conspired against him and had undercut his relationship with the lumbermen who still vehemently opposed the eight-hour day. But Disque's fears proved groundless. He escaped

[67] Disque, *op. cit.*, p. 382.
[68] Hyman, *op. cit.*, p. 203.

blame in the eyes of the lumbermen, and by February, he even considered his position firm enough to suggest that the Loyal Legion locals take up the issue of the eight-hour day for discussion. As the discussion grew heated, Disque returned to Washington, D. C., to report to the War Department on his work. He left behind in Portland a committee of twenty-five prominent lumbermen charged with hammering out some agreement on the eight-hour day. Disque returned to Portland on February 27, after receiving an urgent telegram from the lumbermen informing him that his presence was needed. He returned to Portland not sure in his own mind on what he would recommend to—or impose upon—the lumbermen. On the basis of intelligence gained from his trip to Washington, D. C. and the evidence of the news leak, Disque considered that his colleague Parker had betrayed him to the A.F.L. interests. In a pique, Disque was tempted to retaliate by coming out publicly against the eight-hour day when he got to the lumbermen's meeting. But he knew that such a decision would hopelessly divide the industry and threaten a resumption of the labor troubles as the summer approached.[69]

When he came directly from his train, delayed by a storm, to the meeting, he found the weary lumbermen ready to turn the problem over to him, to abide by whatever decision he made. He immediately appointed a committee and retired with it to a back room to discuss the problem, and before the conference adjourned in the early hours of the morning, he announced the adoption of the eight-hour day, to become effective on March 1, 1918. The conference accepted the decision with only one dissenting vote.[70] "You all know I have been a ten-hour day man, but . . ." he prefaced his announcement to the exhausted lumbermen.[71] Perhaps with this last show of reluctance he wooed the lumbermen and also expressed some of his continuing irritation with Parker. In his press announcement, however, Disque stated that he had always believed in the eight-hour day but had not considered the lumber industry ready for it. No order from federal authorities had prompted his decision,

---

[69] Ibid., p. 203-221.

[70] Clay, op. cit., p. 635.

[71] A recollection of A. C. Dixon, retired lumberman of Eugene, Oregon, and a former district functionary in the Loyal Legion, who was present at the meeting. The author interviewed Mr. Dixon in December 1950.

he said, perhaps to discount a rumor that he had leaped from his train on February 27 and had hurried to the lumbermen's assembly bearing direct orders from the War Department.[72] Thus came the long-argued reform for which bitter strikers had fought the year before and for which they had been branded seditionists and traitors, a reform adopted painlessly by the ukase of a curious "labor leader" in soldier's uniform.

Once the eight-hour day breached the dam, other reforms followed, particularly reforms in the living conditions in logging camps. In the autumn of 1917, the I.W.W. had conducted a referendum among its members on the question of whether to hold a a ceremonial burning of their blanket rolls on May Day, 1918.[73] Wobblies had voted heavily in favor of the proposal. Such a public demonstration of protest, together with the considerable unfavorable comment in the national periodical press on logging-camp conditions, probably hurried Disque's decision to do something quickly about working conditions in the industry. With the support of numerous resolutions passed by the Legion's district councils, he issued the first regulations and reforming decrees. He established first a uniform minimum wage for the industry, the minimums ranging from forty cents an hour for unskilled labor to ninety cents for skilled workers. He ordered logging camps to provide bedding, including regular changes of linen, for all workers, and fixed a fee for linen that could be charged against workers' wages.[74] By the time of the Armistice, other improvements were begun in many camps, and no longer was the worker required to carry his own bed—a rolled blanket, or "bindle"—from job to job.

But it was not only from the expected quarters—the I.W.W. and the Timber Workers—that the Loyal Legion met opposition. Although the Legion's moves were preceded by thorough discussions with lumbermen, it was to be expected that some lumbermen would resent Disque's meddling and the whole idea of such an organization. They had fought strenuously against the I.W.W. for a decade and had resisted the demand of 1917 for the eight-hour day and all such interference with what seemed to them their pre-

[72] Portland *Oregonian*, Mar. 1, 1918, p. 4; Portland *Labor Press*, Mar. 2, 1918, p. 1.
[73] Harrison George, *The I.W.W. Trial* (Chicago, 1918), p. 78.
[74] *Four L Bulletin*, Mar. 1918, p. 5.

107

rogatives of management; then the federal government and the Army appeared and made the same demands, albeit without the abhorrent revolutionary rhetoric. Disque himself admitted later that the first task had been to "sell himself" to both sides, implying that his salesmanship had been directed not exclusively toward the workers.[75] He strengthened his bargaining position with employers at about the same time he was considering his program of reforms. He supported Senator George E. Chamberlain of Oregon, who introduced into Congress a coercive requisition bill—the "Commandeer Bill" as the press termed it—which would empower the President of the United States to take over mills, roads, machinery, and other private properties to insure production under government contracts. The bill also empowered the President to construct and operate such properties in competition with private companies if the need should arise.[76] Disque lobbied discreetly for this bill. He wired Chamberlain during the debate in the Senate to assure the Senator and his colleagues that he needed the bill only to expedite production, not to coerce or punish property owners. He needed the bill, he said, only because some owners of timber lands, for example, were hard to find, or some titles were in probate or were being contested in court.[77] But the political motive, the possible iron fist, was not altogether concealed. Some observers interpreted the Chamberlain bill as a tactical move by Disque to discipline obdurate lumbermen and to give them advance notice of the government's determination to clear the way if necessary for going over their heads completely in a direct appeal to the workers.[78] Even before he made his trip to Washington, D. C., in February 1918, leaving the question of the imminent eight-hour day simmering, Disque had conferred somewhat pointedly, with prominent A.F.L. leaders in Portland.[79]

The United States government achieved its general purposes with this curious excursion into the field of labor-union organization. By the time of the Armistice, the Loyal Legion had recruited over a hundred thousand members, including virtually everyone

[75] Disque, *op. cit.*, p. 380.

[76] *Congressional Record,* 65 Cong.; 2 Sess., Jan. 8, 1918, p. 678.

[77] *Ibid.*, Mar. 21, 1918, p. 3819.

[78] Portland *Oregonian,* Feb. 2, 1918, p. 6; "Colonel Disque and the I.W.W.," *New Republic* (Apr. 6, 1918), p. 284.

[79] Hyman, *op. cit.*, p. 218.

who had worked at all in the industry during the war months. In December 1918, the twelve districts included over a thousand locals.[80] Beyond this quick and spectacular growth, Disque and the founders could point to an impressive record of achievements: the eight-hour day, the marked improvement in working conditions, a system of inspection for the maintenance of the reforms, the restoration of morale, the control of revolutionary and seditious sentiments among thousands of workers. The ulterior purposes of the War Department were served as well. Production of spruce rose to over twenty million feet per month by November 1918, more than enough for all national needs and the need of the Allies. Production and shipping procedures were rationalized to a point never attained before the war.[81]

It appeared the Loyal Legion had succeeded. But its critics and opponents in the I.W.W. and the A.F.L. persisted in opposition throughout the war and after, although their opposition was of necessity restricted more and more to grumbling in the labor press. Most Wobblies or A.F.L. Timber Workers joined the Loyal Legion, probably for much the same reasons that many persons in 1918 bought more Liberty Bonds than they believed they could afford. The opposition of the A.F.L. leaders sprang from a normal suspicion of any trade unionist toward "company unions" that explicitly forbade the right to strike. Organizers for the A.F.L. charged that soldier-organizers of the Loyal Legion had intimidated them and ejected them from mills and logging camps.[82] They charged Disque's soldiers with dispersing union meetings and with spreading overt anti-union propaganda.

Samuel Gompers had initially supported the idea of the Loyal Legion, perhaps seeing it as a shield behind which the A.F.L. Timber Workers could move into an industry hitherto dominated more by the I.W.W. than the A.F.L. But lumbermen did not intend to give Disque support in his eight-hour day reform only to leave the gate open to the hosts of organized labor that might wish to follow in the tracks of the Spruce Production Division and the Loyal Legion. By May 1918, Timber Workers' Union organizers in mills and camps threatened the whole achievement of

---

[80] Howd, p. 84.

[81] *Ibid.*, p. 85.

[82] Portland *Oregon Labor Press*, July 30, 1918, p. 1.

Disque. In response to the challenge, the state and local authorities, obviously on orders from Disque or Suzzallo, began to harass the A.F.L. organizers, arresting them for a variety of petty and obscure violations of law, from peddling without licenses to parking automobiles illegally. In a word, the Army discouraged unionism actively. By the time of the Armistice, the A.F.L.'s disenchantment with Disque had reached the point of filing formal complaints in high places in Washington, D. C.[83]

William Short, president of the Washington State Federation of Labor, attended the first convention of the Loyal Legion after the war as a spectator and newspaper reporter for the Seattle *Union Record*. He reported disdainfully that only fifteen or twenty of the delegates really represented workers, that delegates voting negatively were disfranchised, and that from the speakers platform, Disque ordered two well-known A.F.L. organizers in the gallery out of the convention hall. "Their autocracy was complete," Short said of the Loyal Legion leaders.[84] Several years later, an A.F.L. newspaper, commenting ruefully on the demise of the International Union of Timber Workers, noted that the field had been left clear for a contest between the I.W.W. and the Loyal Legion. Because the I.W.W. was "at least" a body of real workers, the writer hoped it would win the contest.[85] Disque, in defending himself against these blasts from organized labor, claimed that the Washington State Federation of Labor "at no time put the war ahead of its union," and then somewhat disingenuously, "I say this regretfully because I believe in unions."[86] Disque's official position was that the Timber Workers should not be "encouraged" to engage in organizing workers already in Loyal Legion locals, and that, on the other hand, no man should be "forced" to join the Loyal Legion.[87]

Whereas the A.F.L. had no strength and little influence among the rank and file workers in the lumber industry, the I.W.W.'s situation was almost reversed. It had no Samuel Gompers speaking

---

[83] U.S. War Dept., *A Report of the Activities of the War Department in the Field of Industrial Relations During the War* (Washington, 1919), p. 47.

[84] Seattle *Union Record*, Dec. 7, 1918, p. 7.

[85] Portland *Oregon Labor Press*, Apr. 13, 1923, p. 4.

[86] Disque, *op. cit.*, p. 380.

[87] *Four L Convention Minutes*, Aug. 12, 1918 (Spokane, Wash., 1918), pp. 15-18.

for it in high places in Washington, D. C., but it had won the support of many actual workers in the camps and the mills. The I.W.W. leaders, of course, hated the new organization even more vehemently than did the A.F.L. leaders. They charged Disque with being an obvious tool of the lumbermen, interested only in strike-breaking. The crisis in spruce production had been a false issue, they said, because the Spruce Production Division soldiers had gone to logging camps where "not a stick of spruce was produced."[88] The I.W.W. particularly resented the soldiers in the camps and considered them part of a conspiracy to "manipulate mob violence" against the I.W.W. in the Loyal Legion recruitment drive.[89] But the I.W.W. also admitted to finding unexpected allies among the troops. Living under military discipline and occupying a low-status, noncombatant position in the Army, the soldiers often worked as reluctantly as soldiers are reputed to work: they "soldiered" on the job, it was claimed, while the Wobblies "hoosiered" —the same process in a civilian argot.[90] The I.W.W. considered the prohibition of strikes in the Loyal Legion constitution its most objectionable provision, and one Wobbly writer sneered that the Loyal Legion left the workers with only the "gift of gab" as a weapon.[91] Moreover, in the accounts of the strike of 1917 which appeared in its pamphlets and newspapers, the I.W.W. proudly took credit for the eight-hour day, for the disappearance of blanket rolls from the camps, for the newly-built shower rooms—in short, for all the reforms. The public, however, credited the Loyal Legion with the reforms through a process—impossible for the Wobblies to understand—of class collaboration.

After the war, the lumber industry faced a resumption of the antebellum anarchy and labor strife. Lumbermen could no longer rely upon an assured, expanding market, and workers looked fearfully for an offensive by the operators against the eight-hour day and the other wartime reforms. In such a setting, Disque's temporary Loyal Legion polled its members to decide whether to disband or to continue as a permanent, peacetime body. The members voted overwhelmingly in their locals to continue the organiza-

88 Rowan, *op. cit.*, pp. 41, 54.
89 Ralph Winstead, "Enter a Logger: An I.W.W. Reply to the 4 L's," *Survey* (July 3, 1920), p. 476.
90 Rowan, *op. cit.*, p. 54.
91 Winstead, *op. cit.*, p. 476.

tion.[92] Two conventions held in early December 1918, in Portland and in Spokane, chose a new board of civilian executives and empowered it to prepare a permanent constitution. In January 1919, the new board met and drew up the new charter, based on the practices of the wartime organization. The locals retained their conference committees and the principle of joint employer-employee membership; the district boards continued as area conventions of workers' and employers' representatives; the Headquarters Council of Disque became simply the new board of directors; and the new Loyal Legion pledged itself to protect the eight-hour day and to continue and further the other reforms.[93]

The constitution divided the Pacific Northwest into twelve districts, eight in western Washington and Oregon, and four in the Inland Empire east of the Cascades. The constitution provided for annual conventions for each of the twelve districts with one worker and one employer delegate to represent each local in the district. The president, or any member of the board of directors, presided over the annual conventions of the districts. The board of directors, besides serving as the highest court of appeal in settling grievances, selected the president, showing "no predilection" for either workers or employers.[94] Norman F. Coleman, a professor of English at Reed College in Portland, served as the first civilian president after the retirement of Disque and was reappointed through most of the significant life of the organization.[95]

The Loyal Legion, with its ambitious philosophy of class cooperation, for a time did cut away some of the psychic sores in the lumber industry. In 1921, the Jones Lumber Company of Portland, a small mill producing for the local retail trade, cut fifty per cent more lumber on the eight-hour day than it had previously on the ten-hour day.[96] In 1919 a mill in Washington, running at a loss, considered cutting wages or closing down. The Loyal Legion local in the mill held a meeting in which workers were informed

[92] *Four L Bulletin,* Dec. 1918, pp. 3-8.
[93] *Ibid.,* Mar. 1919, pp. 3-8; *Loyal Legion of Loggers and Lumbermen Constitution and By-Laws* (Portland, Ore., n.d.).
[94] *Conference and Cooperation,* Loyal Legion of Loggers and Lumbermen (Portland, Ore., n.d.), pp. 1-2.
[95] Coleman's contract was renewed for the first of several times in Nov. 1921. *Four L Bulletin,* Dec. 1921, p. 26.
[96] *Ibid.,* Oct. 1921, p. 9.

of the company's difficulties. The workers insisted that they could increase production if the management kept the mill open and continued to live up to the Loyal Legion wage-and-hour regulations.[97] The Bonners Ferry Lumber Company, through its Loyal Legion local, gave its workers the alternative of a ten-hour day at three dollars or an eight-hour day at two dollars and sixty cents. The men chose the eight-hour day with reduced pay, and presumably they accepted the cut in wages without the bitterness that would have attended an unexplained announcement by the management.[98] The Loyal Legion promotion literature of the period is, not surprisingly, full of similar accounts of cooperation and good feeling.

The organization also offered a variety of services to its members. In many towns, the Loyal Legion kept a social hall and at least five of the twelve district offices—those in Portland, Seattle, Spokane, Tacoma, and Aberdeen—operated free employment agencies.[99] The number of men placed on jobs through these agencies remained small; probably only the decreasing number of Loyal Legion mills and camps made use of the service.[100] But establishing the agencies was a significant gesture, if nothing else, because of the long tradition of exploitative and fraudulent employment agencies —the "sharks" and "slave markets" of I.W.W. literature—in the region. In 1926, the board of directors negotiated with an insurance company for a sickness-and-accident plan for Loyal Legion members.[101] The reforms of the war months were protected by the board of directors through a corps of traveling inspectors, who, unfortunately, did not have the same kind of influence that Disque's soldier-organizers had wielded in wartime. After the Armistice, the Loyal Legion could only impose its will upon employers by an increasingly futile system of fines and expulsions from the organization.[102]

The early leaders, during the war and after, displayed great zeal. They came to view their organization as some wondrous invention for ending the age-old war of the classes, and its official philosophy

[97] Robert S. Gill, "Four L's in Lumber," *Survey* (May 1, 1920), p. 165.
[98] *Four L Bulletin*, Apr. 1922, p. 17.
[99] *Conference and Cooperation, op. cit.*, p. 4.
[100] Howd, *Industrial Relations*, p. 96.
[101] *Four L Lumber News*, July 1926, p. 13.
[102] *Conference and Cooperation, op. cit.*, p. 2. Ironically, the first local at Wheeler, Oregon, was expelled in June 1922. *Four L Bulletin*, June 1922, p. 9.

—"fourelism," as one enthusiast called it—as the revolutionary idea that would ease social conflict anywhere and any time.[103] "America is showing the way," President Coleman declared in one of his regular editorials in the Loyal Legion journal, explaining that the only way to save civilization itself was to extend "fourelism" to all kinds of social and economic problems, presumably on a worldwide stage. He described the naval disarmament conference then in progress in Washington, D. C., as an example of successful "fourelism."[104] Nothing very precise was ever said, however, in answer to the possible question of how this new philosophy, "fourelism," could accomplish what older moral injunctions under their old names had never been able to accomplish. But the name, together with a few homiletic illustrations of the Golden Rule applied in logging camps and lumber mills, became a kind of verbal magic for many of the Loyal Legion's leaders.

Despite its creditable wartime record of restoring lumber production and its attempts to freshen old ethics with a new name, the Loyal Legion declined rapidly after 1919. During the war, it had administered its membership pledge to over a hundred thousand members; and the first major convention in 1918 had enrolled over four hundred delegates claiming to represent more than sixty thousand members.[105] But by the time of the Great Depression, a little more than a decade later, the organization had dwindled to only a few thousand members and to scarcely more than a nominal existence. The New Deal administered the finishing stroke with Section 7(a) of the National Industrial Recovery Act of 1933 and the Wagner Act of 1935. Although the Loyal Legion jettisoned its employer members, permitted the strike as at least a theoretical possibility, and changed its name to the Employees Industrial Union, all to meet the requirements for recognition by the National Labor Relations Board, it could not survive in competition with the new "untainted" American Federation of Labor or Con-

---

[103] Gill, op. cit., p. 168.

[104] Four L Bulletin, Dec. 1921, p. 3. This curious faith in "fourelism" persisted as late as 1948. A. C. Dixon and several other lumbermen and veterans of the Loyal Legion prepared a history and a statement of "Four L" philosophy to present to Thomas E. Dewey after his anticipated election to the presidency. They hoped that their document might serve as a guide to the labor policy of his administration.

[105] Gill, op. cit., p. 165.

gress of Industrial Organizations unions of the period. Its real *floruit* had come in the troubled war months of 1918, and it had been called into being neither by workers nor by employers, but by the government of the United States. An expedient of Disque and the War Department, created for a temporary purpose during a period of stress when collective labor agreements were needed but no agency was available to supply them, it was only a curious sport in the history of labor. But perhaps it was more a mutant than a sport, reproducing itself rather than dying out. It did, in a sense, reproduce itself in the United States government's positive insistence upon collective agreements under the New Deal legislation.

The Loyal Legion also undercut the I.W.W. quite effectively. In the summer of 1917, the I.W.W. appeared to control an entire industry, but by the end of the war, the I.W.W. was not only suppressed, it had been dispersed and absorbed. The hard facts bore out Carleton H. Parker's theory of "environmentalism." In the minds of all but the most dedicated Wobblies the ferocious ideas of the class struggle evaporated in the atmosphere of patriotism, the eight-hour day, and palpable improvements in living conditions. The Wobblies of hard revolutionary substance had to be driven with the club rather than led by the carrot.

CHAPTER V

THE ATTACK o the "MASTER CLASS"

News of the lumber strike of 1917 and rumors of the I.W.W.'s sabotage and subversion aroused the anger of the country. Earlier disturbances, such as the textile strikes in Massachusetts and New Jersey and the free speech fights, had fixed upon the I.W.W. a reputation for trouble-making, but only with wartime anxieties and their pressures toward conformity did hostile attitudes toward the I.W.W. lead to a concerted, nationwide assault upon the organization. The revolutionary activism of the I.W.W. and its real or imagined subversion of the war effort clearly revealed an enemy within the embattled American society.

The I.W.W. did oppose the war on doctrinaire grounds. Like the socialist movement, of which it was a maverick part, it put loyalty to the international proletariat above loyalty to nation. At the tenth annual convention in 1916, Wobblies declared their views in an unequivocal resolution which called for "anti-militarist propaganda in time of peace" and "the General Strike in all industries" in time of war.[1] But after the American declaration of war Wobblies did not quite live up to this injunction, and the I.W.W. as an organization did not embark upon a general strike solely in opposition to the war. The General Executive Board in Chicago discussed the war, to be sure, and especially whether the I.W.W. should define an official position toward it. Many indi-

---

[1] *Proceedings of the Tenth Convention of the Industrial Workers of the World,* Nov. 20 to Dec. 1, 1916 (Chicago, 1917), p. 138.

vidual Wobblies, of course, faced a practical problem, what to do about registering for the draft or what to do if called for military service. Frank Little, a Board member, advocated a strong, explicit, and official statement by the I.W.W. against the war. Others demurred. As a compromise Ralph Chaplin, editor of *Solidarity*, put a suggestion in the paper that members might register for the draft or refuse to do so according to their revolutionary consciences. Most Wobblies probably registered for the draft as did other citizens, some signing their registrations, as Chaplin himself did, with the note, "I.W.W. opposed to war."[2] Others, like the Wobblies in Rockford, Illinois, refused to register and organized a public demonstration against conscription by parading to the jail to give themselves up for evasion of the draft.[3] Many others opposed war more discreetly by simply avoiding the draft and by fleeing to Mexico to fight in the revolutionary armies of Villa or Zapata.[4] Mexican Communists, after the war, claimed that as many as thirty thousand Americans had sought refuge in Mexico, many of them Wobblies.[5] The I.W.W. press, however, continued for some months to give various unofficial evidences of the I.W.W.'s detestation of capitalist war. The following poem was not intended to ingratiate Wobblies in the eyes of home-front patriots.[6]

> I love my flag, I do, I do,
> Which floats upon the breeze,
> I also love my arms and legs,
> And neck, and nose and knees.
> One little shell might spoil them all
> Or give them such a twist,
> They would be of no use to me;
>   I guess I won't enlist.
>
> I love my country, yes, I do
> I hope her folks do well.
> Without our arms, and legs and things,
> I think we'd look like hell.
> Young men with faces half shot off
> Are unfit to be kissed

---

[2] Ralph Chaplin, *Wobby: The Rough and Tumble Story of the American Radical* (Chicago, 1948), p. 209.

[3] William D. Haywood, *Bill Haywood's Book* (New York, 1929), p. 297.

[4] John S. Gambs, *The Decline of the I.W.W.* (New York, 1932), p. 43.

[5] Portland *Oregonian*, Jan. 12, 1920, p. 1.

[6] *Industrial Worker*, Feb. 10, 1917, p. 1.

I've read in books it spoils their looks,
I guess I won't enlist.

Although Wobblies made no particular secret of their opposition to the war, the I.W.W., as an organization, tried more to ignore the war than to oppose it actively and officially. Anti-militarist action probably smacked too much of political action, something Wobblies could better leave to a political action group such as the Socialist Party.

The Socialist Party indeed did oppose the war more explicitly than the I.W.W., fulfilling thus its obligations to the anti-militarist resolutions passed in various congresses of the Second International from Stuttgart in 1907 to the reaffirmations at Basle in 1912. As the United States Congress acted upon President Wilson's war message early in April 1917, the Socialist Party, meeting in emergency convention in St. Louis, passed a stinging anti-war resolution, much stronger in its language than anything published officially by the I.W.W. The majority report condemned modern war in general as a byproduct of international capitalism and the particular war America was just entering as the most "unjustifiable" of all. The resolution pledged the Socialist Party to try to organize mass political action against the war effort.[7] From a hindsight now possible after two World Wars and a homogenizing Cold War, the Socialist Party's rhetoric seems excessively romantic and a too casual flaunting of reality. But it must be recalled that in 1917 no Americans—including Socialists—had ever experienced those peculiar pressures of "total war." They could not anticipate, of course, the avalanche about to fall on them.

In spite of this indifference of the I.W.W. toward the war—a political indifference it would seem that should have kept the wolves of public opinion from its door—the public perversely considered it the arch-enemy, fearing and hating Wobblies for their past deeds and propaganda and considering everything they did during the war as sedition. Wartime public opinion, of course, tended to lump all the radical anti-militarists together as "slackers" at best and conscious enemy agents at worst. Strikes by Wobblies

---

[7] "War Proclamation and Program Adopted at the National Convention, Socialist Party, Saint Louis, Missouri, April, 1917," in *Revolutionary Radicalism*, Report of the Joint Legislative Committee ("Lusk Committee") of the State of New York (Albany, 1920) I, pp. 613-618.

in the lumber industry or the nonferrous mining industry seemed *prima facie* evidence of sedition. Although investigations by the United States Department of Justice failed to verify the persistent rumors that the I.W.W. received support from the German government, the press continued to print such charges and innuendoes.[8] Many Americans firmly believed that such seditious connections existed between all American radicals, Socialists and Wobblies, and the Kaiser. Samuel Gompers charged that Bismarck had invented the whole international socialist movement to soften the world for the German conquest.[9] Even if many Americans stopped short of branding all radicals as enemy agents, they still viewed them as "foreigners," or as ideologues peculiarly tainted with German *kultur*. Had not Marxism itself come from Germany? Had not the German Social Democratic Party dominated the international socialist movement up to the year of the war? German immigrants, it was generally known, had first brought the un-American doctrines to this country and had promulgated them in a German language press. Milwaukee, a German-American community, had become an enclave of socialism in America. The I.W.W., because it claimed so many foreign members and because it was the ultra-radical left wing of this nefarious "German" movement, suffered the wrath of Americans. Its spiritual kinship as well as its deeds earned for it the enmity of all self-styled patriots.

Many historians and publicists have told and retold the story of the suppression of dissent during the first world war. To repeat the whole story in any detail would require the insertion of an interrupting volume and would shift the focus away from the I.W.W. in the Pacific Northwest. But a brief summary of the suppression of radicalism on the national stage is perhaps required to establish the setting for the regional story. Angry citizens throughout the nation banded together to administer justice as they conceived it without waiting for the more orderly processes of the law. Local governments and the federal government, acting under existing statutes or under new laws passed for the occasion, prosecuted radical dissenters considered dangerous to the national secur-

---

[8] New York *Times*, July 17, 1917, p. 7; Portland *Oregonian*, Oct. 1, 1917, p. 1.

[9] Samuel Gompers, *Seventy Years of Life and Labor: An Autobiography* (New York, 1925), Vol. II, p. 388.

ity. The vigilante actions against Wobblies numbered in the scores. Although many such actions never appeared in the press, the newspapers did publicize, with indulgent editorial comment, a few spectacular acts of suppression. In July 1917, Arizona citizens captured about twelve hundred striking copper miners in the region near Bisbee. They assembled the prisoners in the Bisbee ball park, then herded them into railroad freight cars and unloaded them in the middle of the desert without food or water.[10] Subsequent investigations revealed that most of the men deported had been members of the A.F.L. with families and residences in Bisbee and not Wobblies.[11] A federal grand jury in Tucson returned indictments against twenty-five leaders of the mob—including officials of the Phelps-Dodge mining corporation and prominent Bisbee citizens—for "conspiring to intimidate citizens in the free exercise of rights guaranteed to them by the Constitution." A United States District Court, however, refused to hear the case on the grounds that the deportations were not a federal offense, and an Arizona court found the defendants not guilty.[12]

In Montana, the war-inflamed patriots lynched Frank Little, a prominent I.W.W. organizer who had come to Butte to ply his trade during a bitter copper strike in 1917. The I.W.W. and its liberal friends insisted that "class interests" or the "copper bosses" had inspired the lynching, not patriotic fervor. But the motives were mixed. Wartime patriotism certainly amplified "normal" social and economic antagonisms toward the I.W.W. and special economic interests, as in the lumber industry, were not averse to making use of the patriotic mood and directing it at the I.W.W. and labor unions in general. The lynching of Little followed a bitter strike in the copper mines. In June 1917, a violent explosion at the Speculator Mine destroyed the operation and killed one hundred fifty miners. The miners, charging the company with criminal neglect of safety, went out on strike. They demanded also the abolition of the "rustling card," an employment record that all miners had to carry in order to get work.[13] The I.W.W.

[10] *Report of the Attorney General of the U.S., 1918* (Washington, 1918), p. 58.

[11] *American Labor Yearbook, 1917-1918* (New York, 1918), p. 180.

[12] *Report of the Attorney General of the U.S., 1918*, p. 58.

[13] Charles Merz, "The Issue in Butte," *New Republic* (Sept. 22, 1917), p. 216.

sent Frank Little to Butte to organize the strikers into the I.W.W. Little made himself instantly unpopular with all the citizens of Butte who opposed the strike and considered it a subversion of the war effort. The I.W.W. reconstructed the grisly drama of his death as follows: after he had retired to his hotel room following a strike meeting in the Butte ball park, he awoke to find six masked men in the room. The six intruders trussed him securely, carried him down to the street, tied him to the back bumper of an automobile with a length of rope, and dragged him to the Milwaukee Railroad trestle outside of town. They pinned a note to his coat, a note with scribbled grave dimensions such as frontier vigilantes in Montana had pinned to their victims, and then hanged him from the trestle.[14] Some citizens of Butte, intending a kind of callous gallows humor, suggested the next day to the press that the I.W.W. may have hanged Little, suspecting him of being a private detective.[15]

In November 1917, some citizens and public officials of Tulsa, Oklahoma, calling themselves the "Knights of Liberty," took seventeen Wobblies from their police guard. The "Knights" horsewhipped and tarred-and-feathered the Wobblies "in the name of the women and children of Belgium."[16] The I.W.W. a few months earlier had chartered an Oil Workers' Industrial Union in the Oklahoma fields and had begun their unpopular economic agitation about the time the United States entered the war. In Franklin, New Jersey, the chief of police and several business men of the town captured the local I.W.W. organizer and hanged him from a tree, cutting him down before he strangled but after he had lost consciousness. In Jerome, Arizona, hired gunmen of the United Verde Copper Company captured seventy miners, allegedly Wobblies, and deported them in cattle cars to California.[17]

Indignant Americans also took more orderly action against the Wobblies and other dissenters through the federal government. The United States Congress, shortly after the declaration of war and the enactment of the conscription act, passed the Espionage

---

[14] *Solidarity*, Aug. 4, 1917, p. 1.

[15] Portland *Oregonian*, Aug. 12, 1917, p. 2.

[16] National Civil Liberties Bureau, *The "Knights of Liberty" Mob and the I.W.W. Prisoners at Tulsa, Oklahoma* (New York, 1918), pp. 3-16.

[17] National Civil Liberties Bureau, *War-Time Prosecutions and Mob Violence* (New York, 1919), p. 11.

Act, a law defining many crimes against the security of the nation. It was no accident that this restrictive act came shortly after the passage of the conscription act. Most Congressmen recognized a draft as being the only equitable, or "democratic," means of raising an army quickly. But some also worried over the possibility of mass evasion and political opposition such as the Socialist Party in St. Louis had promised. The only experience of the nation with conscription before 1917 had been with the Civil War law, an experiment that had hardly been a success. Therefore, some special protection against opposition toward the new conscription seemed necessary. The third section of Title I of the Espionage Act was designed to give the government that kind of protection. It made felonious much of the propaganda that Socialists and Wobblies normally disseminated. The section read:[18]

> Whoever, when the United States is at war, shall willfully make or convey false reports or false statements with the intent to interfere with the operation or success of the military or naval forces of the United States or to promote the success of its enemies and whoever, when the United States is at war, shall willfully cause or attempt to cause, insubordination, disloyalty, mutiny, or refusal of duty, in the military or naval forces of the United States, or shall willfully obstruct the recruiting or enlistment service of the United States, to the injury of the service of the United States, shall be punished by a fine of not more than $10,000 or imprisonment for not more than twenty years, or both.

Most of this Espionage Act dealt with the matters that its title would suggest, the control of actual spying and the protection of military secrets, but other parts of the law supported the third section of Title I. The law authorized the issuance of search warrants for the seizure of property used to facilitate the felonious speech or writing. Title XII authorized the Postmaster General to withhold such materials from the mails.

In May 1918, Congress amended and expanded the law. The new amendments, sometimes called the Sedition Act, substituted the phrase "attempts to obstruct" for the simpler but more ambiguous "obstruct" of the original law, and added nine new definitions of offenses such as interfering with Liberty Bond drives and speak-

---

[18] *U.S. Statutes at Large*, XL, Pt. 1, Pub. Laws, 1917-1919, p. 219.

ing or writing against the flag, Constitution, uniforms of the Army or Navy, or war production.[19]

The Attorney General requested the legislation of 1918 because of his dissatisfaction with the word "obstruct" in the original law, a loophole he wished Congress to close because the courts had interpreted the word too narrowly and had thus pulled some of the teeth of the act of 1917. Also, the original law had let too many casual dissenters and critics, unconnected with seditious organizations, slip unpunished through the provisions of the law, and this leniency of the law had led to mob violence. Better to wage the war on sedition with "due process," the Attorney General said.[20]

Though the government had not aimed the Espionage Act specifically at the I.W.W.—at least to the extent of naming the organization—it quickly brought the law to bear upon the I.W.W. The law probably damaged the I.W.W. more than it did any other vulnerable organization, even the Socialist Party. On September 5, 1917, federal agents closed dozens of I.W.W. halls in synchronized raids all over the country and seized tons of records and literature.[21] The government paid minimal attention to the Fourth Amendment, setting an ugly precedent for the later peacetime and more famous "Palmer Raids." The government made no arrests, but contented itself with taking the confiscated papers to government offices where they could be sifted and studied at leisure. The Bureau of Investigation agents of the Department of Justice confiscated with a thoroughness that struck some bemused Wobbly observers as ludicrous. During the raid on the national headquarters in Chicago the agents ordered Ralph Chaplin to open a safe that the I.W.W. had not used since moving it years earlier from the Cleveland headquarters. Inside the safe they found a Mauser 30-30 pistol and several empty Budweiser beer bottles. Their eyes gleamed at the sight of the pistol. They were about to leave the bottles when Chaplin, with tongue in cheek, persuaded them to take them along as evidence of the German influence in the I.W.W. In raiding Chaplin's home, the agents seized a number of *Ladies'*

---

[19] *Ibid.,* pp. 553-554.
[20] *Report of the Attorney General of the U.S., 1918,* p. 18; Zechariah Chafee, Jr., *Free Speech in the United States* (Cambridge, Mass., 1942), p. 41.
[21] *Report of the Attorney General of the U.S., 1918,* p. 18.

Home Journal dress patterns, explaining to Chaplin's astonished wife that they suspected code messages in the perforations.[22]

Three weeks after the raids, the government proceeded to the next step, the arrest of scores of Wobblies. In the interim between raids and arrests investigators had examined the captured literature and had prepared cases under the Espionage Act, dropping hints all along to the press that they had discovered startling evidence of heinous crimes by individual Wobblies.[23] Society women of the Chicago Navy Relief Society patriotically volunteered as chauffeurs to drive the arrested Wobblies from the Cook County jail to the daily grand jury hearings.[24] Ralph Chaplin and George Andreytchine, a young Wobbly intellectual from the Balkans, found themselves manacled together in the back seat of one of the limousines. The Gold Coast debutante at the wheel discussed her two passengers with her companion in the front seat during the ride to the court house, using her best finishing-school French to hide her uncomplimentary remarks. Andreytchine, however, brought blushes all the way to the backs of their necks when, "in the perfectly modulated Parisian syllables that Margaret Anderson so admired," he returned their insults a hundredfold.[25]

The grand jury indicted one hundred sixty-six Wobblies.[26] Over a hundred began their long defense in court in a trial that lasted four and a half months. After the first several days of the trial the press—at least outside Chicago—paid less and less attention, probably because of the tediousness of the proceedings or because the prosecution failed to deliver on its pre-trial promises to reveal new and astonishing evidence against individual defendants. As the prosecution presented its dreary and warmed-over evidence—much of which the government could have obtained by writing to the I.W.W. without the melodrama of the raids—the newspapers in some instances did their best to liven the show. "U.S. Defeat in War the Plan of the I.W.W.," one newspaper announced when the

---

22 Ralph Chaplin, *op. cit.,* pp. 223-224.
23 "The I.W.W. Raids and Others," *New Republic* (Sept. 15, 1917), p. 175.
24 Portland *Oregonian,* Sept. 29, 1917, p. 1.
25 Ralph Chaplin, *op. cit.,* p. 227.
26 *Report of the Attorney General of the U.S., 1918,* p. 53. The government dismissed fifty-one Wobblies before the trial began and sixteen during the trial. The most recent study of the I.W.W. war-time trials is: Philip Taft, "The Federal Trials of the I.W.W.," *Labor History* (Winter 1962), pp. 57-91.

prosecution presented its evidence of the I.W.W.'s attitudes toward the war and militarism.[27] "I.W.W.'s Plans for War on U.S. Bared," the same newspaper entitled its report of the I.W.W.'s plans for the lumber strike of 1917.[28]

The I.W.W. itself lost interest in the trial—or at least its usual breathless tone over an impending martyrdom—and even expected that some or all of the defendants would be acquitted. "All witnesses are giving clear-cut, convincing evidence ... The case is certain to be victory for the workers."[29] Surprisingly enough, Wobblies found no particular fault with the trial judge, Kenesaw Mountain Landis. Haywood even expressed his personal satisfaction with the fairness of the judge's rulings. Landis did show a toleration over procedure exceeding that demanded by judicial impartiality. He permitted seventy Wobblies to go free every day after the court recessed on their own recognizance. He let twenty-one other defendants out of jail on bond, and he kept only nine in jail throughout the trial.[30] During the more tedious stretches of the trial, as the prosecution and the defense waded through the verbal swamps of the literary evidence, Landis permitted the defendants to stretch out on the benches and catch naps.[31] To the Wobblies, connoisseurs of court trials, the case against them seemed unusually weak, and the chief prosecutor, F. K. Nebeker, Assistant Attorney General of the United States, seemed more than a little confused in his own plans and strategies. Before the trial, he had insisted that the government would not prosecute the I.W.W. as an organization; the government rather intended to try particular individuals for particular crimes. But in his examination of witnesses and in his opening speech to the jury he concentrated almost exclusively upon the "nihilism" of the I.W.W. and upon the criminal tendencies inherent in its creed.[32] Even the defense attorneys grew over-confident or bored. They waived their privilege of analyzing and summarizing the evidence when the case went to the jury.[33]

---

[27] Portland *Oregonian*, May 11, 1918, p. 1.

[28] *Ibid.*, May 19, 1918, p. 3.

[29] *Defense Bulletin of the Seattle District*, July 29, 1918, p. 2.

[30] Portland *Oregonian*, Aug. 19, 1918, p. 5.

[31] *Defense Bulletin of the Seattle District*, Aug. 7, 1918, p. 1.

[32] Victor J. Yarros, "The Story of the I.W.W. Trial," *Survey* (Aug. 31, 1918), p. 604.

[33] *Ibid.* (Sept. 14, 1918), p. 663.

Landis gave what sounded to most observers like moderate instructions to the jury.[34] But the jury, whatever the Wobblies may have expected from it, deliberated for less than an hour and returned with verdicts of guilty against all the defendants. Some of the convicted Wobblies claimed they had been able to see into the jury room through a transom—an unlikely feat not fully explained by the Wobblies—and they reported that the jurors had deliberated only fifteen minutes and had then killed time for about forty minutes for appearances' sake.[35] Landis sentenced fifteen Wobblies to twenty years; thirty-three to ten years; another thirty-three to five years; twelve to a year and a day; and two to ten days.[36]

The trial at Chicago constituted the government's main prosecution of the I.W.W. under the Espionage Act, but it also tried Wobblies in two lesser trials in two other cities. In Sacramento, California, a grand jury indicted fifty-five Wobblies for conspiring with Haywood and other I.W.W. leaders to obstruct the war effort.[37] In this trial, the defendants conducted a "silent defense" that somewhat disconcerted the court; they refused to expend money or effort for their own defense in what they announced to be a travesty trial in a tribunal of the "master class."[38] They sat through the trial in complete silence, neither calling witnesses nor cross-examining the prosecution witnesses, sitting sometimes with their backs to the court. In spite of Judge G. H. Rudkin's moderate instructions, the jury found most of the defendants guilty.[39] In Wichita, Kansas, the government prosecuted fifty other Wobblies, including the deceased Frank Little, for violations of the Espionage Act, and won convictions in most of the cases.[40]

Postmaster General Albert S. Burleson made free use of the postal provisions of the Espionage Act, and of free interpretations of other postal regulations, to eliminate most radical material from the mails. In the course of the war, he successfully banned most of the Socialist Party press and most of the I.W.W. press, as well as

[34] *Defense Bulletin of the Seattle District*, Aug. 26, 1918, p. 1.
[35] *Ibid.*, Sept. 9, 1918, p. 5.
[36] Portland *Oregonian*, Aug. 31, 1918, p. 1.
[37] *Ibid.*, Feb. 9, 1918, p. 1.
[38] *Defense Bulletin of the Seattle District*, Nov. 17, 1918, p. 7.
[39] "Ol' Rags and Bottles," *Nation* (Jan. 25, 1919), p. 114.
[40] *Defense Bulletin of the Seattle District*, Nov. 17, 1918, p. 4.

such particular items as one issue of *The Nation* which contained an article he disliked. Radicals had to invent various clever ways of distributing their propaganda, sending it, for example, by express in bulk lots and then distributing it through their own volunteer corps of postmen. The I.W.W. complained, with some justice it would seem, that the control and censorship of its mail hampered its efforts in planning and organizing its own defense. Letters mailed in Chicago to another Chicago address sometimes took six months to be delivered and were delivered with the mark "Officially Sealed" on them. Why did the mark not read "Officially Opened?" the I.W.W. asked with some bitterness.[41]

Although mobs and governments from New Jersey to Arizona joined in this attack upon the I.W.W., the people and governments of the Pacific Northwest—particularly in the State of Washington—led the whole nation in devising the tactics and procedures of suppression. Quasi-legal vigilante groups, with presumably justifying "advisory" representatives from official law-enforcement agencies, launched the first assault upon Wobblies and made the first mass arrests or "round-ups." For a time, in the summer of 1917, the United States Army and the federalized National Guard, with the War Department's authorization, cooperated in making the mass arrests. Federal authorities in Washington next experimented with the new technique of controlling radicalism by arresting and detaining aliens for deportation hearings, an experiment in the control of sedition that was to reach the proportions of a national scandal only after the war and then against the new "Bolsheviks" who replaced the Wobblies as objects of popular fear and anger.

The peculiar problems of the Pacific Northwest and its recent unhappy experience with Wobblies explain the region's dubious distinction of being the laboratory for the national control of subversion. The Pacific Northwest had experienced ten years of I.W.W. agitation, of annoying wildcat strikes, red-flag parades, free-speech fights, jailhouse hunger strikes, and endless soapbox oratory. As the nation entered the war, the trial of Thomas Tracy in Seattle came to an end, a trial in which the prosecution's characterization of the anarchical Wobbly had been widely broadcast. In the summer of 1917, the I.W.W. launched the lumber strike, an act that seemed to come as the final outrage to thousands of

---

[41] *Ibid.*, Aug. 19, 1918, p. 7.

respectable citizens. The leaders of the lumber industry—whom the Progressives of the day were wont to call the "Lumber Barons" or the "special interests"—were not averse to whipping up indignation against Wobblies as a way of quashing the strike and of predisposing the public to general "open-shop" attitudes. The Lumbermen's Protective League, organized to resist the strikers' demand for the eight-hour day, regularly couched the defense of its interests in the rhetoric of patriotism.[42] Lumbermen also offered wide ranging and not unwelcome advice to the authorities on how to manage the "I.W.W. menace."

The wartime attack upon the I.W.W. in the Pacific Northwest came in waves, on the crests, so to speak, of particular fears and anxieties. In the summer of 1917, with the crisis of the lumber strike uppermost in everybody's thoughts, the state governments organized their quasi-legal emergency forces and made use of the United States Army and the National Guard. In the winter of 1917-1918, with the strike in recess, some cities in the region—Seattle especially—developed exaggerated fears about the annual influx of migratory, unemployed workers, all of whom were expected to bring the revolution with them from the logging camps to the cities. Authorities refined their techniques of control and repression and hit upon the new weapon of holding alien Wobblies for deportation hearings. In the spring and summer of 1918 the authorities expected the lumber strike to resume, and this fear set off another wave of repression, with the authorities using their whole array of weapons, the Espionage Act, the Sedition Act, the Immigration Acts of 1917 and 1918, and, by the time of the Armistice and into 1919, the new antiradical criminal syndicalism laws that many states enacted.

The first stage of alarm and suppression saw the organization of vigilante actions. Although the Pacific Northwest witnessed no such spectacular affairs as the deportations at Bisbee or the lynching of Frank Little during the war, it did witness scores of lesser popular actions against the I.W.W. The citizens of Hood River,

---

[42] Retail Dealers Protective Association Form Letter, Oct. 8, 1917, DL File 33-574A. Cited in: William Preston, Jr., *Aliens and Dissenters: Federal Suppression of Radicals, 1903-1933* (Cambridge, Mass., 1963), pp. 97-98. This recent study is the most thoroughly researched of the many books and monographs which study the various phases of the wartime suppression of radicalism, and is based almost entirely upon the pertinent archival materials.

Oregon, took such action against Pete Shad, a solitary and fool-hardy Wobbly who wandered into town to preach the gospel of the One Big Union on the streets of Hood River. Thirty-five masked citizens whisked Shad out of town, terrified him with threats of summary lynching, made him kneel and pray, and then—according to the facetious report in the local newspaper—freed him when he had expressed his new-found love of the United States and had pleaded for a "second chance."[43] In Aberdeen, Washington, a mob of three hundred fifty workingmen broke into the I.W.W. hall, dragged out four cart-loads of papers and furnishings and made a festive bonfire in the middle of the street.[44] Another mob, two days later, captured six Wobblies, carried them out of town, beat them, and made them kiss the American flag. The mob then besieged a "soft-drink parlor" where another Wobbly had taken refuge. The proprietor, fearing for his property, kept the angry men at bay by waving a revolver at them, but he finally allowed a delegation from the crowd to enter and to take out the offending Wobbly. He then posted a sign reading, "No drunks. No I.W.W. allowed."[45] In 1918 in Centralia, Washington, the marchers in a Red Cross parade broke ranks as they passed the I.W.W. hall and charged the hall. They piled the furnishings in the street and made a bonfire, but only after several prominent citizens in the crowd had confis-cated such valuable items as the desk and the typewriter.[46] In the summer of 1917, Spanish-American War veterans in Washington organized groups of vigilantes called the "Minute Men" with a quasi-official status. The group in Seattle, two or three thousand strong, took it upon itself to make arrests, conduct raids, and even hold prisoners. They raided the Pigott Printing Company, the firm that printed the I.W.W. paper, the *Industrial Worker*, and sys-tematically destroyed all the equipment in the shop.[47] But law and order, of a sort, soon pre-empted these individual and vigilante acts of suppression.

As he had urged his policy of moderation and concession to-

---

[43] Hood River *Glacier*, Aug. 30, 1917, p. 1.

[44] Portland *Oregonian*, Apr. 8, 1918, p. 1.

[45] *Ibid.*, Apr. 11, 1918, p. 7. "Soft-drink parlor" later became a newspaper euphemism for "speak-easy." Perhaps this is one of the first uses of the euphem-ism during wartime prohibition.

[46] Ralph Chaplin, *The Centralia Conspiracy* (Chicago, 1924), p. 38.

[47] *Industrial Worker*, Jan. 19, 1918, p. 1.

ward the A.F.L. and the nonunion workers in the lumber strike, Governor Lister of Washington also began the first vigorous and implacable campaign against the I.W.W.'s leaders. He proposed a statewide organization of vigilantes, a "Patriotic League" with a branch in every county. He even suggested the names of prominent men in each county to take the lead in organizing the league.[48] He early assured the public, which had grown more and more restive as the lumber strike progressed, that he would use soldiers stationed at the American Lake post to quell any attempt of the I.W.W. to spread their strike to the harvest fields.[49] Using troops and the eager local authorities, he arrested Wobblies by the scores. Vigilantes and soldiers, working together, stopped men on the streets of Washington towns to search for the incriminating "red cards," the membership cards in the I.W.W. They even made routine checks of regularly scheduled passenger trains in the state and checked hotel registers.[50] This general round-up began in July 1917, as the lumber strike entered its first acute phase. Oregon National Guard troops, stationed in Washington, began the offensive with a raid on the I.W.W. hall in North Yakima and the arrest of thirty Wobblies. By the middle of July, the Army had detained seventy-four Wobblies in North Yakima alone and had put its catch into a temporary stockade.[51] Similar detention camps went up in Pasco, Wenatchee, Cle Elum, Ellensburg, and other towns. The Army held this mounting bag of prisoners as military captives, permitting federal authorities to question the prisoners exhaustively for possible violations of the Espionage Act or the conscription law.[52]

The Army made no formal charges against its prisoners and denied them the right to confer with attorneys.[53] The questionable legality of the detainments posed some very practical problems in administration. The county governments refused to pay the full expense; the military authorities had no funds for the purpose; the State of Washington Council of Defense disclaimed financial responsibility. Bitterly, the Wobblies compained that they had to

---

[48] Spokane *Spokesman-Review*, July 3, 1917, p. 2.
[49] Portland *Oregonian*, July 8, 1917, p. 9.
[50] Rowan, *The I.W.W. in the Lumber Industry* (Seattle, n.d.), p. 39.
[51] Portland *Oregonian*, July 17, 1917, p. 4.
[52] *Ibid.*, July 10, 1917, p. 1.
[53] *Ibid.*, July 17, 1917, p. 4.

pay out of their own pockets for the expenses of their illegal incarcerations.[54]

In most of the comment about the summer round-up—even in the comment of such presumed liberals as Carleton H. Parker—a remarkable lack of indignation over the destruction of civil liberties is apparent. If the attitude toward Wobblies was not uncritical rage, it tended at best to be a kind of dispassionate entomologist's interest in his favorite insects. In the Congress, Senator Wesley Jones of Washington, for example, engaged in a colloquy on the I.W.W. problem in his state. He told how unmanageable the Wobbly prisoners in the Wenatchee jail had become, pounding on the bars and almost tearing the jail down, until National Guard troops in uniform appeared on the scene to cool them down with fire hoses. The uniforms, Senator Jones opined, had done the trick. He thought that the Wobblies feared nothing except the uniform, and consequently troops should be used more extensively against them. He expressed no concern—indeed no awareness—of the gross violation of the due process of law in having the Wobblies imprisoned without charges by the military and without recourse to counsel.[55]

In the internment camps and jails, the Wobblies at least found themselves thrust into well-habituated roles. They rioted, pounded mess kits against the bars, went on hunger strikes, and refused to work, all with the desperate gusto they had learned in earlier free-speech fights.[56] They did not find their imprisonment unmitigatedly grim. Most days, they idled in the sun or swam in nearby irrigation ditches under guard.[57]

The authorities in other states affected by the lumber strike adopted policies similar to those tried by Governor Lister in Washington. In fact, the policies were regional; the governors met and planned their strategy in concert. In July 1917, Governor Moses Alexander of Idaho traveled to Spokane to confer with Governor Lister.[58] He came, it was rumored, to demand that firmer action be taken by Washington authorities against the I.W.W. regional

---

[54] *Industrial Worker*, Aug. 22, 1917, p. 1.

[55] *Congressional Record*, 65 Cong., 2 Sess., Mar. 21, 1918, p. 3822.

[56] Spokane *Spokesman-Review*, July 24, 1917, p. 1; Portland *Oregonian*, July 18, 1917, p. 4.

[57] Portland *Oregonian*, July 18, 1917, p. 4.

[58] Spokane *Spokesman-Review*, July 12, 1917, p. 1.

headquarters in Spokane.[59] While in Spokane, Governor Alexander listened to a few I.W.W. street meetings and even purchased some pamphlets, perhaps to confirm his worst fears or perhaps out of simple curiosity.[60] In August, Alexander and Lister met in Portland, Oregon, with the governors of four other states to devise a common strategy for ending the lumber strike and for pulling the fangs of the I.W.W.[61]

Alexander, like Lister, tried to distinguish the I.W.W. agitators from the rank-and-file striker and to persuade the strikers to abandon their I.W.W. leaders and return to work. He toured logging camps and mill towns in Idaho making patriotic appeals. The strikers, for the most part, listened politely but skeptically to his spiel and insisted in rejoinder that their demands were just and that they were at least as patriotic as their "profiteering" employers.[62] Alexander also cooperated with local authorities and the Army in arresting I.W.W. leaders. They built stockades and "bull pens"— familiar and almost institutionalized features of labor troubles in Idaho—in Moscow and other towns. [63] The Idaho legislature passed the first criminal-syndicalism law in the Pacific Northwest, giving authorities for the first time a specific crime with which to charge their Wobbly prisoners. On August 1, 1917, a grand jury indicted twenty-five Idaho Wobblies for violations of the new law, the first of many subsequent indictments in Idaho and other Pacific Northwest states.[64]

Although Oregon suffered slightly from the strike, Governor James Withycombe nevertheless adopted a policy as stern as that of his fellow governors in Washington and Idaho. The Adjutant General, shortly after the I.W.W. made its effort to extend the strike to Oregon, formed a special battalion of experienced soldiers—most Spanish-American War veterans—to suppress I.W.W.'s revolution.[65] But the battalion, poised for counter-revolutionary combat, actually had little to do. Only in Klamath Falls did the I.W.W. cause much worry and there with agitation unrelated to

[59] Portland *Oregonian*, July 14, 1917, p. 4.
[60] Spokane *Spokesman-Review*, July 9, 1917, p. 1.
[61] *Ibid.*, Aug. 12, 1917, p. 1.
[62] Rowan, *op. cit.*, p. 36.
[63] *Ibid.*, p. 37.
[64] Portland *Oregonian*, Aug. 2, 1917, p. 11.
[65] *Ibid.*, July 13, 1917, p. 1.

the lumber strike. In the middle of July 1917, the large Martin Brothers grain elevator burned to the ground, an act of presumed arson that produced a property loss of over a hundred thousand dollars. Residents of Klamath Falls immediately charged the I.W.W. with arson and listened credulously to extravagant rumors that Wobblies were roaming the countryside poisoning livestock. The sheriff hastily organized a posse to comb the countryside and to patrol the streets of Klamath Falls. The deputies rounded up Wobbly suspects "like cattle."[66] Most of the prisoners were eventually released for lack of evidence or given sentences for vagrancy in municipal court, and only a few were held for any time to be questioned for possible violations of federal laws. While the counties suppressed the I.W.W. in Oregon, the governor adopted a more conciliatory policy toward the A.F.L. and unorganized workers by establishing a mediation board with five members from management and five from the A.F.L. Although the board had no remarkable successes in settling labor strife during the war, the A.F.L. supported it and even expressed satisfaction with the choice of most of management's representatives.[67]

These regional efforts to suppress the I.W.W. by mass arrests and quasi-martial law culminated on August 19, 1917, with the arrest of James Rowan and twenty-six other Wobbly leaders, the closing of the regional headquarters in Spokane, and the declaration of actual martial law in Spokane and environs.[68] This radical action came in answer to a resounding ultimatum published by the Spokane I.W.W. on August 14. Rowan, its author, demanded the immediate release of all prisoners of the "class war" and threatened a general strike in all industries if the establishment did not comply.[69] The bludgeoned I.W.W. could scarcely maintain its waning lumber strike, let alone extend the strike elsewhere, but Rowan's ultimatum nevertheless stirred up considerable fear. In Ada County, Idaho, the anxious sheriff swore in eight hundred deputies in preparation for the ominous strike.[70] Governors Lister and Alexander braced themselves for the shock, ready, if necessary, to im-

---

66 *Ibid.*, July 16, 1917, p. 1.
67 Portland *Oregon Labor Press*, Aug. 11, 1917, p. 1.
68 Spokane *Spokesman-Review*, Aug. 20, 1917, p. 1.
69 *Industrial Worker*, Aug. 18, 1917, p. 1; Spokane *Spokesman-Review*, Aug. 15, 1917, p. 1.
70 Portland *Oregonian*, Aug. 20, 1917, p. 5.

provise new emergency policies.[71] In such a tense atmosphere, the declaration of local martial law seemed only a necessary precaution. The I.W.W. acted on its threat, but its general strike of August 20 fell flat. Hardly any agricultural workers or construction workers heeded the call. The most extensive walkout occured at St. Johns, Washington, where eighty harvest hands left the fields. The press, with obvious relief, reported fully on the collapse of the strike. One cartoon, for example, entitled "A House of Dirty Cards, It Collapsed at the First Touch" pictured a house of cards labeled "I.W.W. Strike" falling on a seedy-looking man labeled "Sabotage."[72]

Martial law in Spokane continued even after the obvious failure of the general strike. Guardsmen under Major Clement Wilkins patrolled the streets and enforced a military order prohibiting street speaking.[73] Major Wilkins, however, was a man who did not want to foreclose all possibilities of reclaiming fallen Wobblies. He permitted the Volunteers of America to hold street meetings, outside his ban, to try to redeem Wobblies and restore them to patriotism and respectability. During one such meeting, the superintendent of the Volunteer's "Industrial Department" noticed a Wobbly incorrigible jabbing a knife into the tires of his parked automobile. Stopping in the middle of a hymn, the angry superintendent charged after the Wobbly vandal and caught him. Immediately a hundred fifty other Wobblies converged upon him and rescued their fellow worker before the soldiers arrived on the scene.[74]

A few days after the August raid on the I.W.W. hall, Major Wilkins released seventeen of his twenty-seven prisoners.[75] Rowan, and the other prisoners still held, petitioned the Washington Superior Court for writs of *habeas corpus*. The court denied them, explaining that it had no jurisdiction over prisoners held by the military. From his cell, Rowan then issued a lengthy, and somewhat plaintive, statement protesting his arrest and the whole campaign to crush the I.W.W. "There is nothing unlawful about demanding clean and sanitary conditions in camps . . . We believe

[71] *Ibid.*, Aug. 16, 1917, p. 3.
[72] *Ibid.*, Aug. 21, 1917, p. 1.
[73] *Ibid.*, Aug. 20, 1917, p. 5.
[74] *Ibid.*, Aug. 27, 1917, p. 5.
[75] *Industrial Worker*, Aug. 29, 1917, p. 1.

that the great mass of the people of the country are in favor of the things which are advocated by the I.W.W."[76] Some people, at least, did sympathize with the I.W.W. and its demands. The Spokane Labor Council passed an irate resolution condemning the authorities and demanding the removal of Governor Lister from office, the removal and demotion of Major Wilkins, the resignation of all labor members on the State Council of Defense, and a general strike to force these demands if necessary.[77] But some A.F.L. unions in the Spokane Labor Council did not subscribe to the fiery resolution or feel such open sympathy for the I.W.W. The Building Laborers and Hod Carriers, for example, withdrew from the Council.[78] The Plasterers, in patriotic protest, refused to march in the Labor Day parade planned by the council.[79]

This first campaign in the war against the I.W.W., in which the military cooperated closely with civil authorities and quasi-legal vigilantes, began in a mood of panic triggered by the lumber strike. Most of the authorities, Governor Lister, for example, undoubtedly convinced themselves that the I.W.W. had instigated the lumber strike as a revolutionary act, as a willful subversion of the nation's war effort, and that the very first necessity was to crush the I.W.W. pitilessly. In such an obvious emergency, no one paid much heed to niggling considerations of constitutional guarantees and due process. The war justified constitutional corner-cutting, just as "national emergencies" from the undeclared war with France in 1798 to the presumed danger from the "Japs" on the west coast in 1942 have seemed to justify such actions. The Bill of Rights is set aside for the duration of the emergency as a kind of peacetime luxury. The war-powers clauses in the Constitution take precedence over the first ten amendments, although, as Zechariah Chafee has remarked, there is no real *legal* reason for such precedence-taking. That the war powers should take precedence is no more warranted than that the Bill of Rights should take precedence over the war powers, if precedences of any kind must be taken.[80]

---

[76] Requoted from Max Eastman, "Revolutionary Progress," *The Masses* (Oct. 1917), p. 12.

[77] *Industrial Worker*, Aug. 25, 1917, p. 1; Portland *Oregonian*, Aug. 22, 1917, p. 1.

[78] Portland *Oregonian*, Aug. 27, 1917, p. 5.

[79] *Ibid.*, p. 2.

[80] Chafee, *op. cit.* (above, note 20), p. 30.

REBELS OF THE WOODS

The intervention of the troops in 1917 rested ultimately upon the authority of Article IV, Section 4, of the United States Constitution and the several federal laws giving this constitutional provision effect.[81] But the lumber strike, in spite of some of the I.W.W.'s ferocious rhetoric, did not really endanger the republican form of government in Washington, Oregon, or Idaho, nor did the Wobblies, in spite of their frequent foreign birth, constitute a foreign invasion. Most of the seeming justification for the military arrests and the kind of "illicit martial law"[82] that came with the arrests derived simply from the climate of panic and crisis, and much of the panic was manipulated by parties whose interests in the lumber strike were being served by the military strike-breaking.

In March, April, and May 1917, the War Department gave orders empowering the Army to suppress civilian acts of seditious intent and to protect all public utilities. President Wilson instructed Newton D. Baker, the Secretary of War, to distinguish carefully between ordinary offenses against law and order—those matters for civilian police authorities to handle normally—and offenses with seditious or disloyal intent. Of course, local military commanders, and the local sheriffs and police with whom they cooperated, could not always make such fine distinctions, and often did not try very hard.[83] The lumber strike itself, although probably neither a civil crime nor a seditious act, seemed crime enough to the Army, the sheriffs, and their vigilante cohorts.

Apologists for the manhunt sometimes claimed it was necessary as a means of protecting Wobblies from the irregular justice of vigilantes and inflamed private citizens. Better, they said, to arrest Wobblies by the hundreds and control them in safe stockades than to let them run free and perhaps be massacred by the people. But this justification, transparently, is sophistical. It makes a person a felon because his neighbors cannot refrain from doing him violence.[84] The Army's role apparently was not to "protect" Wobblies but to suppress the first symptoms of revolution, that first rash on the hypochondriacal body politic that set off the panic. The Army, to continue the figure, treated the symptoms until more systematic, juridical therapy could be brought to bear on the

81 Preston, *op. cit.* (above, note 42), pp. 103-104.
82 *Ibid.*, p. 106.
83 *Ibid.*, p. 105.
84 Chafee, *op. cit.*, p. 151.

I.W.W. virus by the Immigration Bureau of the Department of Labor and by the Justice Department.

In early 1918, Clarence L. Reames, acting as a special deputy of the United States Attorney General, arrived in Seattle to direct the enforcement of the Espionage Act and other national laws in the Pacific Northwest. Before his mission, the Justice Department had been showered with advice from many sides on the dangers of sedition and revolution in the Seattle area. Hugh Campbell Wallas, Democratic National Committeeman from Washington and a friend of President Wilson, had reported on the revolutionary dangers. Colonel M. L. Saville, head of the Military Police at Camp Lewis, sent an even more frightening report to Washington, D. C. Reames thus came to Seattle as a special trouble shooter with a charge to expedite prosecutions under the federal laws and also to bring some semblance of order into a chaotic situation. He found:

> ... every public officer, federal, state, and municipal, including the members of the Fire Department, and all volunteer organizations exercising the privilege of unceremoniously arresting citizens, aliens, and alien enemies and throwing them unceremoniously into jail, where they were booked for investigation by the Department of Justice ... citizens without any semblance of authority at all were arresting men for pro-German utterances and turning them over to the police department where they were being held under the broad charge "Held for Federal authorities."[85]

Reames found his position delicate. He had to curb the wilder enthusiasms of the local authorities, the vigilante groups such as the Minute Men, and the Army and Navy commanders, but he had to do it discreetly and diplomatically. Any public condemnation of the rampant official disregard for the Constitution would be construed as "coddling" the Wobblies and, by the Wobblies, as an admission of grave error that they could exploit in their propaganda to the embarrassment of the government.[86]

Reames at first cooperated with the local authorities in con-

---

[85] Reames to Attorney General, Mar. 4, 1918 and Mar. 16, 1918, DJ File 190159—19, 48. Quoted by Preston, *op. cit.*, pp. 160-161; Portland *Oregonian*, Feb. 10, 1918, p. 3.

[86] Preston, *op. cit.*, p. 161.

REBELS OF THE WOODS

tinuing the routine checks of trains and hotels, and by the middle of February 1918, he had captured and detained over a hundred new Wobbly suspects.[87] In Spokane, he continued the Justice Department's cooperation with the Army in ferreting out possible violators of the law. Wobblies there discovered two microphones concealed in the office of their defense attorney. They followed the attached wires through a vacant office next door and into a third office down the hall where they surprised a soldier assiduously taking notes on their conversation with their lawyer.[88] The same defense attorney later discovered that his stenographic notes of the I.W.W. municipal-court trials, reports he had paid for himself and which he intended to use in drafting appeals, had been stolen from his office. The Spokane police chief denied any knowledge of the burglary, but hinted vaguely that "Army Intelligence" might have been the culprit.[89]

Despite some continuing lapses by police and the military, Reames succeeded in bringing a degree of order out of the chaos. He limited arrests without warrants for mere membership in the I.W.W., and he stopped some of the grosser mob actions, all without losing the confidence of the mob.[90]

Most Wobblies in the Pacific Northwest arrested for suspected violations of the Espionage Act won their freedom in one way or another. In Seattle, a compliant grand jury brought in indictments against fifty Wobblies, but the United States Circuit Court released all fifty prisoners and chastised the grand jury for its sloppy work of including in its true bills only the wording of the Espionage Act without any recitation of particular offending acts.[91] Many other arrested Wobblies similarly won their freedom even before their cases reached the courts. In September 1918, the authorities raided the I.W.W. hall in Tacoma and detained thirty-three Wobblies for violations of the Espionage Act. The government for lack of evidence beyond their mere membership in the I.W.W. had to release the prisoners before prosecution.[92] The sheriff at Bend, Oregon, assisted by deputized business men, arrested Carl

---

87 Portland *Oregonian*, Feb. 10, 1918, p. 3.
88 *Defense Bulletin of the Seattle District*, Sept. 9, 1918, p. 4.
89 *Ibid.*, p. 3.
90 Preston, *op. cit.*, p. 163.
91 *Solidarity*, July 21, 1917, p. 8.
92 *Defense Bulletin of the Seattle District*, Sept. 30, 1918, p. 5.

Svelgrin, the secretary of the local I.W.W. branch. After several days of rough "third degree" Svelgrin came under the custody of the federal authorities in Portland. They tried to organize a case under the Espionage Act with the meager evidence at hand but finally had to release Svelgrin.[93] But the I.W.W. as an organization obviously suffered from these arrests and long imprisonments, even if many individual Wobblies eventually won freedom without standing trial.

Some of the arrests, of course, did culminate in trials and convictions. The case of Dr. Marie Equi of Portland, for example, revealed the kind of offense for which Wobblies were often arrested if not always prosecuted or convicted. Although Dr. Equi was not formally a member of the I.W.W., she had associated with the organization for years and had joined in its agitation. So far as the public was concerned she was a Wobbly even if the technicality of her not being a wage earner, a proletarian, barred her from formal membership. In June 1918, Dr. Equi had spoken in the I.W.W. hall and had called American soldiers "dirty, contemptible scum," comparing them unfavorably to the clean and open fighters in the I.W.W. She had advised the I.W.W. to follow the example of the Irish revolutionaries who were striking their master, the British Empire, when the master was weak and preoccupied. She had also charged that the "ruling class" owned the Army and Navy, and that many American workingmen in the trenches of France fought their German "fellow workers" most reluctantly.[94] Witnesses at her trial also charged her with disloyal remarks not mentioned in the indictment. While watching a military parade in September 1917, she had shouted, "There they go. Nothing to be proud of. Those skunks!" While watching yet another parade, the irrepressible doctor had violently spurned an American flag that some patriot had urged upon her, throwing it into the dirt with obvious contempt.[95]

The jury deliberated two and a half hours and found Dr. Equi quilty. The volatile doctor then created a scene in the court room, crying out, "I will not take an appeal. I will go to San Quentin and write a book." She strode over to the prosecuting attorney and

[93] *Solidarity*, July 21, 1917, p. 8.
[94] United States v. Equi, 261 Fed. 53 (1919).
[95] Portland *Oregonian*, Nov. 15, 1918, p. 3.

demanded that he apologize for calling her an "unsexed woman" in his speech to the jury. "Come on, now, apologize," she demanded. The flustered attorney explained by way of apology that he had meant only "unwomanly." As she walked from the court room, Dr. Equi insisted that she had been "framed" and that her conviction was class persecution. She compared her severe treatment to that of a prominent Portland flour miller of German descent awaiting trial under the Espionage Act for some verbal pro-German indiscretion. The authorities, Dr. Equi claimed, had not even searched his house.[96] Even if the reader discounts the newspaper's possible intent to make Dr. Equi look ridiculous, it is still obvious to him that Wobblies in trouble with the law did not hide their opinions in protective equivocations.

Although the government succeeded in convicting few Wobblies under the Espionage Act, it imprisoned scores, using the law as a means of holding troublesome Wobblies in jail—and thus *hors de combat*—even if convictions did not always follow. When the authorities could not assemble sufficient evidence to prosecute under the Espionage Act, and if the prisoner was an alien, they increasingly fell back upon the deportation provisions of the 1917 Immigration Act and, shortly before the end of the war, the 1918 Immigration Act. Indeed, Immigration Bureau officials had began a dragnet of their own—supplementing that of the Army, the Minute Men, the local sheriffs—even before Reames appeared in Seattle. Reames supported this project although, of course, Henry M. White, the Commissioner of Immigration in Seattle, became its principal advocate and administrator.[97]

The Immigration Bureau arrested and detained scores of Wobblies for possible deportation, but the small number actually deported, like the meager convictions under the Espionage Act, does not measure the damage to the I.W.W. as an organization. During the war the government perforce had to postpone most deportations to enemy nations, and after the Armistice, a number of fortuitous developments saved many detained Wobblies from actual deportation. They escaped because of the uncertain policy of the Department of Labor, an uncertainty arising from court decisions on several belated appeals for writs of *habeas corpus*, and, later,

---

[96] *Ibid.*, Nov. 22, 1918, p. 12; Albers v. United States, 263 Fed. 27 (1920).
[97] Preston, *op. cit.*, pp. 163-164.

because of a squabble within the government between the Justice Department and the Department of Labor. But many Wobblies nonetheless languished in jail for months before their cases were disposed of.

Under the terms of the immigration laws, the various regional commissioners of immigration tried deportable aliens in administrative hearings. Since deportation was not considered punishment for any particular crime, but merely the withdrawing of hospitality, the law did not provide for court trials. Immigration commissioners directed the hearing unfettered by legal rules of evidence or by standard court procedures, and the burden of proof rested upon the prisoner and not the government. Although only the Secretary of Labor had the power to order deportation under the law, he usually followed closely the "verdicts" of the regional hearings and the certifications of his commissioners.[98]

While officials scratched their heads and wracked their brains for "legal" techniques to use in the suppression of the I.W.W., the 1917 Immigration Act, passed in February over President Wilson's veto, presented itself to them as an adventitious weapon to use in the fight. Many Wobblies, of course, were aliens. The 1917 law contained, besides its more well-known literacy test, a strong antiradical clause:

Any alien who at any time after entry shall be found advocating or teaching the unlawful destruction of property, or advocating or teaching anarchy or the overthrow by force or violence of the Government of the United States or of all forms of law or the assassination of public officials . . . shall, upon warrant of the Secretary of Labor, be taken into custody and deported.[99]

By late 1917, the Immigration Bureau began to assume a kind of leadership in the campaign to smash the I.W.W. in the Pacific Northwest. By making its own interpretation of the law, and by virtue of its freedom from having to prove particular crimes against particular persons or from having to prepare tight cases for regular court trials, the Immigration Bureau found itself with a

[98] "The Deportations," *Survey* (Feb. 22, 1919), p. 724; Louis F. Post, "Administrative Decisions in Connection with Immigration," *American Political Science Review*, X (May 1916), pp. 251-261.
[99] Preston, *op. cit.*, p. 83; *U. S. Statutes at Large*, XXXIX, Public Laws, 1917, p. 889.

certain freedom of action that Reames, for example, did not have. As if to make the arrest of alien Wobblies that much easier, the office of the Secretary of Labor, three thousand miles away, granted the Seattle office all the emergency telegraphic arrest warrants it requested, assuming that the Seattle office's version of the emergency was accurate.[100]

The Immigration office in Seattle, needless to say, shared the populace's negative attitude toward the I.W.W. and had no greater reverence for due process than was common in 1917 and 1918. Into every individual record the Seattle office inserted its own specially mimeographed brief on the I.W.W. problem, a document prepared as a guideline for the campaign. In it the Wobblies were freely, if injudiciously for a "legal" document, characterized as "yeggs," as the "scum of the earth," and as persons who recognized no law save "the policeman's night stick."[101]

The Seattle office probably corralled more Wobblies than all the other agencies before it. In only two weeks of January 1918, it arrested a hundred aliens. It quickly filled its own limited detention facilities and began to farm out its prisoners to every cooperating county jail in Western Washington. It offered its services helpfully to employers who came to it asking for the arrest of particular Wobblies, or merely of troublesome aliens on their payrolls. Even the railroad detectives called upon the Immigration Bureau for help and pointed out the persons they wished arrested.[102]

At this promising juncture in the campaign against the I.W.W., with officials thinking in terms of as many as five thousand arrests, the Secretary of Labor far away in Washington, D. C., William B. Wilson, braked the too smoothly running machine. He stipulated in an astonishing memorandum that mere membership in the I.W.W. would not constitute sufficient reason for deportation. The round-up stopped temporarily. But one hundred fifty Wobblies already arrested still waited in jail for their deportation hearings.[103]

The temporary halt to this first deportation campaign in Seattle during the winter of 1917-1918 led the Justice Department and the

---

[100] Preston, *op. cit.*, pp. 168-169.
[101] *Ibid.*, p. 165. From "Mimeographed Summary," 1, IN File 54379/76, and other individual case files examined by Preston.
[102] *Ibid.*, p. 166.
[103] *Ibid.*, pp. 167-169.

Immigration Bureau of the Department of Labor to support a new and stronger Immigration Act that would indeed make mere membership in seditious organizations a deportable offense. The law, passed finally in October 1918, had been aimed at the Seattle Wobblies. The Seattle officials had lobbied for it. But its major consequence was the mass "Palmer Raids" of 1920 which it made possible.

In advance of the new law for which they were lobbying, the Immigration Bureau in Seattle tried again in the summer of 1918 to interpret the 1917 law in such a way as to make possible the deportation of the Wobblies already in custody. Membership in the I.W.W., together with evidence that the alien member knew what the I.W.W. stood for and was up to, would constitute a deportable offense according to the new interpretation by the Seattle office. Because the prisoners were presumed guilty anyway and because they tended to be surly and uncooperative during their hearings, the Seattle Bureau thought its new interpretation might stand up. In September 1918, eighteen of the prisoners were certified for deportation. The Bureau sent their records on to Washington, D. C., hoping that the transcripts would give enough evidence not only of admitted membership in the I.W.W. but also of individual advocacy of illegal doctrines.[104]

But again the campaign stalled. Federal District Judge F. H. Rudkin issued an important writ of *habeas corpus* to a Wobbly prisoner detained for deportation. He argued that the government had presented no proof that this particular Wobbly had advocated, in his own words or actions, the violent destruction of property. Although the law in October 1918, passed after Judge Rudkin's decision, came along to make mere membership in an organization advocating violence sufficient grounds for deportation, the Immigration Bureau could not decide whether to institute new proceedings against its prisoners, to release them, or to make an appeal to the Circuit Court for a more definitive ruling on the 1917 law, under which its first cases had been prepared.[105] As a result of the confusion, some Wobblies were released from custody.

---

[104] *Ibid.*, pp. 172-177.

[105] *I.W.W. Deportation Cases*, Hearings before a Subcommittee of the Committee on Immigration and Naturalization: House of Representatives, 66 Cong., 2 Sess., April 27 to 30, 1920 (Washington, 1920), p. 69.

In 1919, another significant court decision defined for a time the limits of even the new 1918 law. In April 1919, Sam Nelson, a Wobbly long detained for deportation, appealed to Judge Augustus H. Hand for a writ of *habeas corpus*. Judge Hand reviewed the record of Nelson's deportation hearing and issued the writ. He explained his decision as follows:

> In this case the relator explicitly denies that he advocates the destruction of property. Such a denial, of course, may be expected in cases where a relator does in fact advocate active sabotage; but, in the face of his denials, which are uniform, some other evidence must appear substantiating the charge for which he is being deported. The only thing that I can derive from the record is that he believes that there is an irreconcilable conflict between employer and employee and that he believes the fruits and even the instruments of production belong to the laborer. This is a doctrine of socialism which may or may not be worked out by peaceful means, and I find no evidence in the record that destruction of property was advocated or intended by the relator.[106]

During the ensuing months, the immigration authorities again had to release Wobbly prisoners, some on parole, some on their own recognizance, and for several months after the Nelson case deportation proceedings against Wobblies virtually ceased. The Justice Department, assisting the Department of Labor in enforcing the immigration law, began to shift its attention from the I.W.W. to the Federation of Unions of Russian Workers and other radical organizations spawned by the new Bolshevik Revolution in Russia.[107]

Although the I.W.W. left the center of the stage and confusing administrative quarrels within the government began to slow deportations, federal authorities still held scores of Wobblies for deportation, the remainder of the wartime bag. Probably the largest single group of such prisoners waited through most of the months of the war in the Snohomish County jail in Everett, Washington, farmed out there by the Seattle Bureau. Some of the prisoners had been arrested as far back as the first weeks of the 1917 lumber

---

[106] *Ibid.*, p. 4.

[107] American Civil Liberties Union, *Since the Buford Sailed: A Summary of the Developments in the Deportation Situation* (NewYork, n.d.), p. 3.

strike, and had then been passed along by the Army to the Immigration Bureau. Because the county did not want to burden itself unnecessarily with the care of federal prisoners, it supplied the Wobblies with none of their needs except food. In anger, the Wobblies voted to refuse charitable aid from outside sympathizers, insisting with characteristic obstinacy that the government would have to take care of them if it wanted to keep them prisoners. They wore their clothes to tatters and soon exhausted their pocket money.[108] In August 1918, by which time most of them had been in prison for at least thirty weeks, they wired the Secretary of Labor and demanded that he supply their minimal needs. They began a hunger strike to publicize their plight, and they sent a letter to the Everett *Daily Herald* to protest their neglect by the county. The newspaper did not publish their complaint, but did publish a letter from the immigration officials in Seattle praising the county for its exemplary treatment of federal prisoners.[109] The Commissioner General of the Immigration Bureau eventually replied to the Wobblies' telegram, advising them in bureaucratic jargon that the government was studying their complaints and preparing final dispositions of their cases.[110]

One of these Everett prisoners languished in jail for twenty months before eventual deportation in November 1918, shortly after the Armistice. He arrived in England penniless, in rags, and without any relatives or friends in the native land he had not seen for twenty-five years.[111] The day before he embarked from Ellis Island, he wrote to the Commissioner General requesting clothing. He received no clothes, but only a formal request to write complaints on only one side of the paper.[112]

The largest contingent of deportees from the Pacific Northwest left Seattle for Ellis Island on February 7, 1919. Most of the thirty-six men on the sealed train—the "red special," as the newspapers called it—were Wobblies. The authorities routed the train at the last moment through Helena, Montana, rather than Butte,

---

[108] *Defense Bulletin of the Seattle District*, Aug. 19, 1918, p. 4.
[109] *Ibid.*, Sept. 9, 1918, p. 5.
[110] *Ibid.*, Sept. 30, 1918, p. 8.
[111] American Civil Liberties Union, *American Deportation and Exclusion Laws*, Report by Charles Recht to the New York Bureau of Legal Advice (New York, 1919), p. 9.
[112] *Ibid.*, pp. 29-30.

because the I.W.W. branch in Butte had organized a force of three hundred armed men to free the deportees by force. As soon as they reached New York, the Wobblies managed to get word to a New York lawyer retained for them by the Chicago headquarters. Most of the Wobblies after their day in court won writs of *habeas corpus* and were released. Only twelve of the "red special" shipment actually suffered deportation.[113]

With the war over, and the Wobblies for the first time adequately defended by counsel, the full story of their wartime ordeal in the Pacific Northwest began to spread through eastern liberal and radical circles. It all made "excellent atrocity stories for radicals to tell one another." The Wobblies' new defenders prepared an impassioned but closely argued document which they sent to the Secretary of Labor. Secretary Wilson, a former coal miner and a man of a generally liberal turn of mind, may not have known the full extent of the decay of due process in the Pacific Northwest deportation campaign. At any rate the Secretary of Labor and his Assistant Secretary, Louis Post, began to keep much closer tabs on the whole deportations program.[114]

With the beginning of open controversy and of publicity, the courts established precedents that led to the release of many detained alien Wobblies. But as the I.W.W. danger seemed to wane with the end of the war, the new threat of "Bolshevism" assumed its place and the October 1918 Immigration Act, with its seeming acceptance of "guilt by association," became the handy weapon to use against the new danger. Because the Department of Labor had not received an appropriation for the implementation and enforcement of the 1918 law, the Attorney-General, A. Mitchell Palmer, graciously agreed to do the police work. In January 1920, a new "deportations delirium" began with the famous—or infamous— "Palmer Raids" upon the headquarters of various radical, foreign-language associations all over the nation.[115]

Louis Post, the Assistant Secretary of Labor acting for Secretary

---

[113] Seattle *Daily Times*, Feb. 10, 1919, p. 3; Portland *Oregonian*, Feb. 11, 1919, p. 3; Preston, *op. cit.*, p. 206.

[114] *Ibid.*, pp. 200-201.

[115] Louis F. Post, *The Deportation Delirium of Nineteen Twenty* (Chicago, 1923), p. 187; *Investigating Activities of the Department of Justice: Letter from the Attorney General* . . . 66 Cong., 1 Sess., Senate Document No. 153 (Washington, 1919), p. 10.

Wilson during the latter's illness, reviewed almost 4,000 deportation cases presented to him for final disposition by Palmer. Post ordered about seven hundred deported and, to the consternation of Palmer and some Congressmen, cancelled deportation orders on about 2,700 other aliens.[116] This "softness" on the part of the Department of Labor aroused the ire of all patriots eager to get the radical foreigners out of the country. As early as November 1919, before the raids, the Committee on Immigration of the House of Representatives had evinced grave dissatisfaction with the Department of Labor and had traveled to Ellis Island to conduct hearings, interviewing prisoners awaiting deportation and the immigration authorities. The eighty aliens detained on the island chose this time to go on a strike. They objected to a prison-like wire net put up in the visiting room to separate them from their visitors during visiting hours. They refused to leave their rooms to be interviewed by the visiting Congressmen and created a considerable distraction by singing and yelling.[117] Representative Albert Johnson of Washington, an old enemy of the I.W.W., told reporters that he hoped Congress would soon pass a law giving the Justice Department rather than the Department of Labor control over deportations[118] Palmer took up the mounting complaint against the radical-coddling Department of Labor after Post had released the thousands of aliens so laboriously corralled by Palmer's Bureau of Investigation agents. Palmer thus opened a bitter feud within the administration, denouncing Post as an incompetent administrator with, worst of all faults, an excessive sympathy for "social revolutionaries."[119] Post defended himself successfully, however, before a Congressional committee examining possible grounds for his impeachment. He explained his administrative decisions and, in a counter-attack, criticized the unjust methods of the Attorney General. Justice demanded, he insisted, that standards of procedure for judicial trials hold also for deportation procedures even if the

---

[116] Louis F. Post, *op. cit.*, p. 187.

[117] Portland *Oregonian*, Nov. 25, 1919 pp. 1-2.

[118] *Ibid.*, Nov. 22, 1919, p. 2.

[119] Attorney General A. Mitchell Palmer on charges made against the Department of Justice by Louis F. Post and Others, Hearings before the Committee on Rules, House of Representatives, 66 Cong., 2 Sess. (Washington, 1920), p. 6.

immigration law did not specifically prescribe them.[120] But by this time, as we have seen, the attention of patriotic watchdogs had shifted from the Wobblies to a new scent, and the I.W.W.'s ordeal under the 1917 and 1918 Immigration Acts had about come to an end in the Pacific Northwest. The Wobblies in the Pacific Northwest, however, earned the dubious distinction of having been the experimental guinea pigs for the national program by Palmer in 1920.

Municipal governments in the Pacific Northwest assisted the United States government and the governors in the general assault upon the I.W.W. In cases where the evidence did not warrant prosecution under the federal laws, police courts stepped into the breech and convicted Wobblies on lesser charges of vagrancy or disorderly conduct. On February 23, 1918, federal agents raided the I.W.W. hall in Portland and arrested twenty-six Wobblies. The press announced exultantly that the authorities had uncovered evidence of a plot to terrorize the entire region with a campaign of sabotage. But the press was unnecessarily fearful. The twenty-six Wobblies, for lack of real evidence, were handed down to the municipal court. Some received thirty-day sentences; most were freed. After the trials, the police discovered that the defendants had stuck I.W.W. "silent agitators," their gummed propaganda stickers, all over the court room.[121] In Klamath Falls, Oregon, the United States Marshall arrested Dan Sullivan, a Wobbly, for suspected violations of the Espionage Act, but the marshall had to release Sullivan to the municipal authorities for lack of evidence. The Klamath Falls municipal court did its best for God and country by sentencing Sullivan to jail for disorderly conduct.[122]

A few of these many Wobblies passed down from federal custody to the municipal authorities behaved almost as if they resented such a diminution of their "martyrdoms." Some Wobblies convicted in municipal courts tried to dignify this essentially humiliating treatment by making ambitious speeches to the court or by baiting the judge. Herman Smith, standing trial in Portland for vagrancy, declaimed that he was a man without a country, a part of the proletariat without fatherland. "The U.S. can go to hell,"

---

[120] Louis F. Post, *op. cit.*, p. 255.
[121] Portland *Oregonian*, Feb. 27, 1918, p. 5.
[122] *Ibid.*, Aug. 7, 1917, p. 1.

he announced defiantly. "You can't use that kind of language here," the judge said pathetically as he sentenced Smith to forty-five days in jail.[123]

City governments in the Pacific Northwest also joined the hunt by passing special city ordinances aimed at the I.W.W. The Portland city council enacted an ordinance that prohibited the display of the red flag in any public place, and prescribed that all public assemblages display the American flag.[124] The Spokane city council passed a criminal-syndicalism ordinance, the only such municipal law passed anywhere in the United States. The law gave city officials something besides the ordinary vagrancy and disorderly conduct ordinances with which to belabor the I.W.W. if the higher authorities could not take action under criminal laws.[125]

Many states, beginning in 1917, began to pass special laws defining still another crime to be laid at the doorsteps of the I.W.W. These new laws, named criminal-syndicalist acts, in effect proscribed the I.W.W. and made active membership in it a possible felony punishable by really severe penalties.[126] Of the states in the Pacific Northwest, Idaho pioneered with this kind of legislation, passing "An act defining the crime of criminal syndicalism and prescribing punishment therefor" in March 1917, a month before the United States' declaration of war and three months before the beginning of the lumber strike. The law defined criminal syndicalism as "the doctrine which advocates crime, sabotage, violence or unlawful methods of terrorism as a means of accomplishing industrial or political reforms . . ."[127]

The legislatures of Washington and Oregon followed shortly afterwards with similar laws. The legislature of Washington, in fact, passed its first criminal syndicalism law in the same month as the Idaho legislature, but Governor Lister's veto postponed its

---

123 *Ibid.*, Aug. 8, 1917, p. 7.

124 *Ibid.*, Feb. 1, 1919, p. 10.

125 *War-Time Prosecutions and Mob Violence*, pp. 36-37.

126 The United States Congress also tried five times to enact federal criminal-syndicalism legislation. The Senate passed one such bill that subsequently died on the calendar of the House of Representatives. The other four bills never came to the floor of either house. E. F. Dowell, *A History of Criminal-Syndicalist Legislation in the United States* (Baltimore, 1939), pp. 89, 109.

127 *General Laws of the State of Idaho*, Passed at the Fourteenth Session of the State Legislature, Chap. 145, pp. 459-461.

149

REBELS OF THE WOODS

final passage till the next legislative session in 1919. The Washington law defined criminal syndicalism as any doctrine advocating "crime, sedition, violence, intimidation or injury as a means or way of effecting or resisting any industrial, economic or political change." Any person joining or voluntarily associating with any organization formed to further such purposes came under the jurisdiction of the law.[128] In the same session, the legislature passed a supplementary law defining the crime of sabotage and fixing punishments. The lawmakers defined sabotage as the attempt to obstruct or injure any enterprise hiring wage earners with the intent to impair or supplant the owner's control or management over the enterprise.[129] The Oregon law, approved in February 1919, defined criminal syndicalism as "the doctrine that advocates crime, physical violence, arson, destruction of property, sabotage, or other unlawful acts or methods, as a means of accomplishing or effecting industrial or political ends, or as a means of effecting industrial or political revolution, or for profit." The law virtually specified the I.W.W. as its object, stating in Section 5 that "a very active element within the state" was busy organizing lawless and dissatisfied persons. The "very active element" was as obviously the I.W.W. as the "self-created" societies in a famous speech by President George Washington were the pro-French democratic societies of that time. The Oregon legislature also passed a supplementary act during the same session, making unlawful the carrying or displaying of the red flag to flaunt a belief in anarchy or disloyalty.[130]

The Washington authorities used the new laws vigorously against the I.W.W. During the thirteen years following the passage of the criminal-syndicalism laws, Washington courts convicted eighty-six violators of the law.[131] In February 1920, the Superior Court in Tacoma, in one trial, convicted thirty-six Wobblies.[132]

---

[128] *Session Laws of the State of Washington,* Sixteenth Session, Jan. 13, 1919 to Mar. 13, 1919, Chap. 174, pp. 518-519.

[129] *Ibid.,* Chap. 173, pp. 517-518.

[130] *General Laws and Joint Resolutions and Memorials,* Adopted by the Thirtieth Regular Session of the Legislative Assembly (Salem, Oregon, 1919), Chap. 12, pp. 25-26; Chap. 35, p. 49.

[131] H. W. Stone, *Oregon Criminal-Syndicalism Laws and the Suppression of Radicalism by State and Local Officials* (Unpublished thesis, University of Oregon, 1933), p. 2.

[132] Seattle *Post-Intelligencer,* Feb. 2, 1920, p. 1.

In interpreting the law, the Washington Supreme Court brooked no legalistic nonsense from the I.W.W. appellants; it sustained most convictions appealed to it. In one important appeal, the I.W.W. attorney, in attacking the information of the indictment of his client, tried also to attack that interpretation of the law that made mere membership in the I.W.W. a crime. The information had stated simply that the defendant had helped to organize, had joined, and had associated with the I.W.W. Then in the indictment a brief, and somewhat tendentious, description of the aims of the I.W.W. followed. The Supreme Court rejected the appellant's contention that the indictment had given no facts, only conclusions. It also rejected the claim that evidence on the nature of the I.W.W. was, by itself, insufficient to convict a voluntary and knowing member.[133] The Supreme Court did sometimes reverse the decisions of the lower courts over minor irregularities in the trials, but none of these decisions altered in any basic sense the interpretation of the law as a proscription of the I.W.W.[134]

Authorities in Oregon began to enforce the Oregon law in February 1919, almost as soon as the ink in the governor's signature was dry. Portland police arrested Jay Wirth, a Wobbly, for selling radical literature on the streets. They charged him with violation of the new criminal-syndicalism law and with him another prisoner they had arrested on another charge before the law had been approved.[135] Later in February, the police raided the I.W.W. hall—a kind of recurring festivity—in quest of lawbreakers. The mayor notified the owners of the I.W.W. hall that they would be prosecuted under the criminal-syndicalist law unless they evicted their Wobbly tenants.[136] The Deputy District Attorney for Multnomah County, later in the year, informed the public of the policy he had been acting on in dealing with the I.W.W. "All we demand is proof of membership in the Wobbly organization and we will do our utmost to get a conviction."[137] For one reason or another, however, most of the captured Wobblies in this last round-up turned up in municipal court, as they always had, to take their punishments for

---

[133] State v. Lowery, 177 Pac. 355 (1918).
[134] State v. McLennen, 200 Pac. 319 (1921); State v. Gibson, *et al.*, 197 Pac. 611 (1921).
[135] Portland *Oregonian*, Feb. 9, 1919, p. 1.
[136] *Ibid.*, Feb. 26, 1919, p. 1.
[137] *Ibid.*, Nov. 15, 1919, p. 16.

vagrancy or disorderly conduct. Even with the stern criminal-syndicalist law at their disposal, law enforcement officials found it easier and cheaper to try Wobblies in the simple routine of the municipal courts rather than in the most expensive, full-dress state courts.

Late in 1919, the authorities in Oregon prepared cases against twenty-six Wobbly prisoners, the biggest campaign under the new law. In March 1920, the state brought the first of the group, Joseph Laundy, to trial. Laundy had organized the somewhat portentous-sounding Portland Soldiers', Sailors', and Workmen's Council, an organization obviously inspired by the Russian Soviets.[138] A grand jury indicted Laundy for helping to organize, for joining, and for voluntarily associating with the I.W.W. The defense tried to have the more inflammatory I.W.W. literature, published before 1917 and in most cases withdrawn during the war, barred as evidence against the I.W.W. Vanderveer, the defense attorney, claimed that the I.W.W. had ordered circulation of that propaganda stopped during the war.[139] The judge overruled Vanderveer's objection, and the jury eventually found Laundy guilty. The I.W.W. appealed the conviction to the Oregon Supreme Court on a number of counts, claiming, of course, that the criminal-syndicalist law was unconstitutional because it violated the guarantees of the Bill of Rights, that the law was uncertain and indefinite in its wording, and that Laundy's indictment was duplicitous in that it charged him with commission of more than one crime at the same time. The Supreme Court agreed with Vanderveer that the indictment was duplicitous, and remanded Laundy for a new trial, but rejected the I.W.W.'s claim that the criminal-syndicalism law was unconstitutional.[140]

Oregon authorities continued to prosecute Wobblies under the law till about 1923. The indecisive trial of Ole Hendricks in Tillamook and the diminishing of popular agitation over the radical "menace" caused the law to fall into disuse until the 1930s, at which time it was revived briefly for use against Portland Communists. On February 9, 1923, the police arrested Ole Hendricks, "a furtive

---

138 State v. Laundy, 204 Pac. 958 (1922).

139 Ibid.; Portland Oregonian, Apr. 5, 1920, p. 8.

140 William G. Hale, "A Brief Review of the Criminal Cases in the Supreme Court of Oregon for the Year 1921-1922," Oregon Law Review, II (Apr. 1923), 170-171.

little foreigner" who had been wandering through the logging camps of the Tillamook region trying to arouse interest in a projected I.W.W. strike.[141] The trial, the last important prosecution of a Wobbly under the criminal-syndicalism law, gave off some of the heat that had been generated during the more dramatic I.W.W. trials before and during the war. B. A. Green, a prominent Portland lawyer, went to Tillamook to defend Hendricks. Green tried his best to present the trial, somewhat unsuccessfully, as a major struggle between the forces of trade unionism and predatory "lumber interests."[142] He berated the press for distorting the motives of the I.W.W. in its planned strike and for thus stacking the cards against Hendricks in his forthcoming trial.[143] The press, for its part, accepted Green's charged assessment of the trial and saw it also as a supremely important struggle between "I.W.W.-ism and law and order." As the jury deliberated in Tillamook the Portland *Oregonian* commented that the fate of "I.W.W.-ism and red radicalism in the state of Oregon" and the forces of decency waited breathless on its decision.[144] But the war had been over for too long, and the passions of the hunt had subsided by 1923. The jury, after forty-one hours of deliberation, reported itself deadlocked, unable to reach a verdict. The judge discharged the jury, and the authorities prepared wearily to try Hendricks over again at the next session of the court.[145] Hendricks went back to jail to wait but shortly thereafter was set free and the second trial was never held.

The 1917 lumber strike, the first and last real display of power by the I.W.W. in the Pacific Northwest, produced an angry and determined manhunt that ended only years after the war. For two or three years the story of the I.W.W. is a story of dreary and repetitive raids and arrests, trials and appeals, fund-raising for defense committees and recriminatory pamphleteering. The attack of the "master class' jolted the I.W.W., and forced it to turn all of its energies and resources to its own legal defense. The I.W.W. really ceased as a labor union of any kind and became merely a

---

141 Portland *Oregonian*, Mar. 9, 1923, p. 1.
142 *Ibid.*; *Nation*, (Apr. 25, 1923), p. 495.
143 *Ibid.*
144 Portland *Oregonian*, Mar. 9, 1923, p. 1.
145 *Ibid.*, Mar. 10, 1923, p. 9.

harried victim, its actions marked not by the elan of the prewar years but by the desperate preoccupations of a cornered animal. The baited and wounded I.W.W. struck back once with fury in 1919 and then sank gradually into that vast limbo of public forgetfulness. By the 1930s people erroneously talked of the I.W.W. in the past tense.

CHAPTER VI

CENTRALIA

The Centralia Armistice Day riot of 1919, like some abrupt "close-up" in a motion picture of confused conflict, revealed in agonized detail the bitterness and desperation of the beleaguered I.W.W. and the ugly passions of hinterland patriots whose Jeffersonian myths the Wobblies had so long threatened. The riot not only epitomized in one local instance the whole nationwide conflict between the "reds" and the American public; it also marked the climax to the entire career of the I.W.W. in the Pacific Northwest. Its very fury reached a level from which neither Wobblies nor their foes could rise in intransigence or violence. Unlike less climactic or more chronic I.W.W. conflicts, the Centralia riot produced a major *cause celebre*, a case that stirred up for a time the same kind of national involvement as the Mooney-Billings case in California or the Sacco-Vanzetti case in Massachusetts.

The I.W.W. opened its first hall in Centralia during the height of the war fever. In the spring of 1918, a few Wobbly organizers appeared in previously Wobbly-free Centralia to pass out literature and to recruit members.[1] Viewed as little better than German spies, they insulted the patriotic sensibilities of the community with their mere presence, and during a Red Cross promotional parade in May 1918, the marchers rushed into the hall, smashed the doors and windows, dumped the furniture, literature and organizational records into the street, and beat the few Wobblies they

[1] Ralph Chaplin, *The Centralia Conspiracy* (Chicago, 1924), p. 36.

155

REBELS OF THE WOODS

captured inside the hall. James Churchill, the owner of a glove factory in Centralia, confiscated the phonograph from the hall, and E. B. Hubbard, a Centralia businessman and the chairman of the Chamber of Commerce, took the desk.[2] The raiders then put the captured Wobblies in a truck, lifting them into it by their ears, and drove them out of town to beat them and warn them not to return.

The I.W.W. did not try to return immediately, but some Centralians remained vigilant even after they had demolished the I.W.W. hall and expelled the Wobblies. With determination and dispatch, they moved against the only remaining reminder of the I.W.W., a blind newspaper vendor named Tom Lassiter, who sold the Seattle *Union Record* and the I.W.W.'s *Industrial Worker* from a news stand in the street. A group of vigilantes overturned his stand one night and scattered his newspapers in the mud. A few days later, some men in an automobile picked Lassiter himself off the street in the middle of the day, drove him out of town, dumped him unceremoniously in a ditch and warned him not to return.[3] In the absence of real Wobblies after the Red Cross parade of May 1918, Lassiter perforce had to serve as their surrogate in the eyes of aroused patriots in Centralia in late 1918 and early 1919.

In June 1919, at the time of Lassiter's deportation, the businessmen of Centralia gathered at the Chamber of Commerce to meet with organizers of the Employers' Association of the State of Washington. They listened to exhortations on patriotism, the radical menace, and the sanctity of the open shop. At the same meeting they also created a local Citizens' Protective League and chose E. E. Hubbard of the Chamber of Commerce temporary chairman.[4]

After the first raid on their hall, the Wobblies waited more than a year before venturing to return to Centralia. In September 1919, Britt Smith, an I.W.W. functionary, leased a hall on Tower Avenue in Mr. and Mrs. J. C. McAllister's Roderick Hotel building.[5] The I.W.W. rented a part of the ground floor next to the lobby of the hotel. Almost immediately after their return, rumors of another raid began to circulate through the town, and the busi-

---

2 State v. Smith *et al.*, 197 Pac. 770 (1921).
3 Chaplin, *op. cit.*, pp. 42-43.
4 Centralia *Hub*, June 26, 1919, p. 1.
5 State v. Smith *et al.*, 197 Pac. 772 (1921).

nessmen again began to discuss urgently the "I.W.W. problem" in Centralia.

In October 1919, the Citizens' Protective League, organized the previous summer, called a meeting to discuss ways of coping with the I.W.W. One senses even a certain elation at having the enemy back in the arena. The local newspaper urged every employer, whether a member of the League or not, to attend the meeting: "Employers—Your presence at the Elks Club Monday evening at eight o'clock to discuss the I.W.W. problem is earnestly requested."[6] The executives of the League announced that they had a definite proposal to present to the meeting, but they would not divulge it in advance.[7]

The assembled businessmen at the Elks Club meeting discussed the Red Cross parade and raid of the previous year. They called upon the Chief of Police for expert advice, but the Chief disappointed them by insisting that the I.W.W. had a legal right to remain in the town and that the city had no ordinances to silence or expel it. William Scales, newly chosen commander of the American Legion post, then suggested to the meeting, perhaps to revive dashed spirits, that no jury would ever convict men for raiding the I.W.W. hall again. He added, perhaps for the record, that he had no desire himself to raid the hall.[8] The Citizens' Protective League at this juncture of the meeting appointed a special secret committee to formulate tactics. Dr. David Livingstone, the County Coroner, was chosen president of the League, and William Scales of the American Legion vice president. E. B. Hubbard accepted the post of treasurer, a modest post considering he was high in the establishment of Centralia because of his holdings in the Eastern Railway and Lumber Company, the Farmers and Merchants Bank, and coal mines.[9] The meeting adjourned with officers chosen and a secret action committee appointed. In its press announcement, the League justified the secrecy of this special committee on the grounds that its enemy, the I.W.W., was secret and conspiratorial and that one

---

[6] Centralia *Hub,* Oct. 20, 1919, p. 8.

[7] *Ibid.,* Oct. 19, 1919, p. 1. "Members of the committee state that they have a definite plan to advance at the meeting Monday night, which plan will not be made public until that time."

[8] Federal Council of Churches, *et al., The Centralia Case* (New York, Dept. of Research and Education, 1930), p. 10.

[9] Centralia *Hub,* Oct. 21, 1919, p. 8; Chaplin, *op. cit.,* pp. 32-33.

must fight fire with fire.[10] The following day, the editor of the Tacoma newspaper congratulated the Centralia businessmen for their vigorous but somewhat mysterious action against the I.W.W. The secret committee in particular pleased the editor, reminding him of the virile Americanism of frontier vigilantes.[11] The Centralia press, taking up the Chief of Police's complaint over the absence of anti-radical ordinances, urged immediate action by the city fathers and suggested passage of such laws before decent citizens were put at the mercy of a "band of outlaws." The editor asked indignantly, "What are we going to do about it?"[12]

On November 7, the planning committee of the local American Legion post made public the scheduled route of the forthcoming Armstice Day parade. The I.W.W. in Centralia, predisposed to suspicion by previous assaults throughout the state as well as in Centralia, viewed the proposed line of march with great alarm. The parade was to pass the I.W.W. hall twice, once on its way up Tower Street and then again on its way back into town. The Wobblies saw in the proposed route a clear indication of another planned raid on their hall.[13] Other citizens also assumed that the American Legion intended to raid the I.W.W. hall during the parade to top its celebration of Armistice Day. Mrs. McAllister, the wife of the proprietor of the Roderick Hotel, in which the I.W.W. had rented space, became understandably anxious. She visited the Chief of Police and asked him frankly whether he intended to protect her property against the raid, virtually an open secret in the town by then. The Chief told her with equal frankness that he could not guarantee protection for her property, that his police could not last fifteen minutes against the marchers if they really intended to raid the hall.[14]

A few days before Armstice Day, the I.W.W. distributed a circular addressed to the people of Centralia, making the following direct appeal:[15]

---

[10] Centralia *Hub*, Oct. 21, 1919, p. 8.
[11] Tacoma *News-Tribune*, Nov. 7, 1919, p. 4.
[12] Centralia *Hub*, Oct. 29, 1919, p. 2.
[13] Walker C. Smith, *Was It Murder?* (Chicago, n.d.), p. 34.
[14] State v. Smith *et al.*, 197 Pac. (1921). Testimony of Mrs. McAllister, File No. 16354, Clerk of the Supreme Court, Olympia, Wash.
[15] *We Must Appeal*, With File No. 16354, Clerk of the Supreme Court, Olympia, Wash.

To the Law-abiding citizens of Centralia and to the working class in general: We beg of you to read and carefully consider the following: The profiteering class of Centralia have of late been waving the flag of our country in an endeavor to incite the lawless element of our city to raid our hall and club us out of town . . . These profiteers are holding numerous secret meetings to that end, and covertly inviting returned service men to do their bidding . . . Our only crime is solidarity, loyalty to the working class, and justice to the oppressed.

The suspicious Wobblies also turned to a young Centralia lawyer, Elmer Smith, for advice. Smith, a graduate of Macalester College in Saint Paul, Minnesota, and a young man of idealistic radical opinions, had only recently begun the practice of law in Centralia. He had given friendly legal advice to the I.W.W. on other occasions. He told the Wobblies, when they called upon him, that they had a legal right to defend their lives and property with force if they could not secure protection from the law-enforcement officials.[16]

The Armistice Day parade began at about two o'clock in the afternoon with the Centralia Legionnaires leading the march in the first platoons. The Legionnaires, swollen in numbers by contingents from Chehalis and other nearby towns, marched up Tower Street past the I.W.W. hall. About a block north of the hall, at Third Street, the marchers halted and turned around in order to return down Tower Street to the center of town, where a patriotic program would end the festivities. In making the turn at Third Street, however, the platoons became scraggly, and the Centralia Legionnaires leading the parade stopped again at Second Street to allow the platoons behind to catch up and to dress up their ranks. This maneuver placed most of the Centralia Legionnaires directly opposite the I.W.W. hall near the intersection of Second and Tower Streets.[17] As the marchers, their ranks again in order, prepared to move off, someone in the Centralia platoon near the I.W.W. door broke ranks and charged toward the door of the hall. Almost as one man the whole Centralia platoon broke formation and surged toward the door. They kicked in the door, shattered the windows,

---

[16] Seattle *Post-Intelligencer*, Nov. 12, 1919, p. 1.
[17] Ben Hur Lampman, *Centralia—Tragedy and Trial* (Tacoma, Wash., n.d.), pp. 6-8.

and crowded eagerly to get into the hall. As the battered door flew open, the expectant Wobblies, stationed inside the hall, across the street in another building, and on the crest of Seminary Hill several hundred yards away, opened fire with rifles and revolvers. Arthur McElfresh, one of the first Legionnaires at the door, dropped across the threshold with a bullet through his head. Warren Grimm, the new commander of the Centralia American Legion post and the leader of the parade, doubled up suddenly out in the street as a fatal bullet entered his stomach. Ben Cassagranda stumbled onto the pavement, fatally wounded, as he tried to flee from the hail of bullets.[18] Several other Legionnaires dropped out of the attacking mob with lesser wounds.

Reviving quickly from their initial shock, the now furious Legionnaires rushed into the hall. They dragged Britt Smith, the secretary of the I.W.W. in Centralia, Bert Faulkner, Ray Becker, Mike Sheehan, and James McInerney out of a large unused ice box at the rear of the hall.[19] One of the Wobblies who had fired at the mob from the hall, only long after capture identified as Wesley Everest, escaped from the rear of the hall and fled through the streets toward the Skookumchuck River, firing his revolver after his pursuers. He tried to ford the river but found it too deep and the current too swift. Returning almost to the river bank, he waited for the Legionnaires to overtake him. Dale Hubbard, a former athlete and a nephew of a Centralia businessman, outstripped his fellow Legionnaires and rushed up to Everest far ahead of the others. For several tense moments Everest and Hubbard warily surveyed each other. Hubbard ordered Everest to drop his revolver and give himself up. Everest refused, shouting nervously that he would surrender to the police but not to the mob of Legionnaires. He ordered Hubbard to keep his distance. But Hubbard made a sudden and rash charge toward the armed fugitive, and Everest fired, killing him instantly. The other pursuers quickly closed in and overpowered Everest without suffering any other casualties.[20] The I.W.W. Defense Committee, in its detailed history of the entire riot and its aftermath, admitted a generous admiration for Dale

[18] *Ibid.*, pp. 71-72.
[19] *Ibid.*
[20] Chaplin, *op. cit.*, p. 72.

Hubbard: "He was a strong, brave and misguided young man—worthy of a nobler death."[21]

The Legonnaires dragged Everest back to the Centralia jail, venting some of their fury on him by kicking his teeth out and by beating him. In front of the jail they tied a rope around his neck and threatened to lynch him then and there. Everest is reported to have defined them in his agony by saying: "You haven't got the guts to lynch a man in the daytime."[22]

The same night all the lights of Centralia mysteriously went out for about fifteen minutes. During that brief interval of darkness the few guards at the city jail gave up Everest to a small but quietly determined mob. "Tell the boys I died for my class," Everest said as the men dragged him from his cell.[23] The lynchers drove Everest to a railroad trestle over the Chehalis River and hanged him, illuminating their work by automobile headlights. Before he died, however, his executioners pulled him back up onto the trestle to attach a longer rope to his neck and then dropped him over again. Then they repaired to the river bank and riddled his dangling body with rifle fire. All I.W.W. accounts—and most other accounts by now—insist that some of the lynchers castrated Everest with a razor blade during the drive from the jail to the river.[24]

The following morning someone cut down Everest's body, and it lay in the shallow waters of the Chehalis River till that evening. County Coroner David Livingstone—and president of the Citizens' Protective League—then tardily retrieved the body and deposited it in the city jail, in full view of the other Wobbly prisoners. The body lay thus in jail—hardly in state—for two days.[25] The inquest, such as it was, took place under the Justice of the Peace in the absence of Livingstone, who left town on the scheduled day.[26] But later, at the Elks Club, Livingstone gave in his formal and unofficial coroner's verdict: Everest had broken out of jail, had fled to the river, had hanged himself, had then climbed back the rope to

---

[21] *Ibid.*

[22] *Ibid.*, p. 73.

[23] Walker C. Smith, *op. cit.*, p. 40.

[24] *Ibid.* The investigators for the Federal Council of Churches in 1930, however, could uncover no evidence to prove or disprove this atrocity. *Centralia Case*, p. 18.

[25] Walker C. Smith, *op. cit.*, p. 40.

[26] Portland *Oregonian*, Nov. 13, 1919, p. 1.

replace it with a longer one, had jumped again, had then shot himself several times, and finally had drowned in the river after cutting the rope.[27] According to the I.W.W. investigators, Livingstone's car had transported Everest to the lynching.[28]

Although the episode of the lynching of Everest, dramatic and grisly as it was, had only an incidental relationship to the question of culpability for the afternoon riot, it figured prominently in all I.W.W. defense propaganda. Those writers and publicists plead-the cause of the Legionnaires quite understandably did not emphasize the lynching. Ben Hur Lampman, the official historian for the American Legion post in Centralia, referred to the lynching only in passing: "The lynching of Everest was an unlawful error."[29] The Wobbly prisoners in the city jail, although not lynched, lived in terror for over a week. The coroner had placed the sodden corpse of Everest in their midst to terrorize them. For nine consecutive nights, mobs gathered outside the jail, shouting and cursing, thrusting poles and rifles through the barred windows, and hurling violent threats. Loren Roberts, whom a jury later found insane, might well have been precipitated into that condition by the week of acute fear. Tom Morgan, a youth only briefly connected with the I.W.W. before the riot, broke down under the ordeal and agreed to testify for the state, thus earning the eternal contempt of all Wobblies.[30] In 1925, Morgan got into difficulties with the law for statutory rape, and the I.W.W., reporting this misadventure with relish, dismissed him as "poor, weak Morgan."[31]

Meanwhile, all of western Washington fermented with rage. Posses of Legonnaires combed the countryside seeking Wobblies who might have been in Centralia during the Armstice Day shooting.[32] Although most of the posses returned with Wobbly prisoners, one posse produced only another bloodletting. Coming upon a suspicious-looking and uncooperative man in the woods, the Legionnaires opened fire and killed him. The victim, John Haney of Tenino, had not been a Wobbly fugitive as supposed, but rather a Legionnaire from another posse. At first the press reported

---

27 *Ibid.*, Mar. 7, 1920, p. 9.
28 Walker C. Smith, *op. cit.*, p. 40.
29 Lampman, *op. cit.*, p. 15.
30 Chaplin, *op. cit.*, pp. 74-75.
31 *Industrial Worker*, Aug. 8, 1925, p. 3.
32 Seattle *Union Record*, Nov. 12, 1919, p. 1.

that desperate Wobblies had shot Haney.[33] "That John Haney, resident of the Tenino district . . . was slain in a skirmish with refugee I.W.W. suspects . . . has been established almost beyond doubt." The following day, however, the press got the complete story but tolerantly dismissed the violence as an unfortunate accident. The authorities made no legal inquiry into Haney's death; everybody quickly forgot the episode.[34] Haney's twenty-year-old son, Bill, even waxed philosophical about the accident and magnanimously decided to blame no one: "I don't blame you fellows. Don't think that I do for a minute. It's tough to lose dad—but you fellows did your duty."[35]

The roaming posses captured all but one of the Centralia Wobblies who had participated in the armed defense of the hall. The day after the riot, Legionnaires captured Eugene Barnett at his home outside Centralia. Another posse captured O. C. Bland and John Lamb at their homes and arrested Loren Roberts two days after the shooting.[36] Legionnaires arrested the last of the defendants, Bert Bland, a week after the riot.[37]

The authorities throughout western Washington also arrested scores of Wobblies who could not conceivably have participated in the Centralia riot, but who could be prosecuted under the newly enacted criminal-syndicalism law. In Tacoma, police raided the I.W.W. hall and arrested fifteen Wobblies;[38] in Seattle they jailed thirty-eight,[39] and raided other I.W.W. halls throughout the region. In its literature, the I.W.W. referred to the period after the Centralia riot as the "white terror."[40] At the same time the law-enforcement machinery of the state geared itself to suppress once again the newly recognized radical menace. Attorney General L. L. Thompson advised the various prosecutors to rush I.W.W. cases through the courts as rapidly as possible, to try defendants *en masse* in order to save taxpayers' money and to insure the maximum number of convictions. The county prosecutors should also keep a

[33] Portland *Oregonian,* Nov. 17, 1919, p. 1.
[34] *Ibid.,* Nov. 18, 1919, p. 1.
[35] Centralia *Chronicle,* Nov. 19, 1919, p. 1.
[36] Lampman, *op. cit.,* p. 9.
[37] Portland *Oregonian,* Nov. 19, 1919, p. 1.
[38] Seattle *Union Record,* Nov. 12, 1919, p. 1.
[39] *Ibid.,* Nov. 13, 1919, p. 1.
[40] Chaplin, *op. cit.,* p. 26.

close check on jury panels to see that only "courageous and patriotic" jurors were chosen to hear the cases.[41]

Only a few newspapers tried to report the riot at all objectively. The shock and rage that swept through western Washington apparently affected editors and reporters as much as the ordinary citizens of the region. Most newspapers, excepting the radical press and perhaps the labor press, shared the public opinion that the I.W.W. had committed an unforgivable atrocity. The bias appeared in editorials, in the coloration of news stories, and in the national comment on the riot that the press chose to quote. Newspapers, for example, quoted General Pershing, boxing his comment prominently on their front pages: "Too drastic measures cannot be taken to rid our country of the class of criminals who inspire or commit such crimes."[42] The press of the Pacific Northwest quoted also the warning of Mayor C. B. Fitzgerald of Seattle to "anarchists" to stay clear of Seattle. He said that severe vigilante actions against Wobblies would continue so long as the law permitted them freedom to travel about spreading their pernicious doctrines.[43] The *Timberman*, a trade journal, emphasized the issue of patriotism as well as the criminality of the I.W.W.: "The tragedy at Centralia defines for all time the issue between the American and the anti-American." The three dead Legionnaires, the editors said, had died as truly in the service of their country as if they had been slain in the trenches of France.[44] But perhaps the Centralia *Chronicle* summarized the meaning of the outrage to the community the best:

> This country for several years had been drifting toward Bolshevism. This continuous fault finding of social conditions, capitalistic oppression, industrial servitude, socialistic tommy-rot, down-trodden laboring man, must stop. People who peddle this stuff have diseased minds and their propaganda is contagious. This is the most enlightened country the sun ever shone upon and any one who talks slightingly of it is a traitor ... Out here in the far Western Coast red radicalism showed its hand and for years to come Centralia will be referred to as the Lexington of industrial liberty.[45]

[41] Seattle *Union Record,* Nov. 24, 1919, p. 1.
[42] New York *Times,* Nov. 12, 1919, p. 1.
[43] *American Lumberman,* Nov. 22, 1919, p. 54.
[44] *Timberman,* (Nov. 1919), p. 29.
[45] Centralia *Chronicle,* Nov. 15, 1919, p. 2.

The Seattle *Union Record* published the first dissenting opinion on the riot. The newspaper published a statement by the Seattle Labor Council suggesting almost mildly that there might be more than one explanation for the violence at Centralia and that fair-minded persons should perhaps wait for more facts before giving in to the mounting hysteria.[46] Although many in the Labor Council wasted no affection on the I.W.W., they still counseled moderation because they did not want public opinion to congeal into an indiscriminate anti-labor attitude any more than opinion already had since the war. The plea for open-mindedness appeared in the first edition of the *Union Record*; a later "extra" edition the same day announced that the editor and manager of the paper, E. B. Ault, had been arrested for sedition and that the federal authorities had closed the offices of the paper to prevent further sedition.[47] The editors of the *Union Record* published the next several editions—including the afore-mentioned "extra"—on a rented press while the authorities ransacked their regular offices for evidence of sedition.[48] The federal authorities, however, proved to be somewhat more impartial enforcers of the law than Wobblies usually gave them credit for being. A federal court upheld the denial of mailing privileges for one day to the Seattle *Post-Intelligencer* and the Seattle *Star* for printing an inflammatory anti-labor advertisement that tended, in the opinion of the court, to incite readers to violence.[49]

Two days after the first startling news of the riot, the press reported the first hard facts to indicate that two interpretations of the riot were indeed possible. On November 14, the Seattle *Union Record*, in a noon "extra" edition, reported the testimony of Dr. Frank Bickford, one of the marchers in the Armstice Day parade, given at the coroner's inquest over the death of the Legionnaires. Bickford testified that the Wobblies had fired only after the marchers had launched their attack upon their hall. The Centralia platoon, marking time in front of the hall, had prepared to march again when Bickford himself had broken ranks and rushed toward the door of the hall. Another marcher, Dr. Herbert Bill, testified

---

[46] Seattle *Union Record,* Nov. 13, 1919, p. 1.
[47] *Ibid.,* Extra Edition, p. 1.
[48] *Ibid.,* Nov. 15, 1919, p. 1.
[49] *Ibid.,* Nov. 19, 1919, p. 1.

that the entire Centralia contingent had then rushed toward the door before any shots had been fired from the hall.[50] Four days later the *Union Record*, understandably eager to justify its early unpopular appeal for moderation by emphasizing any evidence of provocation by the American Legion, reported that the Legion had forcibly deported the Associated Press representative in Centralia who had released the news of Bickford's testimony.[51] The *Industrial Worker*, as could be expected, made the most of Bickford's testimony at the inquest: "The truth will be vindicated and the guilty agents of plutocracy will be pilloried in the judgment of an awakening working class."[52] Before Bickford gave his testimony, however, the I.W.W. displayed an unusual moderation in its comments upon the bloodshed at Centralia. William D. Haywood, for example, made the surprising statement that the Wobblies, if guilty, should get every punishment coming to them.[53] At least one local post of the American Legion departed from expected form as much as Haywood had. The Legion post in Butte, Montana, published a biting indictment of its fellow Legionnaires: "Mob rule in this country must be stopped and when mobs attack the home of a millionaire, or of a laborer, or of the I.W.W., it is not only the right but the duty of the occupants to resist with every means in their power."[54]

The state decided to try the Wobbly prisoners for the single crime of murdering Warren O. Grimm, perhaps anticipating some of the technical matters of law that were to help the prosecution in trying the Wobblies for this particular crime. After the manhunt had subsided somewhat, a grand jury indicted eleven Wobblies for the murder. The eleven defendants were: Britt Smith, Ray Becker, Bert Faulkner, James McInerney, Bert Bland, Mike Sheehan, Eugene Barnett, Loren Roberts, John Lamb, O.C. Bland, and Elmer Smith, the I.W.W.'s Centralia lawyer. Loren Roberts had turned state's evidence during his imprisonment and had confessed that the Wobblies had conspired for weeks to attack the American Legion's parade. But he also insisted that the Wobblies—particu-

---

[50] *Ibid.*, Nov. 14, 1919, p. 1.
[51] *Ibid.*, Nov. 19, 1919, p. 1.
[52] *Industrial Worker*, Nov. 29, 1919, p. 1.
[53] Seattle *Union Record*, Nov. 12, 1919, p. 1.
[54] *Industrial Worker*, Nov. 29, 1919, p. 1.

larly Wesley Everest—had expected an attack by the Legion.[55] The state charged Elmer Smith with first-degree murder, his advice to the I.W.W. making him a particularly culpable accessory to the crime in the eyes of the grand jury. Before the arraignment, the Lewis County Bar Association had pledged itself not to defend Wobblies in any legal actions whatsoever; consequently, the eleven defendants had difficulty at first in retaining counsel.[56] They eventually retained George Vanderveer, the perennial I.W.W. advocate, and Vanderveer hurried to Washington from Chicago only a few days before the trial, preparing his brief hastily.[57]

The court granted the defense a change of venue and scheduled the trial for Montesano, the county seat of Lewis County. Upon taking charge of the case for the I.W.W., Vanderveer requested a second change of venue, contending that Montesano was just as prejudiced as Centralia. He thought that a jury from Tacoma or Olympia would insure a fairer trial. Judge George Abel of Montesano, orally and informally, granted the defense this second change of venue in spite of increasing pressure from the American Legion to hurry justice along. The prosecution had strenuously opposed even the first change of venue to Montesano, circulating petitions throughout Lewis County affirming that there was no prejudice in Centralia, but at the same time persuading citizens to sign the petition so that "justice" could be meted out to Wobblies at the scene of their crime.[58] Before Judge Abel could officially grant the second change of venue he was removed from the case. The prosecution had hired his brother, W. H. Abel, as one of its attorneys and had then cited the relationship between judge and prosecutor as grounds to petition the state for a new judge. The governor appointed Judge John M. Wilson of Olympia as trial judge, although the other Superior Court Judge of Lewis County, Judge Ben Sheeks, should normally have replaced Abel. Judge Wilson, the new judge, denied Vanderveer's request for another change of venue.[59]

The I.W.W. followed this legal maneuvering closely and charged that the state by all means, fair or foul, was trying to insure

[55] *Ibid.*
[56] Seattle *Post-Intelligencer,* Nov. 16, 1919, p. 1.
[57] Chaplin, *op. cit.,* p. 83.
[58] *The Centralia Case,* pp. 20-21.
[59] State v. Smith *et al.,* 197 Pac. 773 (1921); *The Centralia Case,* p. 21.

a conviction. The prosecution, the I.W.W. charged, had cleverly replaced Abel and had then gone outside the county to select a judge to their liking, a judge who would make sure that the case was tried in Lewis County. The I.W.W. called attention to a speech made by Judge Wilson in Centralia before the governor had appointed him to hear the case. In the speech he had eulogized the slain Legionnaires and had castigated the I.W.W.[60] The I.W.W., however, did not report that Judge Wilson in a different speech in another town had also castigated Washington employers for policies that made I.W.W. troubles inevitable.[61]

The trial opened in a tense and expectant atmosphere. Legionnaires in uniform crowded the streets of Montesano, and the I.W.W. identified scores of other Legion partisans, "pool room characters," by their cast-off Army clothing.[62] All during the trial the uniformed Legionnaires crowded the court room, and the Legion improvised a mess hall and barracks in the basement of the Montesano city hall to attend to the needs of its members. The organization also paid each Legionnaire four dollars a day to stay in Montesano and to appear in the court room every day.[63] The Legion admitted frankly its intentions to intimidate—not the jurors, as the I.W.W. charged—but Wobbly sympathizers who otherwise would have crowded the court room and brow-beaten the jurors.[64] But the jurors in subsequent affidavits claimed that they had interperted the presence of so many Legionnaires as an attempt to intimidate them.[65]

An even more astonishing irregularity, coming one morning late in February, was the arrival of a bivouac of federal troops on the court house lawn. Vanderveer erupted in anger, demanded that Judge Wilson order their removal immediately.[66] Judge Wilson showed his surprise and pique when he learned that Prosecutor Allen had requested the governor for troops without even consulting the court. The governor in turn had asked for the troops from Lieutenant-General Hunter Liggett, the commander of all United

[60] Chaplin, op. cit., p. 85.
[61] The Centralia Case, p. 21.
[62] Industrial Worker, Feb. 7, 1920, p. 1.
[63] The Centralia Case, op. cit., (above, note 8); Lampman, op. cit., p. 39.
[64] Lampman, op. cit., pp. 39-40.
[65] Industrial Worker, May 27, 1922, p. 1; June 10, 1922, p. 1.
[66] Seattle Post-Intelligencer, Feb. 25, 1920, p. 1.

States troops on the Pacific Coast. Allen explained his action to the judge in a private hearing, and Wilson, his annoyance assuaged, somewhat reluctantly allowed the troops to remain. The prosecution explained that they were needed to protect the court and the jurors from an I.W.W. raid on the court hourse. Vanderveer insisted that such fears were insincere or at least ridiculous, that the prosecution had requested the troops only to intimidate the jurors and lead them to think that the I.W.W. endangered their lives.[67] But the soldiers camped on the court house lawn for the duration of the trial in watchful anticipation of attack by the I.W.W. that never came. Perhaps the I.W.W. was theoretically capable of such a romantic act as a jail-raising, but by this time most Wobblies in western Washington either languished in jail themselves or had taken to the woods and were hardly willing to expose themselves in a community crowded with vengeful Legionnaires.[68]

Vanderveer, in his opening remarks to the court, presented the outline of his case for the defense. He would demonstrate, he said, that the defendants had killed the Legionnaires in self defense as justifiable homicide. The businessmen of Centralia had conspired to do violence to the Wobblies, drive them out of town, wreck their hall. After making reasonable efforts to secure police protection the I.W.W. had, as a last resort, killed the raiding paraders in self defense. In his opening statment, Vanderveer even absolved the American Legion of blame; the Legionnaires had only been the dupes of the conspiring Protective League.[69]

The prosecution, in its opening statement, contended that the I.W.W. had deliberately fired upon unsuspecting and peaceful marchers and that the I.W.W. had planned its malevolent attack for days in advance of the parade, motivated apparently by the purest devilishness toward decency and patriotism. As Prosecutor Allen spoke, Vanderveer interrupted him to ask whether he charged that the Wobblies had fired before the Legionnaires had attacked the hall. There had been no attack upon the hall before the shooting, Allen replied unequivocally.[70]

Vanderveer set out ambitiously to try to prove his plea of justi-

[67] Lampman, *op. cit.*, pp. 40-41.
[68] *The Centralia Case*, p. 28.
[69] *Industrial Worker*, Feb. 21, 1920, p. 4.
[70] Seattle *Post-Intelligencer*, Feb. 8, 1920, p. 1.

fiable homicide, presenting as exhibits selected issues of the Centralia *Hub*, the I.W.W. circular, *We Must Appeal*, and a number of crudely lettered cardboard placards threatening violence to the I.W.W.[71] William Dunning, a former vice-president of the Lewis County Trades Council who had attended the October 23 meeting of the Citizens' Protective League, testified that the businessmen at the meeting had discussed making a raid upon the I.W.W. hall.[72] Dr. Bickford repeated the testimony he had given at the coroner's inquest. The prosecutors in their cross-examination of Bickford, however, succeeded in dulling the edge of his testimony. They forced him to admit that he was partially deaf, and with a confident inference for edification of the jury they suggested that Bickford may not have been able to tell whether the shooting came before or after the raid.[73] Another defense witness, Joseph Smith, testified that a Legionnaire in the Centralia platoon had turned to him as the parade turned at Tower and Third and had said, "You'll see plenty of excitement after we turn and come back." Smith also testified that Warren Grimm had assured several of the marchers that there would be "something doing" when the parade started back down Tower Street.[74] Other witnesses testified that two of the marchers, T. H. McCleary, Centralia Postmaster, and H. W. Thompson, a retired minister, had carried ropes during the parade.[75] McCleary explained that he had only picked up the rope from the street to play tug-o'-war during the parade,[76] and Thompson denied having been in the parade at all.[77] Other defense witnesses testified that the shooting had come after the attack upon the hall by the Legionnaires.[78]

Judge Wilson, however, virtually demolished Vanderveer's planned defense with a crucial ruling, making much of the defense's collected evidence irrelevant. Late in February, as Vander-

---

[71] These exhibits are with File No. 16354, State v. Smith *et al.*, Clerk of the Supreme Court, Olympia, Wash.

[72] *Ibid.*

[73] Chaplin, *op. cit.*, p. 94.

[74] *Ibid.*; *These Are the Facts* (Chicago, n.d.), pp. 10-11.

[75] Seattle *Post-Intelligencer*, Mar. 5, 1920, p. 1.

[76] *Ibid.*, Mar. 8, 1920, p. 1.

[77] Portland *Oregonian*, Mar. 6, 1920, p. 7.

[78] *Ibid.*, Mar. 1, 1920, p. 1; Mar. 2, 1920, p. 8; also File No. 16354, Clerk of the Supreme Court, Olympia, Wash.

veer began to bring on his array of witnesses, Judge Wilson ruled that he could not present any more evidence of a "business conspiracy." Such evidence, he ruled, would be admissable only if the defense could also demonstrate that Warren Grimm had been involved in such a conspiracy. The defendants were on trial only for the murder of Grimm.[79] Vanderveer, for the rest of the trial, did the best he could within the restrictions of Wilson's ruling. Elmer Smith took the stand to testify that he had attended a Labor Day celebration where Grimm had lectured on his experience with the United States Army in Siberia. Grimm had at that time referred to the I.W.W. as the American Bolsheviki and had warned American labor to change its radical attitudes. Smith also testified that he had talked privately with Grimm several weeks before the parade and that Grimm had revealed vehemently unfriendly attitudes toward the I.W.W. William Dunning, who had testified to the "business conspiracy," also tried to implicate Grimm in the same conspiracy.[80] Judge Wilson at this point sustained an objection by the prosecution and ruled that the defense with such testimony was not clearly involving Grimm in any kind of conspiracy against the I.W.W. Wilson ruled further that such testimony to be admissable would have to be supported by evidence that Grimm had actively participated in the raid upon the hall before the shooting began.[81] Neither the testimony of Elmer Smith nor of Dunning had clearly implicated Grimm in any conspiracy, whatever his expressed attitudes toward the I.W.W. may have been.

Vanderveer then brought a number of witnesses to the stand to testify that Grimm had indeed been shot at the very door of the I.W.W. hall while patriciating in a raid. Guy Bray, a sixteen-year-old boy and a relative of the prosecution's star witness, stated that he had participated in the raid and that he had seen a "large man" also at the door of the hall. The man had doubled over suddenly, clutching at his abdomen, and had staggered back toward the curb. Ray Cook testified that he had seen a man who could have been Grimm stagger away from the door of the hall and stumble toward the intersection of Tower and Second. Ray Cook's brother testified to seeing the same thing. Mrs. May Sherman said

---

[79] State v. Smith *et al.*, 197 Pac. 770 (1921).
[80] Seattle *Post-Intelligencer*, Mar. 3, 1920, p. 4.
[81] *Ibid.*, Mar. 4, 1920, p. 14; State v. Smith *et al.*, 197 Pac. 770 (1921).

she had seen a "large man" with his arms crossed over his abdomen standing directly in front of the hall when the shooting began.[82] None of these witnesses very specifically identified the "large man" as Grimm. Guy Bray, however, testified that the "large man" had been standing with Van Gilder, a witness for the prosecution, and in his testimony, Van Gilder had placed himself next to Grimm throughout the parade and the shooting.[83]

Whatever effect this evidence might have had on the jury evaporated suddenly when the state arrested two of Vanderveer's nine witnesses for perjury. The state arrested Guy Bray because his testimony had placed Van Gilder, as well as the "large man," in front of the I.W.W. hall, and Van Gilder denied having been in that position. The state arrested Ray Cook because his testimony had placed the head of the whole parade opposite the I.W.W. hall and not at the intersection of Tower and Second where every other witness placed it.[84] Vanderveer again blew up in anger, charging that the state was deliberately trying to intimidate all the defense witnesses.[85] When the sheriff appeared in the court room to arrest the two witnesses, Vanderveer came close to exchanging blows with him.[86]

Vanderveer persisted throughout the trial in trying to prove at least his minimal contention that the business men of Centralia had conspired to raid the I.W.W. hall and that the Legionnaires had attacked the hall before they had been fired upon. On one occasion Judge Wilson threatened him with a contempt citation if he persisted in the face of the court's rulings.[87] Although barred from presenting his case in detail, Vanderveer led his witnesses to state, almost parenthetically at times, that the Wobblies had been victims and not aggressors. The clearest expression of the defense claims came from one of the defendants, Bert Bland, when he took the witness chair. "I heard talk for eleven days prior to the raid of the I.W.W. hall that the hall was going to be raided. I heard it in the hall, I heard it in the streets, and I heard it in the logging camps; it was a general discussion."[88]

---

[82] State v. Smith et al., 197 Pac. 775 (1921).
[83] Ibid.; Eight Men Buried Alive (Chicago, n.d.), p. 22.
[84] Lampman, op. cit., p. 52.
[85] Portland Oregonian, Mar. 3, 1920, p. 1.
[86] Seattle Post-Intelligencer, Mar. 3, 1920, p. 1.
[87] Portland Oregonian, Mar. 2, 1920, p. 1.
[88] State v. Smith et al., 197 Pac. 774 (1921).

Although the state charged all eleven defendants with complicity in the murder of Warren Grimm, it charged one of the defendants in particular, Eugene Barnett, with having fired the fatal shot. The state charged that Barnett had stationed himself in the Avalon Hotel, below the intersection of Tower and Second and almost a block away from the I.W.W. hall. Van Gilder, the key witness for the prosecution, testified that he and his friend, Grimm, had been standing at the head of the parade near Second Street and facing away from the I.W.W. hall behind them. When the firing began, Barnett's fire from the Avalon Hotel had killed Grimm as he stood unsuspecting at the intersection.[89] After the shooting, Barnett had slipped away from the hotel and had fled from town, throwing his incriminating rifle behind a sign board on his way out of town. Barnett established a consistent alibi, presented in his defense by many witnesses and without discrepancies in detail. The McAllisters testified that Barnett had been visiting them in the lobby of the Roderick Hotel, unarmed and disassociated from the armed Wobblies in the I.W.W. hall only a few feet away. After the riot he had left town hurriedly but not guiltily. Numerous other witnesses traced his itinerary out of town, a route that took him nowhere near the sign board behind which he had supposedly thrown his rifle.[90] W. C. Green, a resident of Centralia, testified for the defense that he had spent the Armistice Day afternoon sawing wood in his back yard in easy view of the sign board in question and had seen no one throw a rifle there.[91] Indeed, in the exhaustive appraisal of the whole case published by the Federal Council of Churches, the investigators concluded:

> As to the contention of the prosecution that Barnett fired the fatal shot from the Avalon, this was not definitely established and does not seem to be in accord with the facts. As already stated the weight of the evidence tends to support his own contention that he was in the Roderick Hotel and unarmed rather than the contention of the state.[92]

According to another perhaps more partisan account of the trial, J. C. McAllister was the "semi-senile boniface of the Roderick,"

[89] Lampman, *op. cit.*, p. 33.
[90] Chaplin, *op. cit.*, pp. 102-105.
[91] *Ibid.*
[92] *The Centralia Case*, p. 42.

and his wife was a "fleshy termagent [*sic*] who testified far too eagerly."[93] The authorities had detained Mrs. McAllister as a material witness immediately after the shooting and had kept her under guard in the Centralia jail for three weeks. According to I.W.W. accounts, the authorities had pressed her none too politely during those three weeks to change her testimony.[94]

Prosecution witnesses testified that they had seen Barnett in the window of the Avalon Hotel, but their testimony did not make a very impressive case. Elsie Hornbeck, one of these prosecution witnesses, identified Barnett as the "thin-faced" man she had seen in the window, although Barnett did not have a remarkably thin face. Vanderveer, in his cross examination, maneuvered Elsie Hornbeck into admitting that she had seen photographs of Barnett before she had identified him from the row of defendants in the court room.[95] Vanderveer used a defense-attorney ruse on Leila Tripp, another of the prosecution witnesses against Barnett. He asked for a court recess just as Prosecutor Abel was about to have his witness identify Barnett from the row of defendants. During the brief recess, Vanderveer changed Barnett's position on the bench, and when the court reconvened, Prosecutor Abel, surprisingly, did not ask Leila Tripp to try to identify the man she had seen in the window of the Avalon Hotel.[96]

The confessions of Loren Roberts and Tom Morgan did not seal the case against the defendants, though they did substantiate some facts admitted quite openly by the other Wobblies, admitted facts that brought the last and most crucial of Judge Wilson's rulings from the bench. Roberts testified that the shooting had preceded the raid and that the Wobblies had planned their attack for three weeks. He and two other Wobblies had gone to Seminary Hill overlooking the parade route at about one o'clock on the afternoon of Armistice Day. Other Wobblies had taken posts across the street from the hall in the Arnold and Avalon Hotels.[97] Vanderveer objected perfunctorily to Roberts' testimony on the grounds that his pleas of insanity made him an incompetent witness. Wilson

---

93 Lampman, *op. cit.*, p. 42.
94 Chaplin, *op. cit.*, pp. 112-113.
95 *Ibid.*, p. 98.
96 *Ibid.*, p. 100
97 Centralia *Chronicle*, Nov. 17, 1919, p. 5.

overruled the objection and explained that Roberts' testimony would be expunged if the court did find him insane.[98] In cross-examining Morgan, Vanderveer tried to show that his confession had been extorted from him by terror, but Wilson ruled his questions out of order.[99] Though Roberts' and Morgan's confessions proved no more valuable to the prosecution than the testimony of many other prosecution witnesses, the confessions did, as we have seen, substantiate damaging facts that other defendants admitted before they realized how important they would be to the case. Two of the defendants admitted frankly, for example, that they had stationed themselves in the Arnold Hotel across the street from the I.W.W. hall to wait for the expected attack, and the proprietor of the Arnold Hotel confirmed the fact for the prosecution.[100] The I.W.W. also admitted stationing men on Seminary Hill as Loren Roberts had testified.[101] These admissions, mixing badly with the plea of justifiable homicide, irreparably damaged the case for the defense. In his instructions to the jury, Judge Wilson ruled that the I.W.W. had no legal grounds for pleading self-defense even if the Legionnaires had indeed attacked first.[102] Since Wobblies had admittedly stationed themselves on Seminary Hill and in the Arnold Hotel they could not claim to be defending their lives and property, not even being on the property supposedly defended.[103] Consequently, Judge Wilson advised the jury that it had to bring in verdicts of guilty either for murder in the first degree or murder in the second degree. A verdict acquitting the defendants was legally impossible. In the case of Elmer Smith, an exception, the jury could either acquit him or find him guilty of murder in the first degree.[104]

Vanderveer spoke two hours to the jury, reviewing somewhat futilely the evidence for self-defense, and for the contention that the raid had preceded the shooting. The jury brought in a verdict that Judge Wilson refused to accept, for it found Mike Sheehan and Elmer Smith not guilty, found Loren Roberts insane, found

---

98 Seattle *Post-Intelligencer*, Feb. 12, 1920, p. 1.
99 "Centralia Before the Court," *Survey* (Apr. 3, 1920), p. 14.
100 *Ibid.*
101 Seattle *Post-Intelligencer*, Mar. 2, 1920, p. 1.
102 *Ibid.*, Mar. 13, 1920, p. 17; State v. Smith *et al.*, 197 Pac. 771 (1921).
103 *Ibid.*
104 Seattle *Post-Intelligencer*, Mar. 3, 1920, p. 17.

REBELS OF THE WOODS

Eugene Barnett and John Lamb guilty of manslaughter, and found the other defendants guilty of murder in the second degree.[105] The judge had to explain the law to the jury and send it back. The second verdict, that Judge Wilson accepted, found Barnett and Lamb guilty of murder in the second degree along with the other defendants and again acquitted Smith and Sheehan and found Roberts insane. The jury recommended leniency.[106] Wilson ignored the recommendation for leniency and sentenced all the convicted Wobblies to the maximum sentence under Washington law, twenty-five to forty years in prison.[107]

Both Wobblies and Legionnaires, for obviously different reasons, found the verdict unsatisfactory. One of the defendants as he left the court room under guard commented disgustedly, "A bone-headed jury!"[108] Vanderveer expressed his disgust with the whole case and the verdict in particular. How could a conspiracy to murder, he asked, possibly be judged second-degree murder when conspiracy implies premeditation and second-degree murder expressly excludes premeditation?[109] This disgust must have been for public consumption, because Vanderveer must have known how such a verdict was legally possible. The American Legion, on the other hand, considered the verdict much too lenient. But the Legion commended Judge Wilson for at least giving the maximum sentence. Perhaps it was all patriots could hope for, they reflected, considering that at least two of the jurors had been "reds."[110]

Vanderveer appealed the decision to the Washington Supreme Court almost immediately. On April 14, 1920, only a few weeks later, the Supreme Court upheld the verdict at Montesano and sustained all of Judge Wilson's critical rulings, accepting Wilson's arguments and citations of precedents and rejecting Vanderveer's.[111] The Supreme Court also punctured Vanderveer's contention that murder in the second degree and conspiracy are

---

[105] Portland *Oregonian*, Mar. 14, 1920, p. 7. The other defendant, Bert Faulkner, had been released during the trial upon a motion by Vanderveer. Seattle *Post-Intelligencer*, Feb. 19, 1920, p. 1.

[106] Portland *Oregonian*, Mar. 13, 1920, p. 1.

[107] *Ibid.*, Mar. 14, 1920, p. 1.

[108] *Ibid.*, Mar. 15, 1920, p. 1.

[109] *Ibid.*, Mar. 14, 1920, p. 9.

[110] Lampman, *op. cit.*, p. 70.

[111] State v. Smith *et al.*, 197 Pac. 771 (1921).

incompatible. The court reminded the appellants that any homicide, admitted or proved, is presumed by the law to be murder in the second degree unless otherwise demonstrated to be murder in the first degree by the prosecution or manslaughter by the defense. Vanderveer had geared the defense to prove justifiable homicide, not manslaughter.

A "labor jury," so called, heard most of the testimony of the trial while sitting with the spectators in the court. This jury published its verdict after the trial and took sharp exception with the official verdict, finding that Grimm had indeed been implicated in the conspiracy to raid the I.W.W. hall, that he had personally taken part in the raid, and that Judge Wilson had prejudiced the whole defense with unwarranted and restrictive rulings from the bench.[112] Ben Hur Lampman, the author of the official American Legion account of the trial, ridiculed this self-appointed "jury"—and with some justification. One of the "jurors," for example, had devoted most of his time during the trial not to hearing the testimony but rather to scouting throughout Lewis County for possible defense witnesses. None of the "labor jurors" heard most of the trial.[113]

The aftermath of the Centralia riot and trial consumed years, and all of the "martyrs" sentenced to Walla Walla penitentiary suffered their martyrdoms through years that saw the I.W.W. dwindle and virtually disappear from the American scene. But the sense of injustice born by radicals and liberals did not depend upon the continuing importance of the I.W.W., and the case became in radical and liberal circles one of the postwar *causes célèbres*.

Elmer Smith, after his acquittal, became more and more committed to the defense of the I.W.W., perhaps feeling something like the guilt of a soldier survivor whose buddies are all wiped out. He traveled throughout the region, organizing meetings, raising funds, lecturing on the evils of the criminal-syndicalism laws, and trying always to win the release of the Wobblies in Walla Walla. Before the riot, he had acted as the volunteer high-school football coach, had been a promising young lawyer in Centralia with a considerable following among the people of the town despite his noticeable propensity for unpopular causes. He began to become

[112] *Industrial Worker*, Apr. 23, 1920, p. 1.
[113] Lampman, *op. cit.*, p. 64.

persona non grata with the local establishment even before the Armistice Day parade by assuming the legal defense of bankruptcy cases and, worst of all, by associating with the I.W.W. After he returned to Centralia from the Montesano trial, his landlord trebled his rent, and he began to receive threatening anonymous telephone calls and letters advising him to leave town. In 1922, he could take his new status in Centralia no longer and moved to Eureka, California, to practice law and to continue his efforts in the campaign of the I.W.W. for amnesty.[114] When he accepted the job as defense counsel for ten Wobblies being tried in Sacramento under the California criminal-syndicalism law, the California bar withdrew its courtesy permission to practice law in California.[115] The next year, 1923, the Washington State Bar Association disbarred him in Washington,[116] and he made an unsuccessful appeal to the Washington Supreme Court for reinstatement in 1925.[117] He died some years later still disbarred, a casualty of the Armistice Day violence despite his acquittal.

Several years after the trial, a somewhat unusual American Legionnaire became prominent in the campaign in Washington to win commutation of sentences or pardons for the Wobbly prisoners. "Captain" Edward Patrick Coll, a blood relative of Eamon De Valera, came to Hoquiam and Aberdeen in 1928 to sell insurance. He was surprised at the number of working people in Washington who hated the American Legion. He decided to investigate the whole Centralia affair himself to satisfy his curiosity and to persuade his own conscience as a Legionnaire. In his investigation, he satisfied himself of the Legion's sin and of the I.W.W.'s innocence, and thereafter became a persistent thorn in the side of the Washington American Legion. He first requested a discussion of the Centralia affair at a forthcoming state convention of the Legion, but Legion officials told him that the question was still too explosive to be brought to the floor of the convention. Much to Coll's surprise, however, this same convention did discuss the riot and it even passed a resolution opposing pardons for the prisoners. C. D.

---

[114] "The New Wild West," *Liberator* (Jan. 1920), p. 21; *Industrial Worker*, May 27, 1922, p. 1.

[115] *Ibid.*, July 8, 1922, p. 2.

[116] *Federated Press Letter*, Mar. 11, 1925, p. 4.

[117] *Ibid.*, Mar. 4, 1925, p. 2.

Cunningham, a Centralia Legionnaire and one of the prosecutors at the Montesano trial, introduced the resolution. In the course of his investigation, Coll gathered thirty affidavits from marchers in the fateful parade, all to the effect that the Legionnaires had rushed the hall before the Wobblies had opened fire. Even old friends of Warren Grimm confided to Coll that Grimm had raided the hall with the other marchers. Coll also claimed to have uncovered evidence on who lynched Wesley Everest. In one interview with the press he named a prominent Centralia lawyer, calling him a "murderer," and daring him to sue for libel.[118]

"Captain" Coll's personal collection of affidavits only swelled the number of such statements secured by other amnesty workers. In May 1922, two of the jurors came to Elmer Smith before his departure for California and made signed statements to the effect that the pressure of public opinion and prejudice had forced them to give their verdict of guilty. At about the same time, another of the jurors swore to a similar statement before a notary public in Montesano.[119] Other jurors, as though feeling some collective need to absolve themselves of the responsibility for the severe sentences, hastened to sign affidavits.[120] The few jurors not making formal affidavits admitted to a change of heart after the trial when interviewed by Bert Carpenter from the Legal Bureau of the Seattle Central Labor Council. One juror visited by Carpenter stated that he had been shocked by the severity of the sentences; he had expected the defendants to get about five years, and he had acquiesced in the verdict of guilty on this expectation.[121]

The appellants and the authorities, without perhaps fully realizing it, talked at cross-purposes. The I.W.W. General Defense Committee and its increasing number of liberal sympathizers tended to ignore the legal irrelevancy of their affidavits and "new evidence" in the face of Judge Wilson's rulings. The appellants considered the exclusion of evidence of a conspiracy against the I.W.W. a blatant injustice. The successive governors of Washington, hearing the appeals, could find nothing in the spate of

---

[118] C. E. Payne, "Captain Coll—Legionnaire," *Nation*, (July 10, 1929), pp. 38-39.

[119] *Industrial Worker*, May 27, 1922, p. 1.

[120] *Ibid.*, June 10, 1922, p. 1.

[121] *Ibid.*, June 24, 1922, p. 1.

affidavits and "new evidence" to change those legal interpretations that had undone the defense at the trial and had made a guilty verdict mandatory. All the campaigners for amnesty could do, in effect, was plead for pardons despite the legalities and disseminate their argument that the state had perpetuated a legal injustice. *"The defendants stood accused of doing a legal thing in an illegal manner!"*[122] Not given to legal hair-splitting, the I.W.W. considered its plea of justifiable homicide very cogent. Could not a man defending his home from a mob station a relative in a strategic tree on a neighbor's lawn? Would the position of such a defender make the defense of the home any less justifiable? To the Wobblies the answer was obvious. Judge Wilson's precedents, supported by the Washington Supreme Court, said otherwise.

But the I.W.W. continued to collect affidavits and new evidence to present to the meetings of the parole board or to the governor. Governor Louis Hart, in 1924, showed indifference to three affidavits by witnesses to the riot. Cecil De Witte, a high-school student, swore that he had seen Warren Grimm lead the attack upon the hall, and P. M. Crinion confirmed the story, and added that he had presented himself to the prosecution during the trial but had never been called as a witness.[123] He did not explain why he had not taken the next obvious course and presented his evidence to the defense. The obdurate attitude of Governor Hart did not dampen the spirits of the defense groups, for later in 1924 they were back with more affidavits. Cecil Draper, a Centralia veteran, swore that the Legionnaires had planned a raid long in advance of Armistice Day. Another veteran, a resident of Spokane, swore that a former Army captain had approached him at his home in Spokane and had asked him to go to Centralia to help intimidate the jury. The captain had promised to pay all his expenses.[124] However trustworthy this belated evidence may have been, it had little effect in melting the hearts of the governors or members of the parole board.

The official I.W.W. defense committee for several years could not devote much energy to the defense of the prisoners from Centralia; it was much too occupied with the amnesty campaign for

---

[122] Walker C. Smith, *op. cit.* (above, note 13), p. 45.
[123] *Federated Press Bulletin*, Sept. 13, 1924, p. 6.
[124] *Ibid.*, Dec. 13, 1924, p. 7.

all the wartime federal prisoners.[125] In the years following the trial, the General Defense Committee in Chicago did publish a number of pamphlets presenting the I.W.W.'s version of the riot and urging popular action to free the prisoners. In early 1927, the I.W.W. established a Washington branch of the General Defense Committee—the federal Espionage Act prisoners had long since won their freedom. Ed Delaney, the acting secretary of the Washington branch, announced that his principal task was to free the prisoners from Centralia.[126] In addition to pressing for amnesty and organizing liberal support, the I.W.W. also assumed some responsibility for the support of the prisoners' families and dependents.[127]

Besides arguing at cross-purposes over questions of law, the amnesty campaigners and the authorities clashed over more personal matters. The I.W.W. soon added a new charge of injustice in its propaganda, arguing that the governors refused pardons not on the merits of the cases but because they disliked the "radicals" making the appeals. Upton Sinclair published an exchange of letters between Governor Hartley and an amnesty worker in the *New Republic* to make this new point. One amnesty worker, Mrs. Kate Crane-Gartz, exchanged acrimonious letters with the governor. The governor expressed his irritation with Mrs. Crane-Gartz's petition and stated bluntly that the prisoners had received a fair trial and that they did not deserve pardons. But the operation of the law, he continued, was difficult to explain to the likes of Mrs. Crane-Gartz. "No one, who is without prejudice and familiar with the facts in the case, will contend that these men did not receive a fair trial . . . The quicker these men in Walla Walla cut loose from the agitators and propagandists, the brighter their future."[128] Mrs. Crane-Gartz replied to the governor with indignation. What about the affidavits of the jurors? she asked. And if the laws of the State of Washington put men in jail for defending their lives and property while allowing lynchers to go unpunished, then the laws of Washington needed considerable explaining to the likes of her, or to anyone else.[129]

The I.W.W. and its radical supporters bore the full load of

---

125 John S. Gambs, *The Decline of the I.W.W.* (New York, 1932), p. 151.
126 *Industrial Solidarity*, Jan. 19, 1927, p. 1.
127 *Ibid.*, Jan. 5, 1927, p. 3.
128 *New Republic* (Jan. 15, 1930), p. 226.
129 *Ibid.* (Sept. 17, 1930), p. 129.

the amnesty campaign throughout the 1920s. The Centralia case dropped out of sight after the decision at Montesano; it ceased to be urgent enough news to get back into the commercial press. Not till 1929 and 1930, at the ten-year anniversaries of the riot and the trial, did the case make news for the second time. The Federal Council of Churches made its careful investigation at this time and published its authoritative report. Although moderate in tone, and morally critical of both the I.W.W. and the American Legion, the report left some questions unanswered as before. The I.W.W. press, as might be expected, took issue with the moderation of the report. The pamphlet, the I.W.W. scoffed, was merely more evidence of where church people and their ilk inevitably lined up in the class struggle.[130] The report did revive a more general interest in the fate of the Wobbly prisoners in Walla Walla, and the press published many "anniversary" accounts of the trial.

With the subsiding of the "red menace" and the publication of the report by the Federal Council of Churches, public sentiment toward the Centralia prisoners underwent a change. More "respectable" persons came out for clemency. The New York City Willard Straight American Legion Post even petitioned Paul V. McNutt, the national commander, to investigate the case to make sure that no injustice had been done, but the national officials of the American Legion took no action on the petition.[131] W. H. Abel, one of the prosecuting attorneys at Montesano, appealed for a pardon for the prisoners.[132] Over two thousand citizens of Centralia signed a petition asked the governor to pardon the men. In 1929, the state convention of the Washington State Federation of Labor voted unanimously for a resolution requesting clemency.[133] In the more favorable atmosphere, the I.W.W. recruited more and more such "bourgeois" workers in its amnesty campaigns, and in Washington, many clergymen actively entered the campaign for pardons or commutations. The Puget Sound Conference of the Methodist Church appointed a special committee to investigate the case.[134] The Centralia American Legion post volunteered to assist the

---

130 *Industrial Solidarity*, Oct. 21, 1930, p. 1.
131 "The Centralia Case Again," *New Republic* (May 14, 1930), p. 341.
132 Payne, *op. cit.*, p. 38.
133 *New Republic* (May 14, 1930), p. 341.
134 *Christian Century* (Oct. 2, 1928), p. 1279.

Methodists in their inquiry, but also expressed its opinion that the inquiry was unnecessary. The Methodist church in Centralia, however, refused to cooperate in the investigation.[135]

This more and more respectable pressure for clemency won paroles for all but one of the prisoners. Ray Becker refused parole and held out grimly for complete vindication, but in September 1939, Governor Clarence D. Martin commuted his sentence to the time served, eighteen years and three months. In 1935, Becker had written out in longhand a one-hundred-fifty-page plea for a writ of *habeas corpus* which his attorney, Irvin Goodman of Portland, had presented to no avail to the federal district court.[136] After his release in 1939—still without the complete vindication he had struggled for—Becker went to Portland to live. The Klamath Falls, Oregon local of the C.I.O. Woodworkers made him an honorary member in recognition of his work in organizing lumber workers in the Pacific Northwest. During the Second World War, he opened a small leather goods store in Vancouver, Washington, and in March 1950, he died. His obituary appeared as a nostalgic news story in the Portland *Oregonian*.[137]

The other Centralia prisoners, upon being released on parole, settled down to more or less bourgeois lives in or near the community that had so fatefully shaped their lives. John Lamb opened a Turkish bath in Centralia and made a living massaging the well-fed bodies of the "master class." Only Eugene Barnett maintained a close connection with the labor movement, organizing for the C.I.O. in Washington.[138] The I.W.W. had almost disappeared by the time of their release, and political and social changes had already made it and its program little more than a curious relic. If the prisoners reflected at all on their brief careers as revolutionaries, they probably saw that the savagery and fury on the streets of Centralia on Armistice Day 1919, had brought the whole career of the I.W.W. to a climax as much as it had suddenly altered the course of their private lives.

---

[135] *Ibid.*, p. 1301.

[136] Letter to the author from Irvin Goodman, Portland attorney, Mar. 3, 1952; Portland *Oregonian*, Mar. 9, 1950, p. 13.

[137] Portland *Oregonian*, Mar. 9, 1950, p. 13.

[138] Letter to the author from C. D. Cunningham, Centralia attorney, Jan. 25, 1952.

World War I marks a great dividing line in the history of our civilization, and in American history, as well, it brought to an end the age of American innocence. If the frontier ended as a statistician's concept with the census of 1890, it did not end as a cultural reality, as a potent myth, till the war. In 1919, citizens of Centralia, determined to live their version of the Jeffersonian pastoral, could still, figuratively speaking, take the musket down from the mantle to oppose the Wobblies. They saw the Wobblies, unrealistically, not as neighbors but as "Bolsheviks," as the agents of an alien, corrupt, un-American class consciousness. On the other hand, the Wobblies viewed themselves in their hearts as a kind of latter-day Regulator and could defend their eccentric version of the American myth with equal violence. By the 1920s—certainly by the 1930s—both the Wobblies and their provincial enemies seemed peculiarly out of style, and the Wobblies in Walla Walla suffered the additional indignity of being "martyrs" to a cause that had become an anachronism.

CHAPTER VII

BATTLE SCARS

━━━━

During World War I, and during the troubled xenophobia of the postwar period, Americans withheld all tolerance towards the I.W.W. Federal, state, and local governments, and various vigilante irregulars, attacked the organization and gave it no quarter. It is not surprising that the I.W.W. declined rapidly after the war. With its first and second echelon of leaders in jail—and with hundreds of its rank and file members under indictment in state and municipal courts—the I.W.W. became almost exclusively an organization devoted to its own legal defense. The bludgeoning inevitably induced a certain caution and loss of *élan*, and many Wobblies understandably sought ways to further the revolution without bringing the police down on themselves. Moreover, the I.W.W. acted in a ritualistic manner when it did act, going through the motions of its earlier triumphs. It seemed at times to be operating from a manual, without the dash and improvisation of the old days.

The I.W.W. also found itself, in this time of travail, face to face with a potent rival, the new Communist movement. The former left-wing Socialists whom Wobblies had disdained before the war attached themselves to the prestigious Bolsheviks of Russia. Odd as it might seem to observers outside the entire Left, the new Communists possessed not only prestige but also an apparent realism from their identification with a successful revolution. Some Wobblies abandoned the I.W.W. and went over to the new movement. In responding to this unexpected threat to its existence, the I.W.W.

had to defend the correctness and relevancy of its anarcho-syndicalism against the philosophers of the Left. In the process, the I.W.W. fell further out of action and into the hair-splitting and schismatics that had marked its early history in the days of its conflict with Daniel De Leon before 1908.

To further the work of its enemies and rivals, the stream of history itself cast the I.W.W. high and dry. Social and economic conditions changed with war and growth, ending once and for all the frontier conditions of the lumber industry, of nonferrous mining, and of agriculture. As the society changed, the migratory labor force underwent a change, and the hobo worker—the Wobbly "type"—gave way to a "home guard" or sedentary worker. The lumber worker, in particular, became less migratory, more attached to place and community. If farm labor remained migratory and seasonal, the laborers became increasingly "home guard" types, family men moving from harvest to harvest with wife and children in battered automobiles or the trucks and busses of a labor contractor.

Thus the I.W.W. faced a bewildering array of problems after the war, how to defend itself against persecution, how to demonstrate its relevancy in the face of the world-shaking Communist movement, and how to recruit members and maintain its membership in a society that was destroying the reservoir of manpower from which it had previously drawn.

Besides helping to change the I.W.W. into a society of debaters, the ordeal of the war made the I.W.W. noticeably less militant and more cautious. Communists liked to point out that the I.W.W. had "gone soft" or had lost its nerve.[1] The I.W.W., for example, began to edit its most violent propaganda even before the war had ended, and during the criminal-syndicalist trials in the Pacific Northwest it complained with some justification that its members were being convicted on the basis of prewar pamphlets and circulars that had been repudiated or softened after the first assault of the courts.[2] Wobblies also ceased to advocate sabotage as openly or as unequivocally as they once had, and they devoted pages of print to explain that sabotage, or "direct action," did not really entail the violent acts envisioned in the public accusations. With the possible

---

[1] John S. Gambs, *The Decline of the I.W.W.* (New York, 1932), p. 205.
[2] Portland *Oregonian*, Mar. 25, 1920, p. 8.

exception of the furious but essentially defensive struggle in Centralia on Armistice Day 1919, the I.W.W. ceased to provoke the same kind of disturbance that it had before the war.

During the famous Seattle general strike of February 1919, Wobblies as individuals may have acted in accordance with their revolutionary principles but with unusual circumspection. Although anxious conservatives came to blame the strike on Wobbly conspirators in the Seattle unions, the Wobblies had little to do with the inception of the strike. The trouble began after the Shipping Board refused to allow a wage increase to the Seattle A.F.L. Metal Trades Council, a raise that the Council had begun to negotiate with the local ship builders. The I.W.W. during these maneuvers seemed content to blend its distinctive voice into the radical chorus of the Seattle labor movement. For almost two years prior to the strike, Wobblies by the scores had been arrested and rearrested, detained without trial or without charges being brought against them by soldiers, police, sheriffs, vigilantes, and Immigration Bureau officials. It is understandable perhaps that many Wobblies became "two-card" union men, radicals who revealed only their membership in one or another of the Seattle unions affiliated with the A.F.L.

Workers in Seattle's shipyards had been restive all through the war months. After a threatened strike in 1917, the Shipbuilding Labor Adjustment Board—more commonly called the Macy Board after its chairman, V. Everit Macy—had granted a wage scale very unsatisfactory to the militant Seattle workers who thought a West Coast cost-of-living differential wage was just. But the Macy Board kept to its principle of a uniform national wage scale, although it did try to placate the West Coast shipyard workers by allowing them a "temporary" ten per cent "bonus." Charles Piez, head of the Emergency Fleet Corporation, in July 1918, also agreed, under the pressure of Seattle labor leaders, to permit the Seattle workers to negotiate directly with their employers for a wage increase, as long as any such wage increase did not obligate the Emergency Fleet Corporation in any way.[3] Later, however, he reversed himself and insisted that the workers were "under agree-

---

[3] Robert L. Friedheim, *The Seattle General Strike* (Seattle, Wash., 1964), pp. 64-65. This book is the most recent and the most authoritative history of the strike.

REBELS OF THE WOODS

ment, not with shipyards, but with the Emergency Fleet Corporation not to strike and to accept the award of the Macy Board . . ."[4]

The Seattle Metal Trades Council, representing all the shipyard workers, waited with somewhat impatient patriotism for the war to end, and then, shortly after the Armistice, decided to invoke Piez's original permission to negotiate for a wage increase. The Council began, under the threat of a strike, to negotiate directly with the shipbuilders. Piez thereupon sent an indiscrete telegram to the employers of Seattle, to the Metal Trades Association, urging them to hold firm against any increase in wages on pain of losing their metal allotments from the government. This peremptory telegram to the employers was delivered by mistake to the workers' organization of similar name, the Metal Trades Council.[5] The negotiations, of course, came to an abrupt halt. On January 21, 1919, the shipyard workers went out on strike, much more angry with Piez and the United States government than with their local bosses with whom they had been negotiating.[6]

Up to this point, the conflict in Seattle showed nothing unusual to distinguish it from ordinary labor-management disputes ending in strikes, except perhaps for the *faux pas* of the Piez telegram. But on January 22, in a noisy meeting of the Seattle Central Labor Council, the extension of the strike to a general sympathy strike began, and with the general strike came that confusion of ends and that rhetorical hint of revolution which gave off the scent of the I.W.W. to the nervous bourgeoisie. At the meeting of January 22, the crowds in the galleries sang I.W.W. songs and shouted heckling advice. Even on the floor of the meeting, Seattle labor leaders rose to their feet to propose that Seattle unions "go industrial" and cut loose from the parent A.F.L. The representative from the Metal Trades Council, amid the militant hubbub, got the Central Labor Council to pass a resolution for polling all union members in Seattle on the question of a general sympathy strike. The Metal Trades Council speaker tried to specify his intent very

---

[4] *Ibid.*, p. 67. Requoted from Piez to Hurley correspondence, Feb. 26, 1919; File 18252-1 National Archives, RG 32.

[5] *Ibid.*, p. 70; Anna Louise Strong, *I Change Worlds* (New York, 1935), p. 75.

[6] Seattle *Times*, Jan. 21, 1919, p. 1; Seattle *Post-Intelligencer*, Jan. 22, 1919, p. 1.

carefully. The proposed general strike, he said, should not be considered as a revolutionary act, but only as a just demonstration of labor's power, as a way to insure labor's future in Seattle. His appeal for such a definite, stated objective for the general strike went largely unheeded.[7]

As the sentiment for this amorphous general strike mounted through late January, the conservatives and unorganized workers of Seattle reacted with honest puzzlement. Why were *all of* Seattle's local unions voting so overwhelmingly for the strike? Was a kind of test-tube revolution being planned? Why did not the leaders specify what they hoped to accomplish and what would have to be done by whom to bring the strike to an end?

On January 29, the Central Labor Council met again to discuss the question. With its regular leaders back from a Tom Mooney protest meeting in Chicago, the Council conducted its business in this second meeting in a more orderly manner. James A. Duncan, secretary of the Council, led the self-styled "Progressive" faction of Seattle's union labor. Duncan and his Progressives wrested control of the strike from the hands of the "Radicals." Duncan and his followers approved the idea of the strike but only if they led it.[8] But the Radicals—many of them open or covert Wobblies—succeeded in keeping the objectives of the strike vague. The "General Strike," of course, as a concept, was a central part of anarcho-syndicalist ideology. The Radicals therefore considered it in their interests to urge the general strike without pettifogging limitations on what it might produce. Although the Progressives won the day by grabbing the reins of leadership, the Radicals won their point to the extent that they kept the purpose of the strike ominously vague.

Last-minute efforts at mediation failed. Piez wired his last word on the matter, an unyielding support of the Macy Board award.[9] Efforts at mediation very likely would have failed without the damper by Piez because the first mediator, Henry White, had antagonized the Seattle unionists. He had been during the war the local Commissioner of Immigration responsible for the rounding up of Wobbly aliens. Moreover, he had destroyed his usefulness

---

[7] Seattle *Star*, Jan. 23, 1919, p. 1.

[8] Seattle *Post-Intelligencer*, Jan. 30, 1919, p. 1; Friedheim, *op. cit.*, p. 88.

[9] Seattle *Post-Intelligencer*, Feb. 2, 1919, p. 1.

as a mediator by stating publicly that the shipyard workers' vote to strike had been dishonest.[10] Although he would not give an inch on the issue of the Macy Board award, Piez tried to woo rank-and-file strikers at the last moment by placing advertisements in the local press. The workers, he charged, were being duped by their leaders. They should return to their jobs as patriotic Americans.[11] The advertisements had little effect in Seattle. Perhaps Upton Sinclair expressed a common reaction, a rhetorical hope, based on some obvious suspicions, that Piez had paid for the advertisements himself rather than using public Shipping Board money.[12]

On February 3, the Central Labor Council made its official call for the general strike. The *Union Record* tried to win the support of Seattle small businessmen in an inept appeal by holding out the lure of a much greater payroll in the city if the strikers won, but most middle-class elements in Seattle easily resisted this bread-and-butter appeal. Rather, they watched the strike develop with foreboding.[13] Radical handbills and circulars spread through the shipyards did little to allay their fears. Harvey O'Connor's "Russia Did It," for example, urged the strikers to seize the shipyards as the Bolsheviks in Russia had done.[14] It was Anna Louise Strong, however, who published in the *Union Record* the most famous, and frightening, of the radical exhortations. The breathless and exalted tone, the hint of revolution in the document was cited frequently thereafter to "prove" that the I.W.W. or the Bolsheviks had fomented the strike. She ended her editorial with the ominous coda: "And that is why we say that we are starting on a road that leads—NO ONE KNOWS WHERE!"[15]

A front page editorial in the Seattle *Star*, a paper hitherto neutral or even on occasion sympathetic to labor's cause, expressed early some of the concern of the middle class in Seattle:

This is plain talk to the common-sense union men of Seattle. You are being rushed pell-mell into a general strike. You are

[10] Seattle *Union Record*, Jan. 31, 1919, p. 3; Seattle *Times*, Jan. 30, 1919, p. 1.
[11] Seattle *Star*, Feb. 3, 1919, p. 9; Seattle *Post-Intelligencer*, Feb. 3, 1919, p. 16.
[12] Seattle *Star*, Feb. 4, 1919, p. 16.
[13] Seattle *Union Record*, Feb. 3, 1919, p. 3.
[14] Harvey O'Connor, *Revolution in Seattle: A Memoir* (New York, 1964), p. 143.
[15] Friedheim, *op. cit.*, p. 111.

being urged to use a dangerous weapon—the general strike, which you have never used before—which, in fact, has never been used anywhere in the United States. It isn't too late to avert the tragic results that are sure to come from its use . . . Confined to Seattle or even confined to the whole Pacific coast, the use of force by Bolsheviks would be, and should be, quickly dealt with by the army of the United States. These false Bolsheviks haven't a chance on earth to win anything for you in this country, *because this country is America—not Russia.*[16]

The next day the *Star* became even more outspoken against the strike and adopted in large part the extreme position of the most frightened conservatives in Seattle:

The general strike is at hand. A general SHOWDOWN—a showdown for all of us—a test of Americanism—a test of YOUR Americanism.

As the Star stated yesterday, this is no time to mince words. A part of our community is defying our government, and is, in fact, contemplating changing that government, and not by *American methods.* This small part of our city talks plainly of "taking over things," of "resuming under *our* government." . . . *Under which flag do you stand?*[17]

On February 6 the strike began. Seattle grew very quiet as street cars stopped running, as stores closed, as the streets emptied of people. What economic life continued—such tasks as delivering milk to hospitals or carrying on the minimal public services—was done with the permission of the Strike Committee. The citizens of Seattle, for the most part, stayed in their homes and waited apprehensively. But nothing much happened. The essential work went on under the sufferance of the Strike Committee, and the streets remained silent, ominously silent perhaps, but nonviolent.

On the second day of the strike, February 7, Mayor Ole Hanson issued his first proclamation.[18]

By virtue of the authority vested in me as mayor, I hereby guarantee to all the people of Seattle absolute and complete protection. They should go about their daily work and business

---

[16] Seattle *Star*, Feb. 4, 1919, p. 1. Reprinted also in Friedheim, *op. cit.*, pp. 108-109.

[17] Seattle *Star*, Feb. 5, 1919, p. 1.

[18] Friedheim, *op. cit.*, p. 131.

in perfect security. We have fifteen hundred policemen, fifteen hundred regular soldiers from Camp Lewis, and can and will secure, if necessary, every soldier in the Northwest to protect life, business, and property.

THE TIME HAS COME for every person in Seattle to show his Americanism. Go about your daily duties without fear. We will see to it that you have food, transportation, water, light, gas and all necessities. The anarchists in this community shall not rule its affairs. All persons violating the laws will be dealt with summarily.

Ole Hanson, Mayor

Two days later, Hanson issued another even stronger proclamation to the nation through the local United Press representative in Seattle. Curiously enough, he did not release it to the local press, perhaps because he realized he would not be believed by his own constituents. In this second proclamation, Hanson branded the strike as revolution. He announced that he would not treat with such revolutionaries, and he implicitly took credit, with his announcement of February 7, for having saved America from red anarchy.[19]

In spite of Hanson's blustering advice to Seattle citizens to ignore the strike and to go about their business, the strike continued. Life and liberty were protected more by the Strike Committee than by Mayor Hanson. But strikers began to defect after the second day, not so much in deference to Mayor Hanson's plea but in response to weariness and confusion. As the workers, local by local, began to abandon the strike, the authorities finally struck forcefully at the edges of the strike, not at the Central Labor Council or the A.F.L. unions still loyal to the strike but at the I.W.W. They arrested Walker C. Smith, editor of the *Industrial Worker*, on February 8. On the same day, the Central Labor Council voted thirteen to one in favor of a recommendation to the Strike Committee that it take steps to end the strike. The Strike Committee debated the question inconclusively into early Sunday morning, February 9.[20] On Sunday, Seattle was quiet for more normal reasons, while the strike leaders had a brief respite in the struggle to reflect on their purposes. On Monday, February 10, the Strike

[19] New York *Times*, Feb. 9, 1919, p. 1.
[20] Seattle *Post-Intelligencer*, Feb. 9, 1919, p. 1.

Committee resumed its deliberations and voted to end the strike at noon on Tuesday, the following day.[21]

As workers returned to work, the authorities stepped up their attack upon the I.W.W., now the scapegoat. They raided and closed the Equity Printing Company, the shop that printed the I.W.W.'s propaganda. They arrested under the newly-enacted criminal-syndicalism law thirty-one Wobblies and eight others. James Bruce, the first of the accused, was brought to trial but acquitted on June 5, and the other prisoners were thereupon released.[22]

The general strike, awesome in its brief effectiveness but vague in its purposes, virtually destroyed the labor movement in Seattle. The unions that survived were to be harder, more pragmatic, and were to eschew the dangerous firewater of Socialist or I.W.W. ideology. An organization called the Associated Industries stepped up its campaign for the open shop, for the "American Plan," after the general strike. The I.W.W., emboldened by the acquittal of James Bruce under the first test of the state's new criminal-syndicalism law, briefly doffed its protective coloration of A.F.L. memberships. Wobblies gave up being "two-card" union men, gave up their footholds in many of the local unions in Seattle and began again to organize open "dual" unions. Perhaps they were not even too unhappy over the debacle of unionism in Seattle after the general strike because they hoped to pick up the pieces and put them back together again in I.W.W. unions. But if such were the conscious strategy of the I.W.W., it proved an illusion. No open shop, anti-union counter revolution would destroy the A.F.L. and then placidly deal with the I.W.W. The I.W.W. could never hope to fill the vacuum left by the diminishing A.F.L., because Wobblies as individuals and their organizations were *persona non grata*. By the end of the year the new assault upon the I.W.W. occasioned by the Centralia riot—the "White Terror" as the I.W.W. called it—virtually eliminated the I.W.W. as a force to be reckoned with in Washington. The postwar collapse of Seattle's industrial boom also tended to throw both the A.F.L. and the I.W.W.—indeed, any labor organization—into the discard.[23]

---

[21] *Ibid.*, Feb. 11, 1919, p. 1.
[22] *Industrial Worker*, June 11, 1919, p. 1.
[23] Friedheim, *op. cit.*, pp. 158-162.

In post mortem, the strike leaders, the I.W.W., Mayor Ole Hanson, the press, and the frightened public all agreed that the Seattle general strike had somehow *really* served radical ends. The I.W.W. probably did play a more important role in the strike than the record immediately reveals, and many of the open leaders of the strike admitted to vague, revolutionary motives.[24] The I.W.W. claimed that concealed Wobblies—the "two-card" union men—controlled all of the major Seattle unions.[25] Mayor Hanson insisted that a secret "soviet" or "Workers' Council" of Wobblies in the Metal Trades Council had planned and directed the strike.[26] The conservative press agreed that the strike had been the work of radicals and Wobblies in control of the A.F.L. unions. "Whatever may have been the motives of the rank and file of the strikers, those who engineered the strike did so with the hallucination that the whole country would flame into revolt."[27] Both the I.W.W. and Mayor Hanson, of course, had their own reasons for either emphasizing or exaggerating the role of the I.W.W. in the strike. In order to advertise himself as the greatest possible "Chamber of Commerce hero," Mayor Hanson had to make the strike as threatening and sinister as possible.[28] The I.W.W., for its part, wanted to take credit for a historic and spectacular strike. But discounting the gaudiest exaggerations on both sides, Wobblies apparently played a significant role in the famous Seattle general strike of 1919, and for the first time they chose to hide their talents under a bushel rather than shout them from a corner soap box. Only in retrospect did the I.W.W. claim that the strike had been theirs.

The I.W.W. revealed its greatest caution and loss of militancy in a grandiose educational and research program it initiated after the war. In 1920 and 1921, it embarked upon a program of educating the workers in the technical and managerial problems of industry, of trying to attract engineers and technicians into the organization, of preparing itself "realistically" for the problems it would face

[24] History Committee of the General Strike Committee, *The Seattle General Strike* (Seattle, Wash., n.d.), p. 28.

[25] *New Solidarity*, Mar. 1, 1919, p. 1.

[26] Ole Hanson, "Fighting the Reds in Their Own Home Town," *World's Work* (Jan. 1920), p. 302.

[27] Seattle *Post-Intelligencer*, Feb. 11, 1919, p. 1.

[28] G. R. Leighton, "Seattle, Washington: The Edge of the Last Frontier," *Harper's* (Mar. 1939), p. 432.

after it expropriated the nation's industries. From such an organization as the I.W.W.—that had won renown for its bombast and
soap box oratory, for "direct action" tactics, for provoking curious
violence—the new policy evidenced an obvious change in temper,
a significant change from heedlessness to intellection.

Significantly, Wobblies conceived the new policy while imprisoned in Chicago's Cook County jail awaiting trial under the
Espionage Act. The prisoners whiled away their time by conducting informal "educational meetings" in their cells, giving each
other the benefit of their practical experience. Facetiously they
dubbed these meetings their "Industrial Congress." But they also
talked more seriously of pursuing the idea out of prison, of someday compiling their collective knowledge of American industry
into a workers' "Industrial Encyclopedia."[29] One of the prisoners
did pursue the idea when released from prison. While free on bond
and touring the country speaking for the I.W.W. defense committee, Ralph Chaplin, Wobbly poet and executive board member,
made the acquaintance of Howard Scott, a visionary engineer
living in Greenwich Village and a man later to win fame as the
seer of Technocracy, Inc. During the course of an evening's conversation in Scott's studio, Chaplin heard many shocking but
trenchant criticisms of the I.W.W. Scott convinced him that the
I.W.W. needed a "research bureau" to compile information on
American industry. Chaplin, though impressed, did not leave the
studio without misgivings. He felt uneasy about Scott's obvious
bohemianism and his remoteness from the proletariat. "All the
time he was discoursing so plausibly about tear-drop automobiles,
flying wing airplanes, and technological unemployment, I was
looking at the other side of the studio where an appalling phallic
water color was displayed among blueprints and graphs on a big
easel."[30]

Haywood and Tom Boyle, other executive board members,
showed little enthusiasm for Scott's ideas or for the establishment
of a research bureau in the I.W.W., but Chaplin won them over
to the idea, convincing them that a "high class educational program
would add to the prestige of the I.W.W. while it was under attack

[29] Ralph Chaplin, *Wobbly: the Rough-and-Tumble Story of an American
Radical* (Chicago, 1948), p. 233.
[30] *Ibid.*, p. 296.

from so many quarters."[31] The argument would seem to establish, if only tacitly, a connection between the program and the persecutions of the war. Perhaps also Chaplin had in mind the "prestige" of such a program as a competitive advantage over the vaguely "intellectual" Communists. The delegates to the 1920 convention created a new Bureau of Industrial Research.[32]

In 1920, Scott presented his ideas to the entire membership of the I.W.W. in its press, identifying himself merely as an "industrial engineer." Scott criticized Wobblies' reliance upon sabotage, arguing that in terms of the socialist philosophy it was self-defeating. If the revolution was to come as the result of economic crises in the capitalist system, then the withdrawal of efficiency by workers would only cripple and slow production and delay the crises. Scott also pointed out that it made little sense to sabotage an industry you intended to seize and use. He also criticized the traditional emphasis within the I.W.W. of organizing the transient and unskilled workers. He argued that realistic revolutionaries should even agitate for restriction of immigration and Oriental exclusion, since the more scarce, productive, and skilled the labor force the more rapid and severe would be the economic crises.[33]

During the brief period of Scott's association with the I.W.W.,[34] the Department of Industrial Research published a number of articles on such technical matters as economic waste and management theory.[35] The *One Big Union Monthly*, the I.W.W.'s journal of opinion, became in 1921 the *Industrial Pioneer*, a name more suggestive perhaps of the new technocratic preoccupations of the I.W.W. By 1922, the I.W.W. had terminated Scott's services and had abolished the Department of Industrial Research, but Scott's influence remained with the I.W.W. for years. In a curious pam-

---

[31] *Ibid.*

[32] Gambs, *op. cit.*, p. 158.

[33] *One Big Union Monthly* (Oct. 1920), pp. 6-10.

[34] Scott denies any "association" with the I.W.W., denies ever being the "research director." He admits only to having supplied the I.W.W. with a technical paper. Norman Frank Benson, *The Origin and Impact of an American Radicalism: Technocracy, Inc.*, Unpublished dissertation, Ball State University, Muncie, Indiana, 1965.

[35] "Report on Waste," *Industrial Pioneer* (Feb. 1921), pp. 33-37; "The Wastes of War," *Industrial Pioneer* (Mar. 1921), pp. 31-34; "Wastes in the Coal Industry," *Industrial Pioneer* (July 1921), pp. 53-58; *et al.*

phlet published in 1923 by the Department of Education of the Agricultural Workers' Industrial Union, the I.W.W. still urged an alliance of technicians and proletarians. In the pamphlet, an engineer discusses the I.W.W. preamble with a boyhood friend who is a manual laborer. The two men chew over, almost word for word, the primitive Marxism of the I.W.W. preamble and eventually come to agree that engineers and workers share a revolutionary interest and that greater cooperation from "technician down to the laborers" will be needed to build the new society.[36]

Even the commercial press noted this new shift in I.W.W. propaganda; the new educational and research program of the I.W.W. impressed one reporter as evidence of an unexpected practicality among radicals. "One's conception of the visionary type of mind that directs these radical forces gives way to a conception of decided practicality, as he observes the close attention to the minutiae of industrial organization and operation."[37] Another writer described the new program as a peculiar new "conspiracy." Wobblies had outlined for him a variant of their new "practical" approach to revolution. They intended to hire efficiency experts and engineers to study a selected American industry. With the findings of the experts in their hands, the Wobblies then intended to approach the managers of the plants and say, in effect, "We can increase your production by, say, sixty per cent. How about dividing the increased profits with us?" Wobblies explained that by using this kind of approach in *all* industries they could eventually seize the means of production "not by mere right of ownership but by the right of knowing what to do with them." If these tactics failed to deliver the actual ownership of the means of production into the hands of the workers, it would make no real difference. "Huh! It don't matter who owns these things if we use them. What do I care who owns the cigar if I smoke it?"[38]

Most Wobblies after 1921 lost their delight in such speculations and in the ambitious research and education program, and most Wobblies in all probability remained anchored to the simpler revo-

[36] *What Is the I.W.W.?* (Chicago, 1923).

[37] C. S. Watkins, "Present Status of Socialism in the United States," *Atlantic* (Dec. 1919), p. 825.

[38] C. W. Wood, "I.W.W.'s Plan to Strike," *Collier's* (Sept. 23, 1922), pp. 5-6.

lutionary ideas of the prewar era. One historian of the I.W.W., however, thought that Howard Scott had permanently disillusioned many Wobblies with the simple-minded orthodoxy of the early I.W.W.[39] The brief excursion into scholarship, whatever its lasting effects upon individual Wobblies, did bespeak a seepage of militancy and a desire to further the revolution without risking jail. After all, Wobblies did not go to jail, nor did they get lynched and beaten, for making economic studies, even if the studies were rationalized as steps toward the ultimate revolution.

The *Industrial Worker*, the I.W.W.'s newspaper in the Pacific Northwest,[40] returned periodically to this early infatuation with technocratic ideas. When in the winter of 1932-1933, Technocracy burst onto the scene from the national magazines and the front page of the New York *Times* as a depression phenomenon with which all kinds of prominent Americans toyed hopefully, the I.W.W. again took up the matter of revolution and technology. The *Industrial Worker* covered Howard Scott's speeches sympathetically, under such headlines as: "Howard Scott Strikes Hefty Blows at Price System." The paper also ran a boxed advertisement urging technicians and industrial engineers to acquaint themselves with the I.W.W., as if to remind all the persons jumping on the bandwagon of Technocracy that the half-forgotten I.W.W. had been through it all before and had even helped to fashion the bandwagon.[41] Wobblies of the Pacific Northwest seemed to attach themselves to the technocratic idea more eagerly than the Wobblies of the Chicago headquarters did, perhaps because the Northwestern Wobblies reacted most negatively to the Communists and felt the need for some "ideology" at least as "intellectual" as the Communists' "Marxism-Leninism." Perhaps there is some tortuous and obscure pattern of causation—not really worth the effort to dig for—which would explain why Wobblies of the Pacific Northwest became the most "technocratic" as well as why Technocracy itself made its last organizational stand in the region.[42]

But the Wobblies did not retreat completely into the A.F.L. as "two-card" union men, nor did they devote all their time to safe

---

[39] Gambs, *op. cit.*, p. 162.

[40] From 1909 until 1931, the *Industrial Worker* was published in the Pacific Northwest and may be considered an organ for the I.W.W. of the region.

[41] *Industrial Worker*, Feb. 7, 1933, p. 1.

[42] Norman Frank Benson, *op. cit.* (above, note 34).

armchair-theorizing about the role of engineers in the class struggle. As the most severe repressions of the war eased, as even the fury accompanying the Centralia trial subsided, the I.W.W. did try to resume its open organizing of workers and did try to conduct strikes as of old. In 1922, for example, its Marine Transport Workers Industrial Union became entangled in a complicated struggle on the docks of Portland, Oregon, a struggle involving both the employers and the International Longshoremen's Association of the A.F.L.

Before May 1, 1922, Portland shipowners had worked more or less amicably with the I.L.A. and its union hiring hall. But in April 1922, the shipowners, lining up in the nationwide struggle for the open shop, or the "American Plan," announced that on May 1 they would establish their own nonunion hiring hall, the "fink hall" as both the I.W.W. and the A.F.L. came to call it. The I.L.A. called a strike in protest. The employers hired strikebreakers and kept them in a special "hotel" ship towed into the harbor, the J. T. Potter.[43] The I.L.A. agreed late in April to end its strike and to go back to work on United States Shipping Board ships. At this partial capitulation, the independent longshoremen and the I.W.W.'s Marine Transport Workers charged that the I.L.A. had pusilanimously ended the strike—or half of it—and had agreed to scab on itself. Since that was the case, the I.W.W. would go back to work on all ships and ignore the I.L.A. pickets. In fact, on June 6 fifty Wobblies did go back to work through the picket line, escorted by Portland policemen.[44] According to the I.W.W., the I.L.A. was saved from its own stupidity by the even greater stupidity of the shipowners—and, one might add, the Wobblies themselves were saved from the shameful appearance of being strikebreakers protected by the Portland police, when the employers stubbornly decided to boycott the Shipping Board ships worked by I.L.A. crews. At this impasse, with all the parties hurling accusations at each other around a triangle, the moderates worked out a compromise. An I.L.A. man would be permitted to work in the "fink hall" to see that half of all men hired were I.L.A. members. On the ships, the strikebreakers and the I.L.A. workers would work in separated crews at separate hatches.[45]

---

[43] *Industrial Solidarity*, Jan. 6, 1923, pp. 5-6.
[44] Portland *Oregon Labor Press*, June 9, 1922, p. 1.
[45] *Ibid.*, June 22, 1922, p. 1.

The compromise outraged many militant I.L.A. members as well as the Wobblies. The Wobblies' Marine Transport Workers local grew rapidly to two hundred and seventy-five members, and some I.L.A. workers and the I.W.W. began to plan a jointly sponsored strike. By a close vote, however, the I.L.A. rejected the proposal to strike in partnership with the I.W.W.[46] The employers, with the tacit support now of the moderate I.L.A. majority, announced a policy of hiring no "known" Wobblies. It seemed a clever way to control and discipline Wobblies and militant I.L.A. members. The I.L.A. representative in the "fink hall"—a gun-toting former secretary of the Portland local—could insure quiet Wobblies and I.L.A. radicals, because if they complained they immediately became "known" and thus unemployable.[47]

But the control broke down. In October, the I.L.A. radicals and the I.W.W. went out together on strike. It was almost like old times for the Wobblies. On October 18, the police arrested three hundred and fifty Wobblies, the whole membership of the Marine Transport Workers local. The press trumpeted like a nervous elephant that twenty-five thousand angry Wobblies were bound for Portland to "teach the town a lesson." The mayor got an appropiration of $10,000 from the council to hire seventy-four special officers.[48] On October 19, sixty-five more Wobblies were arrested, many of them aliens, the press announced darkly. Even the native-born prisoners, it said, "possess names with a decided foreign tinge."[49]

The Wobblies hung improvised red flags from their cell windows, sang songs to crowds of sympathizers crowded outside. The A.F.L. somewhat reluctantly came to the defense of the I.W.W., pointing out correctly enough that Wobblies had done nothing to deserve their imprisonment. In the previous strike of the summer, Wobblies had, of course, acted as strikebreakers and tools of the shipowners, but now they were being used by shipowners in a different way to discredit and destroy the whole labor movement.[50] The K.K.K., a new party to an I.W.W. conflict, offered its services

---

46 *Ibid.,* Oct. 2, 1922, p. 1; *Industrial Solidarity,* Jan. 6, 1923, pp. 5-6.
47 *Industrial Solidarity,* Jan. 6, 1923, pp. 5-6.
48 Portland *Oregonian,* Oct. 19, 1922, pp. 1, 14.
49 *Ibid.,* Oct. 20, 1922, p. 1.
50 *Ibid.*

to the mayor.[51] Among supporters of labor, if not of the I.W.W., the suspicion grew that the mass arrests and the "emergency" had been carefully staged as a tactic in the 1922 election, the campaign that was to see the K.K.K. win control of the Oregon legislature.[52]

Wobblies kept at their strike doggedly, pleading regularly for financial aid in the I.W.W. press, but their strike was doomed to slow failure. The picket lines grew progressively thinner, the membership in the Marine Transport Workers local dwindled, and eventually the strike ended without many noticing it. The waning dock strike faded into the ambitious 1923 "general strike." Perhaps the only achievement of the strike was literary, a new Wobbly song by "Dublin Dan" Liston, entitled "The Portland Revolution":

> The Revolution started, so the judge informed the Mayor,
> Now Baker paces back and forth, and raves and pulls his hair,
> The waterfront is tied up tight, the Portland newsboy howls,
> And not a thing is moving, only Mayor Baker's bowels.
>   . . .
> They were ushered to the court room, bright and early
>   Tuesday morn,
> Then slowly entered "Justice," on his face a look of scorn,
> Some "Cat" who had the rigging, suggested to his pard,
> "Here's a chance to line up 'Baldy,' " so they wrote him out a card.
>
> When he spied the little ducat, his face went white with hate,
> And he said, "I'll tell you once for all, this court won't tolerate
> You Wobblies coming in here," and he clenched his puny fists,
> " 'Cause Mayor Baker has informed me that an emergency exists."
>
> The One Ten Cat then wagged his tail, and smiled up at the "law,"
> He said, "I am a harvest hand, or better known as 'Straw,'
> I'm interested in this wheat, in fact I'm keeping tabs,
> I'm here to see, twixt you and me, t'aint loaded by no scabs."
>
> The One Ten Cats were jubilant, and fur flew from their tails,
> "His Honor" rapped for order, and the next man called was "Rails."
> "I belong to old 'Five Twenty,' I'm a switchman in these yards,
> And I'm here to state, we'll switch no freight,
> 'Cause we've all got red cards.
>
> We're here to win this longshore strike, in spite of all your law,
> That's all I've got to say, except we're solid behind 'Straw.' "
>   . . .
> "Now I can't send you men to jail, I can't find one excuse,

---

[51] *Ibid.*, Oct. 21, 1922, p. 16.
[52] *Federated Press Bulletin,* Nov. 4, 1922, p. 9.

REBELS OF THE WOODS

> I'll wash my hands of this damn'd mess," and turned the whole
> bunch loose,
> Then "dirt" and "sticks" walked arm in arm, with "flirts" and
> "skirts" and "rails,"
> While the One Ten Cats brought up the rear, fur flying from
> their tails.[53]

Of course, Wobblies responded variously to persecution and the changing social scene, by softening their tactics and rhetoric, by tinkering with their "ideology," by pressing ahead as best they could in alliance or out of alliance with the A.F.L. But they also "regressed," as a psychoanalyst would say. They began to cope with their frustrations by reverting inappropriately to tactics that had once, under different circumstances, served them well. During the latter part of 1922 and the first four months of 1923, the I.W.W. made elaborate plans to call a truly great strike, larger in scope even than the 1917 lumber strike. Delegates to the 1922 convention first discused the need for a "general strike,"[54] and Wobblies all over the country soon took up the hue and cry. The I.W.W. press featured articles on the proposed strike, this time to be truly a general strike and to dwarf all previous I.W.W. strikes. In March 1923, the *Industrial Worker* published an article by a veteran of the 1917 strike, an article giving the most detailed advice on tactics and methods based on the experience of 1917. The writer, in fact, displayed so much reverence for the strike of 1917 that the proposed strike of 1923 seemed less like a plan to redress present grievances than an effort to recapture past glory in some kind of ritual repetition.[55] The I.W.W. could not see that 1923 was not 1917 and that conditions that had made the strike of 1917 a fleeting success had altered by 1923. The strike of 1923 was primarily a revivalistic venture, but the I.W.W., finding some of the bad conditions of 1917 still to protest, added economic demands to the principal demand for the release of wartime political prisoners. "The blanket roll shall go! Rooms and cottages shall be built instead of bunk houses crowded with double-decked bed-bug hatcheries."[56] Where working conditions and wages had already improved to meet the

---

[53] Joyce Kornbluh, Editor, *Rebel Voices* (Ann Arbor, Mich., 1964), pp. 32-34.
[54] *Federated Press Bulletin*, Nov. 18, 1922, p. 1.
[55] *Industrial Worker*, Mar. 10, 1923, p. 1.
[56] *Lumber Workers' Bulletin*, Feb. 15, 1923, p. 1.

most minimal standards, Wobblies merely made their demands more extensive. In one Oregon logging camp, where the "bindle" or blanket roll had long since disappeared, the Wobblies demanded that the sheets be changed three times a week. The management exploded in wrath, charging that the outrageous demand came from Wobblies who lived in Portland flop houses where the linen was not changed "once a month."[57] Ole Hendricks, the defendant in the 1923 criminal-syndicalism case in Oregon, had been carrying a printed circular of I.W.W. demands at the time he was arrested. The circular listed amnesty for political prisoners as the first demand, but also listed demands for the end of piece-work or "gyppo" systems, for the eight-hour day to include time required to get to and from the job, for clean sheets, for time and a half for Sunday work, for closer observance of safety rules, and for the end of companies' censorship of workers' mail.[58]

The 1923 strike failed to achieve its grandiose purposes and nowhere in the nation or the region approached the effectiveness of the 1917 strike. But Wobblies religiously applied the old tactics. The I.W.W. had to admit a few weeks after the beginning of the strike that the "strike off the job" had been more "noisy" than effective but advised Wobblies that the "strike on the job"—just as in 1917—would be the real test.[59] As for the "noisy" strike off the job, in Coos Bay, Oregon, only a few hundred workers out of forty-five hundred left their jobs, and elsewhere in Oregon the strike failed as completely.[60] In Washington, the Wobblies put on a somewhat better show; an estimated twenty to fifty per cent of all loggers in the Inland Empire left their jobs for at least a few days, but many of these workers stayed home only to avoid possible trouble.[61] For several days, sixty-five per cent of the lumber workers between Chehalis and British Columbia stayed away from their jobs.[62] The Marine Transport Workers' Industrial Union, the Wobblies' sailors' and longshoremen's union, joined the "general strike" without greatly extending its scope or effectiveness. Wobbly longshoremen in San Pedro, California, stirred up some excite-

---

[57] Portland *Oregonian,* Apr. 23, 1923, p. 1.
[58] *Ibid.,* Mar. 6, 1923, p. 1.
[59] *Lumber Workers' Bulletin,* June 1, 1923, p. 2.
[60] Portland *Oregonian,* Apr. 19, 1923, p. 5.
[61] *Ibid.,* Apr. 26, 1923, p. 1.
[62] *Ibid.,* p. 4.

ment, but in the Pacific Northwest they scarcely added a ripple to the strike. In Portland, a few lonely pickets, veterans of the longshoremen's strike of the previous fall, distributed handbills and circulars but persuaded few workers to leave their jobs.[63]

Although their great general strike failed, Wobblies tried hard to convince themselves that it had succeeded spectacularly. "Old timers of the 1917 days were surprised. The strike committee was surprised," one Wobbly publicist wrote, perhaps unwittingly giving away that few Wobblies had really expected much of the strike from the beginning.[64] Other Wobbly journalists claimed sweeping success, all the while comparing the strike to the strike of 1917.[65] Wobblies mesmerized themselves into viewing the strike as a success because they had repeated, however inappropriately, the same tactics and rhetoric of the strike of 1917 that had established the eight-hour day, abolished the worst conditions in logging camps, and made their name feared in almost very middle-class household.

Only once during the 1923 strike did the I.W.W. show any signs of its former *élan*, its former improvising spirit. In the Grays Harbor region of Washington, early in the strike, Wobblies published and distributed an unusual circular. "Notice to all bootleggers and gambling houses: You are hereby given notice to close up during the strike or drastic action will be taken against you."[66] The I.W.W. distributed similar handbills in Seattle, Portland, and Spokane the following day. I.W.W. "dehorn squads" volunteered their services to the Seattle mayor to help the city close speakeasies. Then, without waiting for sluggish police cooperation, the I.W.W. temperance fighters and law enforcers closed most of the illegal saloons in lower Seattle.[67] In Portland, the Wobbly defenders of the Eighteenth Amendment and the Volstead Act embarrassed public officials and provoked unusual street riots. A thousand Wobblies and laughing sympathizers staged a demonstration in front of one speakeasy that the reporters chose to call, according to standard practice of the era, a "soft-drink establishment." Police

[63] *Ibid.,* Apr. 27, 1923, p. 4.

[64] Vern Smith, "Smashing the Chains of Slavery," *Industrial Pioneer* (June 1923), p. 6.

[65] John Griffiths, "The General Strike," *Industrial Pioneer* (Sept. 1923), p. 26; *Lumber Workers' Bulletin*, Apr. 15, 1923, p. 1.

[66] Portland *Oregonian*, Apr. 26, 1923, p. 4.

[67] *Nation* (Oct. 3, 1923), p. 338.

broke up the demonstration and arrested two Wobblies, both women. Scores of demonstrators then crowded around the patrol wagons crying to be arrested also as the police tried to push them away. The festive crowd even followed the patrol wagons to the police station and continued its agitation outside the building, refusing to disperse when ordered to. The following day, the police and city officials realized that the I.W.W. had made them the butt of a joke, and the mayor, in injured tones, suggested that Wobblies could present complaints and evidence in an "orderly, American fashion" if they wished to help the officials enforce the law. The chief of police left town for a few days to escape the reporters.[68] Citizens of Portland began to fashion jokes about the episode, the incongruous spectacle of the I.W.W. as a defender of the law. In sentencing a number of defendants on bootlegging offenses, a Federal judge in Portland wryly interjected an *obiter dictum* that commended the I.W.W. as a more efficient upholder of the prohibition amendment than the local officials.[69] Wobblies explained their temperance policy as a practical measure to keep strikers sober and out of mischief. Booze was a weapon of the master class.[70] But everyone recognized the tactic as a novel, typically I.W.W. way of making trouble. The *Nation* commented appreciatively: "The wicked, law-less I.W.W. asked to help enforce the law which crooked or incompetent officials fail to respect! Was there anything more comic?"[71]

In this one tactic, of not much significance to the strike, the I.W.W. revealed some of its former spark, the spark that had once kindled free speech fights and all the rowdy and irreverent songs and folklore of the prewar era. But even this comic improvisation revealed the changed temper of the I.W.W. The essence of the humor lay in provoking disorder by defending the law against the constituted law-enforcers, a surprising tactic but at the same time peculiarly "safe" and of little relevance to the "class struggle."

But the authorities apparently took the I.W.W.'s claims for its proposed strike at face value and prepared for an impending revolution. The prosecution's case against Ole Hendricks under the

---

[68] Portland *Oregonian*, Apr. 30, 1923, pp. 1, 6.
[69] *Ibid.*, June 5, 1923, p. 13.
[70] *Industrial Solidarity*, Sept. 15, 1923, p. 2.
[71] "The I.W.W. Close the Saloons," *Nation* (May 23, 1923), p. 588.

criminal-syndicalism law revealed, for example, the real anxiety of governmental authorities. The press, of course, saw Lenin and Trotsky as the instigators of the strike and the Wobblies as puppets of the Comintern.[72] An Oregon official proposed the establishment of machine-gun units all over the state to cope with I.W.W. revolutionary violence.[73] The governor of Oregon sent Adjutant-General George A. White and Captain Thomas E. Rilea into the logging camps as spies to gather intelligence on the extent of the revolutionary ferment.[74] Somehow the Wobblies got their hands on a photograph of the two secret agents, staring into the camera and looking vaguely uncomfortable and theatrical in their brogans and overalls. The photograph was published in the I.W.W. press under the uncomplimentary headline: "Disguised As Men." Underneath the photograph the Wobbly headline writer put the revolutionary lesson: "Keep Them In Overalls!"[75] But, of course, the strike of 1923 fell far short of any such revolutionary overturn of the master class. White and Rilea returned to their bourgeois lives intact.

One historian of the I.W.W. considered the inroads of the new Communist Party a major cause of its decline.[76] The Communists did indeed have glamour and the smell of success from their identification with the Bolshevik revolution in Russia, a glamour that the I.W.W. could hardly match. The Communist Party attracted new and old revolutionaries more readily after 1919 than did the I.W.W. The American Communist Party probably accounted for as many lost members as did the persecutions of the war. William D. Haywood, the most famous Wobbly in the country, deserted to the Communists, skipping bond and fleeing to Russia in 1921 while I.W.W. defense attorneys were appealing to the United States Supreme Court his 1918 conviction under the Espionage Act. Eight other prominent Wobblies fled to Russia with him, not only draining the I.W.W. of valuable leadership but also burdening it with $80,000 of forfeited bonds. Communists had assured Haywood that the Soviet government would reimburse the I.W.W. for his forfeited bond out of money from captured Rom-

---

[72] Portland *Oregonian*, Apr. 27, 1923, p. 6.
[73] *Ibid.*
[74] Portland *Oregonian*, Apr. 28, 1923, p. 7.
[75] *Industrial Solidarity*, Jan. 19, 1924, p. 1.
[76] Gambs, *op. cit.*, pp. 89-90.

anov jewels. But the I.W.W. never saw the money and had to repay it from its own slender defense funds.[77] Many other less prominent Wobblies also emigrated to the new socialist state, some of them settling in the short-lived Kuzbas cooperative; others like Bill Shatov, the Soviet railroad builder, rising to positions of subaltern importance in the regime. When the I.W.W. decided not to affiliate with the Communist Third International, many Wobblies who up to that time had been both Wobblies and Communists chose to become Communists only rather than Wobblies.

In coping with this problem of Communist competition and rivalry, the I.W.W. displayed a noticeable inability to adapt, a hardening of the arteries that the wartime troubles had certainly helped to produce. The I.W.W. reacted to the Communists by simply purifying and dogmatizing its own traditional anarcho-syndicalism, by sanctifying its opposition to all politics when it was obvious that most radicals surviving into the anti-radical 1920s chose communism rather than the I.W.W. because of communism's apparent political success in Russia. The I.W.W., even in opposition to communism, might have competed more successfully had it been willing to adapt more creatively to the changing temper of American radicalism, had it "gone into politics" in some ideological sense, at least.

Before the American Communist Party—under the label of the Workers' Party of the 1920s—appeared as a positive threat to many Wobblies, most of them reacted to the Bolshevik revolution with great enthusiasm. In 1918, the I.W.W. press published eulogistic reports on the progress of the revolution, reprinting a *Pravda* article of Lenin's entitled "The Main Problem of the Times,"[78] and viewing the November revolution as the "Herald of a New Era."[79] Wobblies did not equivocate in choosing sides between the Bolsheviks and the ousted provisional government of Alexander Kerensky. They called Kerensky a "hysterically screaming petit bourgeois masquerading as a social revolutionary."[80] Harrison George, a member of the I.W.W.'s general executive board, wrote an enthusiastic pamphlet on the revolution, *The Red Dawn*, that the

---

[77] Benjamin Gitlow, *I Confess* (New York, 1939), pp. 468-469.
[78] *Defense Bulletin of the Seattle District,* Oct. 7, 1918, pp. 2-3.
[79] *Industrial Worker,* Feb. 16, 1919, p. 4.
[80] *Defense Bulletin of the Seattle District,* Sept. 30, 1918, p. 1.

I.W.W. circulated approvingly with its other propaganda until 1920.[81]

In 1919, during this initial glow of approval, the I.W.W. general executive board voted to establish connections with the new Communist Third International, the Comintern. The board selected a special "Committee of Foreign Relations" to represent the I.W.W. in Comintern affairs and to correspond with the Comintern.[82] In its intial proclamation from Moscow, the new Comintern had specifically invited the American I.W.W. to join. In the call for the new international of January 1919, the Bolsheviks proposed that the I.W.W. take a constituent part along with the Spartacus League of Germany and other parties and factions of the international Left that had not besmirched themselves with chauvinism during the first world war.[83] But with an invitation in hand, with a clear decision to make—to join or not to join—Wobblies began to lose their initial enthusiasm. They procrastinated. In 1920, Zinoviev, the chairman of the Comintern, sent the American I.W.W. a lengthy "personal" invitation to join:[84]

The Executive Committee of the Communist International in session at Moscow, the heart of the Russian Revolution, greets the revolutionary American proletariat in the ranks of the Industrial Workers of the World . . .

History does not ask whether we like it or not, whether the workers are ready or not. Here is the opportunity. Take it—and the world will belong to the workers; leave it—there may not be another for generations.

Now is no time to talk of "building the new society within the shell of the old." The old society is cracking its shell. The workers must establish the Dictatorship of the Proletariat, which alone can build the new society.

---

[81] Gambs, op. cit., p. 76; Harrison George, Red Dawn (Chicago, 1918).

[82] Gambs, op. cit., p. 77.

[83] Bolshevik Movement in Russia, Senate Document No. 172, 66th Cong., 2nd sess. (Washington, 1920), p. 24.

[84] One Big Union Monthly (Sept., 1920), pp. 27-30. Also in: Revolutionary Radicalism; Its History, Purposes and Tactics, Pt. 1; Vol. II, Report of the Joint Legislative Committee Investigating Seditious Activities (Albany, 1920), 1933-1946. This latter collection is sometimes referred to simply as the "Lusk Committee Report."

An article in the ONE BIG UNION MONTHLY, your official organ, asks, "Why should we follow the Bolsheviks?" According to the writer, all the Bolshevik Revolution in Russia has done is "to give the Russian people the vote."

This is, of course, untrue. The Bolshevik Revolution has taken the factories, mills, mines, land and financial institutions out of the hands of the capitalists and transferred them to the WHOLE WORKING CLASS . . .

And you, fellow-workers of the I.W.W., with your bitter memories of Everett, of Tulsa, of Wheatland, of Centralia, in which your comrades were butchered; with—your thousands in prison—you who nevertheless must do the "dirty work" in the harvest fields, on the docks, in the forests—you must see plainly the process by which the capitalists, by means—of their weapon, the State, are trying to inaugurate the Slave Society . . .

In order to destroy Capitalism, the workers must first wrest the State power out of the hands of the capitalist class. They must not only SEIZE this power, but ABOLISH THE OLD CAPITALIST APPARATUS ENTIRELY . . .

And in place of the capitalist State the workers must build their own WORKERS' STATE, the Dictatorship of the Proletariat.

Many members of the I.W.W. do not agree with this. They are against the "State in general." . . .

The Communists are also opposed to the "State." They also wish to abolish it—to substitute for the government of men the administration of things.

But unfortunately this cannot be done immediately. The destruction of the capitalist State does not mean that capitalism automatically and immediately disappears . . .

The aim of the I.W.W. is "to build the new society within the shell of the old." This means, to organize the workers so thoroughly that at a given time the capitalist system will be burst asunder, and the Industrial Commonwealth, fully developed, shall take its place.

Such an act requires the organization, the discipline, of the great majority of the workers. Before the war there was reason to believe that this might be feasible—although in the fourteen years of its history the I.W.W. had been able to organize comparatively only a small fraction of the American workers.

But at the present time such a plan is utopian. Capitalism is breaking down, and the Social Revolution is upon us and HISTORY WILL NOT WAIT UNTIL THE MAJORITY OF THE WORKERS ARE ORGANIZED 100 PER CENT ACCORDING TO THE PLAN OF THE I.W.W., OR ANY OTHER ORGANIZATION . . .

In the face of the Social Revolution, what is the immediate important work of the Industrial Workers of the World? . . .

The Communist International holds out to the I.W.W. the hand of brotherhood.

January, 1920

President of the Central Executive Committee,

G. Zinoviev.

The burden of Zinoviev's letter, rendered in a slightly lecturing tone, was the error of the I.W.W.'s anti-political bias. But he did the I.W.W. the signal honor of addressing a special several-thousand-word plea to it. The I.W.W. press threw its columns open to a general debate on the question of affiliation with the Comintern. The advocates of affiliation argued that the Comintern did not expect Wobblies to "go into politics" but only wanted the I.W.W. to bring its doctrines up to date. The I.W.W. should realize, they argued in echo of Zinoviev's letter, that the building of the new society solely through economic action required the creation of a too perfect majority organization of workers paralleling capitalist organization. The Bolsheviks had shown that revolutions were not made that way, but rather by militant minorities capturing state power.[85]

Opponents of affiliation argued with anger or moderation but always from the same tacit assumptions. These assumptions, never expressed explicitly nor perhaps even recognized clearly by the debaters, rested as much on sentiment as on logic. The I.W.W. was an older and more experienced radical group on the American

---

[85] *Solidarity,* Oct. 9, 1920, p. 3.

scene; it had forged its program in the heat of actual battle in the American environment; it had suffered pain and martyrdom for its beliefs; to capitulate to the old "political" brand of radicalism would be vaguely contemptible or treasonable. "We view the Russian Revolution with the greatest interest and sympathy," one Wobbly prefaced his remarks, but Wobblies, he continued, should not try to duplicate Bolshevik tactics in America. Wobblies were not insurrectionists; they were evolutionists in the deepest meaning of the term.[86] Another opponent of affiliation resented the Communists' criticisms of the I.W.W. What had Zinoviev meant when he cited I.W.W.'s errors? Did he think "soviets" could manage the industrial society of the United States? If the I.W.W. had erred in its diagnoses or programs, Zinoviev should be more explicit in telling how and where.[87] The Wobblies of the Pacific Northwest, always the region of greatest anarchical sentiment in the I.W.W., rejected affiliation early, refusing "to permit the I.W.W. to become the tail of the kite of any political organization . . ."[88] Indeed, while the debate raged in 1920 within the organization, the *Industrial Worker* kept its silence. The editor explained that the Western Wobbly had little to do with the debate. His mind was made up, and he had rejected the Communist "politicos."[89]

The general executive board finally took a referendum of the membership on the issue of affiliation. It was a complicated referendum, asking the members whether they wished the I.W.W. to join the Comintern outright, whether they wished the I.W.W. to join some other new body such as a "Economic Industrial International," whether they wished the I.W.W. to join with reservations.[90] The general executive board voted first and voted not to join the Comintern outright, but voted affirmatively on the other two motions. The membership, in a small vote, accepted only the third proposition, to join "with reservations."[91]

---

[86] Abner Woodruff, "A Letter to the Professors," *One Big Union Monthly* (Aug. 1919), p. 26.

[87] E. W. Latchem, "Where Do We Belong?" *One Big Union Monthly* (Oct. 1920), p. 30.

[88] *Industrial Worker*, Sept. 11, 1920, p. 2.

[89] *Ibid.*, p. 3.

[90] *Solidarity*, Aug. 28, 1920, p. 2.

[91] *Ibid.*, Dec. 18, 1920, p. 4.

Recognizing the depths of the I.W.W.'s feelings against political involvement, the Comintern next tried to interest it in a new international organization of radical labor unions, the Red International of Labor Unions, or the Profintern. The I.W.W. sent George Williams, a member of the general executive board, to the first congress of the organization in July 1921. Williams returned to the United States and published his first reports on the congress in December 1921, several weeks after the general executive board, without waiting for his advice, had already decided not to join.[92] Their invitations spurned, the Communists grew cooler toward the I.W.W. and eventually, during the ferocious Third Period of Comintern policy, the Communists lumped it with other socialist and noncommunist radical groups as "social fascists."[93] Some independent radicals, without accepting the Communist's orthodox interpretation of the I.W.W. as "objectively" reactionary, noted its increasingly crotchety behavior. One such observer, Max Eastman, attributed the I.W.W.'s troubles to senility rather than the wounds of war. "We have been a little saddened of late years to see the rigidity and lethargy of age creeping over the I.W.W. It seems as though all organizations that do not achieve within ten or fifteen years the purpose for which they were formed begin to be more interested in themselves than they are in their purpose."[94] The I.W.W., for its part, grew increasingly hostile toward the Communists in the following years, and it cherished the purity of its pre-Communist radicalism all the more closely as the radicalism receded in influence and relevancy.

The wartime ordeal of the I.W.W. and its rivalry with Communism revived an old, partially-submerged trait of Wobblies, their liking for contention and factionalism, a trait that had, of course, marked the early history of the organization. Even after the refining schisms of 1906 and 1908, factionalism did not end. In 1913, a new schism threatened when Western delegates to the national convention moved to abolish the general executive board and give the constituent industrial unions complete autonomy. Even the "bummery" of 1908, that had found De Leon's politics

[92] Gambs, *op. cit.*, pp. 83-84.
[93] *Ibid.*, pp. 96-97.
[94] Max Eastman, "Bill Haywood, Communist," *Liberator* (Apr. 1921), pp. 13-14.

too rich, thought this decentralizing proposal too extreme and managed to defeat it on the floor of the convention. But the Western decentralizers had warned the convention that their proposal had not been finally defeated.[95] During the time of troubles between 1917 and 1920, Wobblies called a truce on internal squabbling, but the final effect of the persecution during the war was not to end such internal disputes but rather to direct the I.W.W. into such safe but sterile conflicts over principle and doctrine, both among themselves and in arguments with Communists. The decentralist dispute of 1913 revived in this postwar atmosphere of Talmudic hairsplitting, and in 1924 it divided the I.W.W. again into two groups.

The charges and counter-charges, the elaborated differences of opinion that arose out of the 1924 schism, make little sense unless related to the impotence of the I.W.W. The heat of the dispute came not from momentous intellectual differences but from the bitterness of defeat, from those urgent compensatory feelings of being "right" if no longer important. As late as 1953 an aging Wobbly expressed with clarity the state of mind that began to characterize the I.W.W. during the 1920s. "But what our union lacks in numbers is amply compensated for in purity of thought."[96]

The quarrel came out into the open in 1924. In the summer, five members of the general executive board asked for a special meeting of the full board to discuss the mounting conflicts within the I.W.W. The majority of the board members, probably suspecting disruptionist motives in the proposed "discussions," refused to call the special meeting. The five petitioners thereupon called the meeting on their own authority. When their rump session of the board convened, the other members, led by Tom Boyle, ejected it from the headquarters, using armed "goons." The five outraged board members immediately rented a headquarters in Chicago and set themselves up as the "real" I.W.W. The regular executive board—called by the ousted dissenters "the Communist liquidators and their union-wrecking allies"—continued to occupy the old headquarters.[97]

---

[95] Stenographic Report of the Minutes of the Eighth Annual Convention of the I.W.W., 1913 (Cleveland, Ohio, 1913), pp. 82, 163.

[96] *Industrial Worker*, Feb. 27, 1953, p. 4.

[97] *Industrial Unionist*, May 23, 1925, p. 3.

Other Wobblies on the sidelines, witnessing this unseemly fracas within the executive board, hastily called a special emergency convention. The delegates arrived in Chicago from I.W.W. branches all over the country and found two other "conventions" representing the two antagonistic factions of the board already in session. The delegates to the convention representing the regular executive board, however, voted to join the national convention called by the membership. But the five ousted members of the board, led by James Rowan of the Lumber Workers' Industrial Union No. 500, remained aloof and held their own little convention in splendid contempt for the joint convention. The joint convention polled all I.W.W. branches to test its authority and then suspended Rowan and his followers, together with the few locals of four industrial unions supporting them. This expelled faction prepared an "Emergency Program" for submission to all I.W.W. branches and continued to call itself the "real" I.W.W.[98]

In 1925, Rowan began to published a weekly newspaper, the *Industrial Unionist,* in Portland, Oregon. In it, Rowan belabored the majority of the I.W.W., ran an interminable serial history of his own reforming faction, and tried to persuade all Wobblies to join his "Emergency Program" to save the I.W.W. In less than a year's time, however, Rowan had to suspend publication of the paper because the membership in his faction had all but disappeared. In 1930, he could claim only two hundred supporters.[99] But even without an official newspaper, the "E. P.," as Rowan's faction came to be called, persisted with inflexible self-righteousness. The I.W.W. made several attempts to lure it back into the fold, and in 1930 the E. P. unbent sufficiently to send a delegation to a futile unity conference. In 1933, the E. P. finally died, with Rowan very likely its only member at the end.[100]

These bitter arguments of 1924 revealed unmistakably the kind of vicarious militancy that many Wobblies began to experience in mere talk. Rowan's purists pulled all the stops, charging the execu-

---

[98] *Ibid.,* May 11, 1925, p. 2; *American Labor Yearbook, 1925* (New York, 1925), p. 105; "Official Statement from Sixteenth Constitutional Convention of the Industrial Workers of the World," *Industrial Solidarity,* Oct. 22, 1924, p. 4.

[99] Gambs, *op. cit.,* p. 123.

[100] *Ibid.,* p. 125; letter to the author from W. H. Westerman, Secretary-Treasurer of the I.W.W., May 23, 1952.

tive board with fostering political machines, with temporizing with Communism, with cynically betraying I.W.W. principle, with harboring careerists—or "pie card artists" in Wobbly slang.[101] The leaders of the I.W.W. majority in turn charged Rowan and his followers with disruption, anarchism, braggadocio, personal spite.[102] The whole intense argument, against the background of I.W.W. weakness and inaction, sounded like sound and fury, a pathetic substitute for action.

When the Western migratory workers captured the I.W.W. after the expulsion of Daniel De Leon in 1908, they molded the peculiar culture of the organization and at the same time saddled it with some of its unique problems. The I.W.W., for example, could never decide whether to be a labor union or some kind of militant, class-conscious elite leading the working class to revolution. Most Wobblies probably never recognized a practical conflict in these two aims, but considered industrial unionism *and* revolution almost identical. Let us organize the whole working class into "one big union," Wobblies said, and the natural conflict of the classes, the social war between the workers and the parasites, would insure the revolution. The "one big union" would be organizing itself as the new society "within the shell of the old." Only once in the Pacific Northwest, during the first several weeks of the lumber strike of 1917, did the revolutionary I.W.W. become also an operating labor union, and this success, cited thereafter by Wobblies as proof of their program, proved really fleeting and accidental. The very effectiveness of the strike, coming as it did while the United States girded for war, stimulated the nationwide assault upon the I.W.W., the bludgeoning from which the I.W.W. never recovered.

More subtly the war created—or revealed—a highly organized and inter-dependent society mobilizing its complex industries for a vast collective effort. Even without the violent suppression, the I.W.W. would have stood "unmasked" in the face of this monstrous reality as romantic and childish, as a body of "infantile leftists," to use a phrase of Lenin's. The I.W.W. needed for its

---

[101] *Industrial Unionist,* Apr. 11, 1925, p. 2; May 9, 1925, p. 3; June 6, 1925, p. 3.

[102] John I. Turner, "Why the I.W.W. Will Not Die," *Industrial Pioneer* (Apr. 1926), pp. 5-9.

setting the "frontier," the myth of Jeffersonian yeomen and Jack-
sonian small enterpreneurs against which to perform. The first
world war, alas, made much of that old Americanism obsolete, for
Wobbly as well as anti-Wobbly.

But even in its lusty youth, the I.W.W. had never succeeded in
building stable unions among settled industrial workers—the "home
guards" of its slang. Though it preached industrial unionism and
organized itself as a federation of industrial unions, the I.W.W.
could never sacrifice its revolutionary principles to the mundane
and compromising policies necessary to build durable unions. As
a consequence, it attracted mostly those transient workers with
chronic grievances against society but without any particular
stake in job or community. At the height of its career, the I.W.W.
could draw members from a considerable body of such persons in
the population. The lumber industry of the Pacific Northwest—
especially its logging operations—relied upon the floating worker
for much of its labor force, as did other seasonal industries of the
region. Before World War I, the farmers in America's great
wheat belt relied upon young transient workers who travelled
north following the harvest from Oklahoma to Alberta. On the
west coast, similar transients followed the truck and orchard crops
from California to British Columbia.

After the war, economic and social changes, the maturing of
the American economy, diminished the size of this labor reservoir
and altered its character. As Southerners migrated to the mills and
camps of the Pacific Northwest, as the population grew, as roads
and automobiles made logging camps less isolated from towns and
cities, more and more lumber workers became "home guards,"
joining those part-time farmers, or "stump ranchers," who had
always supplied logging camps with labor. Agricultural expansion
during the war months brought farm machinery into more general
use, making the large army of migratory wheat harvesters less
necessary. Farm laborers on the west coast and in the wheat belt
travelled from job to job increasingly in "jalopies" with wives and
children rather than in empty freight trains as hoboes. Though
still obviously casuals, the new "jalopy tramps" were more like
"home guards" than the young rebels who had once joined the
I.W.W.[103] The number of hoboes—unmarried transient workers

---

[103] One authority on migratory labor, commenting on these changes, did

not to be confused with nonworking tramps or sedentary and derelict "bums"—declined after the war. One investigator of migrant labor found that, "In their place came 4,000,000 new migrants, mostly families, and a third of them children."[104] These social changes the I.W.W., of course, could neither hold back nor alter, and the organization's increasing rigidity precluded its adapting its program and appeals to the new kind of worker with his new kind of problems.

Successful labor unionism in the American environment has always emphasized job control rather than class consciousness. On this thesis most historians of American labor agree. But the I.W.W. defied this pressure of reality by working stubbornly for both revolution and unionism, approaching success in neither goal. Such quixotism probably doomed the I.W.W. to failure from the beginning, and the severe beating it suffered during and immediately after the first world war sealed its fate. As we have seen, the scars and bruises made the I.W.W. even more unadaptable to reality, even more doctrinaire and disputatious, and it destroyed whatever chance the organization might have once had to make changes in itself to meet new conditions, to evolve perhaps into a real industrial union. During the 1920s, the I.W.W. almost disappeared from the American scene, living on as the half-forgotten custodian of a curiously mixed radicalism of "American" individualism and "un-American" class conflict. It seemed to fade into the wallpaper as if part of the decor of that older America, changing painfully from "frontier" to metropolis.

---

not even bother to note that an attenuated I.W.W. still existed when he wrote. "The I.W.W. passed out of existence during the period between the World War and the 1929 depression. They receded from the scene with the passing of the hobo worker." Nels Anderson, *Men on the Move* (Chicago, 1940), p. 292. Other sources take notice of these changes in the character of the migratory labor force: L. F. Shields, "The Problem of the Automobile Floater," *Monthly Labor Review* (Oct. 1925), pp. 699-701; L. F. Shields, "Migratory Workers in Agriculture," *Proceedings* of the National Conference of Social Work, 1925, pp. 347-353.

[104] Henry Hill Collins, Jr., *America's Own Refugees: Our 4,000,000 Homeless Migrants* (Princeton, 1941), p. 303.

CHAPTER VIII

A
RELIC

———

The author of the last scholarly history of the I.W.W., who published his work in 1932, predicted that the I.W.W. would survive,
if at all, "as did the Blanquist Party or the Knights of Labor—for
futile decades after its hour of lustihood."[1] The career of the
I.W.W. since 1932 has, in large part, borne out the prediction: it
has indeed survived, but only like a relic from a young and different America. It continues out of a kind of organizational inertia,
prodded perhaps by memories of its own past, but inactive. But
it still defends every jot and tittle of its syndicalist orthodoxy. The
stubborn I.W.W. has become something of an anachronism.

During its more than thirty years of virtually posthumous existence, the I.W.W. did try occasionally to rouse itself. In the early
years of the Depression some Wobblies—or former Wobblies—
joined the various organizations of the unemployed that sprang
up in many American cities. In Seattle, they helped to create the
Seattle Unemployed Citizens' League, an organization that interested journalists from all over the country. The League invented
unusually successful self-help programs, cooperated for a time
with city and county relief administrators, and made its influence
felt in local politics. The Communist Party had its "Unemployed
Councils" all over the country and its publication, *The Unemployed Worker*. The Party agitated the unemployed of Seattle as
well as the unemployed of other cities. For a time, the Seattle

———

[1] John S. Gambs, *The Decline of the I.W.W.* (New York, 1932), p. 206.

218

"I.W.W. element" and the Communists worked together as a bloc within the Seattle Unemployed Citizens' League, but they soon broke apart and brought the whole enterprise down with their sectarian squabbling and their unproductive but competitive militancy.[2]

The father of the Seattle Unemployed Citizens' League was Carl Brannin of the Seattle Labor College, the publisher-manager of the college's organ, *The Vanguard*. Brannin helped to organize a group of unemployed workers, the Olympic Height Community Club, in the summer of 1931. From the beginning, the group included a wide range of political opinion, from Brannin's own Marxism to the syndicalism of the few Wobblies. But the predominant political mood was probably the inertia and demoralized apathy of the typical unemployed worker. Other locals formed, and a federation of all the locals followed. One of the early locals, the Capital Hill group, became identified as the center of "I.W.W.-ism."

At first, the League devoted its energies to its own growth and in devising ingenious means of self-help: collecting and distributing truck-farm products acquired in exchange for volunteer labor, collecting surplus food and supplies donated by sympathetic grocers and restaurant owners, negotiating for higher "wages" with the Mayor's Commission for Improved Employment—the "Dix Commission," named thus after I. F. Dix, a vice-president of the Pacific Telephone and Telegraph Company, who served as chairman of the commission. Locals of the League established their own commissaries throughout the city and appointed their own committees to do the work of collecting, supervising, and distributing all the food and supplies donated or earned.

In January 1932, the League took on a semi-official status when it entered into a formal advisory relationship with the County Relief Administration. But this more or less amicable relationship with officialdom did not last long; it began to dissipate quickly after the spring mayoralty election. The candidate elected in March 1932, John F. Dore, had campaigned vigorously among the League

---

[2] Arthur Hillman, "The Unemployed Citizens League of Seattle," *University of Washington Publications in the Social Sciences*, Vol. V, No. 3, Feb. 1934, pp. 181-270. The story of the League told here is drawn largely from this monograph, unless otherwise noted.

locals, but once in office his conservative "economy" measures antagonized the League. The Mayor and the League soon came to criticize each other openly and bitterly. As might be expected, the League's working relationship with the official city and county relief authorities came to an end. Politicians came to fear and respect not only the verbal radicalism of the League but also its potential political power in delivering votes, a power not to be lightly discounted as the November elections of 1932 indicated. The most famous—and curious—beneficiary of the League's support in the 1932 elections was Marion A. Zioncheck, a young radical lawyer elected to Congress from the First District of Seattle and its environs.

In the late summer of 1932, on the eve of the elections, the League's radical power reached its zenith. The Communists and the I.W.W. apparently cooperated as a bloc and between them they succeeded in crushing the moderate center. They thus destroyed the constructive and practical core of the League, as Hulet Wells, an old but somewhat sobered Seattle radical, charged. In August, W. H. Murray of the Capital Hill local, the I.W.W. enclave, ascended briefly to the presidency of the League. Mayor Dore thereupon took to the radio and sounded the alarm. He asked all loyal Seattle citizens to support his counter-revolutionary Home Defense League.[3]

But this supremacy of the radicals, effected by an unstable alliance of Communists and Wobblies, ended in one of those usual internecine struggles of the Left. The Communists succeeded in capturing more or less exclusive control of the League. The organization, in the meantime, had lost most of its practical functions in administrating relief and self-help projects and was doomed anyway by the forthcoming New Deal measures, the Federal Emergency Relief Administration, the Civil Works Administration, the Works Progress Administration, et al. The attenuated League, under Communist control, devoted most of its energies increasingly to futile protests against capitalism and in unproductive militancy. In February 1933, the League protested the end of the city's cooperation with its commissaries by sending four thousand angry members to occupy the City-County Building. Masses of police and sheriff's deputies drove the crowd from the building,

---

3 Seattle *Times,* Oct. 10, 1932, p. 1.

but as the police arrested the most obstreperous demonstrators, the crowd surged back to rescue them from the police.[4] On May Day 1933, the League cooperated with others in a parade of four thousand persons through the streets of Seattle. The Communists organized and led the parade, but eighteen hundred Wobblies followed the Communist vanguard behind their own I.W.W. banners. And all the marchers sang Wobbly songs.[5] As the political revolution of the New Deal progressed, the leaders of the Seattle Unemployed Citizens' League slipped into the mainstream of Washington state politics. Radicalism prevailed—leading James Farley in 1936 to make his celebrated remark about the "soviet of Washington"—but the specific I.W.W. ingredient got lost more and more in the general mixture. It would seem that even those considerable numbers of Americans seeking radical solutions to the Depression forsook the I.W.W. idea to chase after Communism—or even more curious growths such as Technocracy, Share the Wealth, Social Justice, the Townsend Plan, or what have you.

Where the labor force kept some of its prewar character and where conditions of work remained largely unchanged, the I.W.W. maintained a local influence well into the 1930s. On irrigation construction projects or among old-style transient agricultural workers, the Wobblies continued their agitation, occasionally striking sparks of rebellion, but never inflaming public opinion generally to the degree they had before the war. The days of the I.W.W. as a national "menace" had passed.

In the early summer of 1932, Wobblies working for the Lahar Construction Company on the Lake Cle Elum irrigation dam near Ronald, Washington, went out on strike. The employees on such government-contract work usually received at least fifty cents an hour in wages, but the Lahar Company had cut the rate to forty cents. On May 5, Wobblies in one of the outlying camps called a meeting to demand restitution of the fifty-cent rate and to demand better camp facilities. The meeting then proceeded in a body to the main camp. The Lahar Company superintendent became understandably nervous as the angry workers converged on his camp and began their vehement orations. He fired his revolver over the head of an I.W.W. speaker. He claimed that the speaker had

[4] *Industrial Worker*, Feb. 28, 1933, p. 1.
[5] *Ibid.*, May 16, 1933, p. 1.

insulted his wife—by using the word "damn" in his speech, said the I.W.W. report. The following morning, the whole labor force of the construction project stayed away from work. The company tried to import new workers from Ellensburg, the county seat, but could not recruit enough workers. The whole county was sympathetic toward the strikers. Even the local bourgeoisie saw the advantages of having the striking Wobblies back at work rather than replaced and left to drift about through their towns.[6]

But the company held out against the strikers in spite of the difficulty in maintaining a working crew. The company discharged the obvious Wobbly militants and kept the work going with reduced crews and the forty-cent rate. In July, however, when the company reduced the wage rate further to thirty-five cents, the strike resumed with more enthusiasm.[7] This time the company backed down after a long siege. Striking Wobblies surrounded the company's camps and "discouraged" new workers brought to the job. The Lahar Company lawyer asked for police protection for a body of one hundred strike breakers, but he was turned down. On October 9, 1932, the company capitulated and restored the forty-cent rate.[8]

Arthur Boose of Portland, a Burnside Street orator and organizer, toured the strike area in his "side-door Pullman," and a Wobbly correspondent accompanied him on the tour, sending back his reports to the I.W.W. press with the dateline, "Aboard the Boose Special."[9] In his speeches, Boose urged the triumphant strikers to keep the strike won, to stay organized. As he spoke in the little Washington towns near Ellensburg, it became clear why the Lahar Company had thought it necessary to pay such miserly wages. Besieged by all sorts of creditors, the company failed to meet a November payroll. The I.W.W. quickly threatened legal action and forced the reluctant company to pay its wages ahead of its other obligations. The Lahar Company apparently did not want to be assessed several additional thousands of dollars in court costs if the matter came to court.[10]

In 1933, the I.W.W. carried on a long and complicated struggle

[6] *Ibid.,* May 11, 1932, p. 1.
[7] *Ibid.,* Aug. 8, 1932, p. 1.
[8] *Ibid.,* Oct. 18, 1932, p. 1.
[9] *Ibid.,* Nov. 22, 1932, p. 3.
[10] *Ibid.,* p. 4.

with hop and fruit growers in the Yakima region of Washington, reminiscent of—but perhaps *only* reminiscent of—the prewar *élan*. In May, the I.W.W. led hop pickers out on strike. The first day of the strike produced a scene of rural violence as the striking migrants along the highway jeered and shouted at "scabs" going to the fields to work. One rancher sped his automobile, in a fit of pique, toward a knot of strikers on the highway approach to his property, scattering men and women before him and knocking down one striker not quite agile enough to get out of the way. As the strikers converged on the car in anger, the rancher's son leaped out of the car and waved the crowd back with a gun. He and his father refused to take the injured striker to a hospital and left him for the state police to pick up.[11]

The strike continued with mounting tension. But the I.W.W. could not sustain its effort. Early in June, at a mass meeting in Coleman's Auto Park in Yakima, the strikers decided to discontinue the highway picketing.[12] Although the picketing thus came to an end, the general sense of outrage among farm workers continued, and the I.W.W. succeeded in holding a series of organizational mass meetings throughout the region to keep the fires of discontent stoked.[13] On August 11, the strike resumed, this time on the ranch of D. O. Traubargers near Buena, Washington. A mass meeting two days later in the Yakima city park agreed to extend the walk-out to all the farms of the region.[14] Tension again mounted. Three hundred armed farmers, organized as a flying vigilante squadron, dispersed a hundred pickets at the Condon Ranch on August 24. The state militia took over the city of Yakima the next day as martial law was imposed. The troops set up their ominous machine gun emplacements at downtown street corners. Deputies patrolled the railroad yards as in the old days of free-speech fights to prevent the expected influx of Wobblies.[15] The jails accumulated prisoners as of old, and the Yakima authorities built a stockade to hold the overflow.

The I.W.W. defense attorney sent a disabled war veteran, Mike

---

11 *Ibid.*, May 30, 1933, p. 1.
12 *Ibid.*, June 13, 1933, p. 1.
13 *Ibid.*, July 4, 1933, p. 1.

14 *Ibid.*, Aug. 22, 1933, p. 1.
15 *Ibid.*, Sept. 5, 1933 , p. 1.

Capelik, to the Yakima city jail with credentials to confer with the prisoners. But Mike was detained by the District Attorney, and his credentials were confiscated. That same night a group of Yakima citizens, some in National Guard uniforms, taped and bound Mike and drove him forty miles out of town, ostensibly to hang him. Instead they contented themselves with beating him and with pouring glue into his shoes and over his head. The City Health Department cooperated with authorities by condemning the strikers' camp as unsanitary and by ordering the site vacated and burned.[16] The flying squadron of vigilantes worked efficiently. In Grandview, the Chief of Police learned of trouble at an outlying ranch. He alerted the Grandview vigilantes like a latter-day Paul Revere, and they all raced to the scene of the trouble in a motor caravan of ten to fifteen cars. But at the ranch they found only a domestic squabble—an "eternal triangle"—involving two men and a woman.[17]

The conflict came to its climax on October 14 when the authorities brought thirty-three Wobbly prisoners before Superior Court Judge A. W. Hawkins for arraignment on assault charges. The defense lawyer asked for a change of venue, which was denied. He then asked to have the case transferred to a Federal District Court where, he claimed, the Constitutional rights of his clients would be better protected, and this somewhat dubious request was of course denied. He then asked to have the assault charges quashed on the grounds that the defendants had not been arrested by "any process known to law," and again he was denied.[18] The judge set the trial for December 11, 1933, and the I.W.W. press, typically, announced the forthcoming tribunal with the headline, "Legal Lynching Opens."[19] A "labor jury" appeared in Yakima to hear the case as in Montesano in 1920 for the Centralia trial. It was expected to give its dissident verdict on the "lynch" justice anticipated.[20] But the I.W.W. was denied new martyrs, for a somewhat humiliating reason. The city decided it did not want to shoulder the $30,000 burden of the trial. The prosecutor offered a "deal" to the I.W.W. defense lawyer whereby the defendants would plead guilty to a

---

16 *Ibid.*, Sept. 12, 1933, p. 1.
17 *Ibid.*, Sept. 26, 1933, p. 1; Yakima *Daily Republic*, Sept. 1, 1933, p. 1.
18 *Industrial Worker*, Oct. 17, 1933, p. 1; Oct. 31, 1933, p. 1.
19 *Ibid.*, Dec. 5, 1933, p. 1.
20 *Ibid.*, Dec. 12, 1933, p. 1.

minor third-degree assault charge. The I.W.W. turned down the offer indignantly. The city reluctantly released all the prisoners without trial.[21]

The I.W.W. and its postwar rival, the Communist Party, clashed unexpectedly during the troubles at Yakima. A seventeen-year-old Communist girl, Mary Goold, an honor student at the local high school, was arrested during the picketing and demonstrations. After her middle-class relatives had freed her on bail, she traveled through Washington for the International Labor Defense, a Communist "front," to raise money for the defense of the imprisoned strikers. The I.W.W. prisoners repudiated her efforts vehemently. Wobblies claimed that they never saw any of the defense money ostensibly collected in their behalf. Indeed, the only aid they received from the International Labor Defense were some packages of peanut brittle sent to their prison cells. The Wobblies scornfully returned the peanut brittle. One anti-Communist Wobbly said, "I never want to see a United Front between the I.W.W. and these Communist snakes . . ." Such alliances with snakes, he said, only inject "yellow venom of disruption into the red blood of proletarian revolution."[22]

In 1936, the I.W.W. led sporadic and local strikes in some of the logging camps of northern Idaho, reminiscent again of the old days but not matching the extent or fervor of the strike of 1917. In April, Wobblies launched a brief strike at the Weyerhaeuser Company's "Camp L" in Idaho and won the restoration of a five-dollar-a-day wage rate.[23] At the end of April, Wobblies won another small logging camp strike in the Clearwater district.[24] In May they won yet another victory at the Winton Lumber Company on the Coeur d'Alene River with only the threat of a strike.[25] In July 1936, I.W.W. strikes broke out all over northern Idaho, the heart of the contagion being near Pierce, Idaho, at the biggest pine mill in the world.[26] The governor declared martial law in early August in Clearwater County to control the incipient violence. This largest of the strikes of 1936 did not succeed. On August 19, the

21 *Ibid.*, Feb. 2, 1934, p. 1.
22 *Ibid.*, Feb. 16, 1934, p. 1.
23 *Ibid.*, Apr. 18, 1936, p. 1; Apr. 25, 1936, p. 1.
24 *Ibid.*, May 9, 1936, p. 1.
25 *Ibid.*, May 16, 1936, p. 1.
26 *Ibid.*, Aug. 1, 1936, p. 1.

defeated Pierce strikers voted to go back to work after the troops
had deported a series of I.W.W. strike committees and had protected the importation of strike-breakers from the Midwestern and
Southern lumber regions.[27] The chairman of the I.W.W. executive
board in Chicago boasted, with perhaps more bravado than accu-
racy, that the strike had really succeeded, had raised wages and
improved working conditions, and had generally reactivated the
I.W.W. in the Northwestern woods.[28]

Because the I.W.W. disdained the whole pragmatic philosophy
of "pure and simple unionism," it could not benefit from the policies of the New Deal designed to protect the right to organize
into unions and to bargain collectively. The attempts by the A.F.L.
in 1935 to take advantage of the protection afforded by Section 7 (a)
of the National Industrial Recovery Act met with only hoots of
contempt by the I.W.W. The I.W.W. press, however, did follow
very closely the whole story of the lumber industry and the National Recovery Administration. It also reported in detail the
A.F.L. strike of May 1935. The negotiations and maneuverings of
1935 seemed mostly "hot air" to the Wobbly observers.[29] It was
all quite different, without dispute, from the *élan* of I.W.W. class
warfare, from the "smashing victory won by the I.W.W. in 1917,"[30]
in the words of a Wobbly journalist.

But the labor provisions of the National Industrial Recovery
Act, and later the Wagner Labor Relations Act of 1935, did tempt
some Wobblies who were willing to change their organization
into a more normal union in order to compete under the new dis-
pensation with the A.F.L. and the C.I.O. In 1938, the General
Secretary-Treasurer, W. H. Westman, reaffirmed the traditional
policy of the I.W.W. that forbade all time-contracts with the
"boss."[31]

[27] *Ibid.*, Aug. 29, 1936, p. 1; "Wobblies in the Northwest," *Nation* (Nov.
13, 1937), p. 543.
[28] Report of the Chairman, Charles Velsek, General Executive Board, *Minutes of the Twenty-Second Constitutional General Convention of the I.W.W.*,
1936, p. 1.
[29] *Industrial Worker*, June 15, 1935, p. 1.
[30] *Ibid.*, June 8, 1935, p. 1.
[31] Report of the General Secretary-Treasurer, W. H. Westman, *Minutes
of the Twenty-Third Constitutional General Convention of the I.W.W.*, 1938,
pp. 2-3.

If the I.W.W. is going to change about face and admit that its past thirty-five years of revolutionary teaching have all been wrong and adopt so-called sensible business-like unionism, then the I.W.W. may as well forget about its ultimate aim, "the abolition of capitalism" . . . I do not agree with those who call signing time contracts a mere change of tactics . . .

During World War II, the I.W.W. stirred in its sleep, and some observers, noting signs of activity in the nonferrous mining regions of the West and along the waterfronts of San Diego, New York, and New Orleans, predicted a postwar revival. In Cleveland, Ohio, for example, the I.W.W. represented the 1,600 workers of the American Stove Company. The I.W.W. boasted that it had recruited 7,000 members during the war.[32] The New York *Times* even suggested that the I.W.W. "might be in the process of rejuvenation" and reported that it had a membership of 20,000.[33] Other observers, however, saw the wartime revival as a poignant joke, and reported the I.W.W.'s convention of 1946 with cruel irony. Thirty-nine middle-aged men and one woman met in a sooty, third-rate office building on the north side of Chicago to pass resolutions denouncing the United States government, Communism, Fascism, Nazism, the C.I.O., the A.F.L., and World Wars I and II. "With that off their chests, the Industrial Workers of the World went home."[34] The threatened revival died quietly. The I.W.W. even speeded the process with revolutionary but suicidal puritanism. It expelled its vigorous Cleveland branch when the Cleveland Wobblies petitioned the executive board and all I.W.W. officers to take the noncommunist oath prescribed by the Taft-Hartley Act of 1947. Unless the Cleveland Wobblies took the oath, they could not enjoy the protections of the National Labor Relations Board.[35]

In 1949, Attorney-General Tom Clark placed the I.W.W. on his list of subversive organizations without giving the organization warning or opportunity to plead its case to be omitted. Shortly thereafter, the government ruled that the I.W.W.—no longer a

---

[32] "I.W.W. Revives," *Business Week* (Jan. 6, 1945), pp. 96-98.

[33] New York *Times*, Mar. 24, 1946, p. 31.

[34] "Again the Wobblies," *Time* (Apr. 1, 1946), p. 24.

[35] Letter from W. H. Westman, General Secretary-Treasurer, May 23, 1952.

bonafide labor union— would have to pay a corporate income tax.[36] Periodically, the I.W.W. has protested its inclusion on the Attorney-General's list. In 1965, it began to accumulate a "legal fund" to take its case to court.[37] About the only practical harm being done to the organization by the stigma of subversion seems to be the embarrassment that superannuated Wobblies feel when in the presence of their affluent and conformist grandchildren.[38]

In spite of its listing as subversive, its tax burden, its loss of 1,600 metal workers in Cleveland, Ohio, and its chronic impotence, the I.W.W. still looked to the future. In 1952, one Wobbly writer revived in somewhat new dress the old plan to woo the technicians and engineers, to wed the I.W.W. to scientism. The writer noted that the popular cult of science fiction seemed refreshingly free from the usual American commitment to "free enterprise." Science-fiction authors, for example, often envisioned futuristic or interplanetary societies that were obviously "anti-capitalist." The writer therefore suggested that the I.W.W. either go into the science-fiction field itself in order to extend its influence or ally itself in some way with the leaders of the cult.[39] If this proposal seemed too outlandish for even latter-day Wobblies, the I.W.W. leaders planned a more conventional attack on the organization's decline. They called a regional conference in Seattle where Wobblies could discuss the problems of the organization and propose solutions. The delegates who attended this regional conference did discuss the problems of the organization but proposed no very radical solutions. They reaffirmed traditional I.W.W. policies, lambasted again the oligarchic A.F.L. and C.I.O., and republished a hoary 1919 resolution warning all Wobblies of *agents provocateurs* and of the activities of internal wreckers.[40]

The surviving I.W.W. halls are fit settings for anachronism. The I.W.W. hall in Seattle finally closed its doors in the spring of 1965, but the visitor before that time could find it in the dismal low-rent district near the railroad stations. Behind the grimy shop

---

[36] Report of W. H. Westman, General Secretary-Treasurer, *Minutes of the Twenty-Sixth Constitutional General Convention of the I.W.W., 1950*, p. 2.

[37] *Industrial Worker*, July 1965; New York *Times*, Feb. 14, 1965.

[38] Conversation with Carl Keller, Editor, *Industrial Worker*, Aug. 23, 1965.

[39] *Industrial Worker*, Aug. 29, 1952, p. 3.

[40] *Ibid.*, Feb. 27, 1953, p. 1; Mar. 6, 1953, pp. 1, 4.

windows, Wobblies had arranged a display of I.W.W. pamphlets and books, many of them I.W.W. classics published forty years ago. They also had attached current issues of the hardy *Industrial Worker* to the window with pieces of Scotch tape, one of the few evidences from the street that the year was not 1915.

Inside the hall in the 1950s, near the door, stood two battered roll-top desks stacked high with yellowing piles of papers and newspapers. A naked light bulb hung by a cord from the ceiling over the desks. In the rear of the hall, several elderly men in rough clothing played cribbage at a heavy oak table. Against the wall near the desks stood a book case, the library of the Seattle I.W.W. branches. A few titles were readily distinguishable: Karl Marx's *Capital* in the Modern Library Giant edition, the Bureau of Corporations' investigation and report of the lumber industry published in 1913 and 1914, Gustavus Myer's *History of the Great American Fortunes,* Darwin's *Origin of Species,* and, oddly enough, T. S. Eliot's *Collected Poems.* Above the book case, the Wobblies had hung three ancient photographs, portraits of the three principal I.W.W. martyrs, Joe Hill, Frank Little, and Wesley Everest. They made a curious ikon-like impression on the observer. Underneath the picture of Wesley Everest the Wobblies had printed his last words, "Tell the boys I died for my class."

All the occupants of the hall, the men at the roll-top desks and the cribbage players, appeared to be considerably beyond middle age. At the height of the I.W.W.'s career the typical Wobbly had been under twenty-five. The Wobblies at the desks were gentle and helpful, and they paused periodically in their conversation to rummage through the piles of newspapers seeking documentation on some point they made.

Next door to the hall, an independent cannery workers' union had its headquarters, and the sidewalk was crowded with knots of Japanese cannery workers apparently waiting for job placements. One old Wobbly behind the desks praised them and contrasted their vigorous and democratic union with the powerful and oligarchic Teamsters' Union of Dave Beck, the Seattle union leader of the day. When asked why the I.W.W. did not try to incorporate the cannery workers' union into the I.W.W., the Wobbly mused for a moment as if the idea had not previously occurred to him and then explained that the I.W.W. was not imperialistic. If workers had satisfactory unions, militant and democratic, the I.W.W. gave them its blessing without trying to "muscle in" or take over. When asked about the future of the I.W.W. the old Wobbly offered friendly but essentially vague replies, offering instead to hunt further through the files for a missing pamphlet or scrapbook entry that would throw light on the Centralia riot or the 1917 lumber strike.

Leaving the darkening hall, preserved unwittingly like a museum display, a visitor then strolled uptown toward the neon lights and the bustle of modern Seattle, convinced that the I.W.W. could scarcely survive its aging membership. Ten years later, in the national headquarters in Chicago, the impressions were similar. The I.W.W. that survives to the 1960s is a society for the sharing of memories, esconced in an obscure second-floor office on North Halsted Street. Although some of its youthful culture has been adopted by the young radicals of the civil-rights movement, the I.W.W. as an organization seems to offer little to the continuing stream of American radicalism. Only its spirit, its history, seems appropriate as mute criticism of the megalopolis of slum, freeways, and skyscrapers in which it now lives out its last years in forgotten obscurity. Perhaps the final irony to the story of the I.W.W. is precisely this: the rampaging and revolutionary I.W.W., preaching its advanced "proletarianism" and tough-minded, nonpolitical, collectivist "industrialism," became finally useful to the society that sired it as a reminder of a dream of independence, freedom, optimism, and self-help.